From There To Here

FROM THERE

A Guide to English-Canadian Literature Since 1960
Our Nature-Our Voices II

Frank Davey

TO HERE

Press Porcepic Erin, Ontario 1974

The book has been published with the help of a grant from the Humanities Research Council of Canada, using funds provided by the Canada Council.

Printed and Published by Press Porcepic
70 Main Street, Erin, Ontario, N0B 1T0

ISBN 0-88878-036-2 Hard
ISBN 0-88878-037-0 Soft

Table of Contents for Volume 1

Our Nature - Our Voices Volume I by Clara Thomas provides an examination of English-Canadian writing from the settlement period to the present, with bibliographies and useful suggestions for further study. It is available from New Press, 553 Richmond Street West, Toronto, Ontario.

Contents

Preface

From There to Here, Volume II of Our Nature/Our Voices, is a guide
to the work of English-Canadian writers (excluding dramatists, for
whom there will be a separate volume) who have emerged since
1960, as well as to that of slightly earlier writers, not covered in
Volume I, who have had significant influence on recent work. Its
orientation is more interpretive and explanatory than historical — not
only because of the small period of time with which it deals but also
because of the limited amount of criticism available on most of the
writers.

Those writers discussed here are by no means the only ones who
have made contributions to the shape of English-Canadian writing in
the past fifteen years. Most readers — especially those who are also
writers — will be able to think of many possible additions and
substitutions. I established the present list only after many reluctant
exclusions. Our country today swarms with poets, novelists, short
story writers, editors; each addition that I contemplated threatened
to bring down on the volume a dozen or more writers with approximately equal claims for recognition. Those whom I have not
recognized here will perhaps be comforted by the fact that
throughout literary history contemporary evaluations of writers have
usually been wrong.

I have made my selections on the basis of various criteria, including the writers' pre-eminence as artists, their influence on the
shape and direction of recent writing, and their presence on contemporary high school and college curricula. Except in the case of
authors of established classics, I have passed over writers without a
substantial body of work. I have similarly passed over younger

writers whose work to date offers little variation on that of earlier writers or periods. The sixties and seventies have been a period of intensive experimentation in both English-Canadian poetry and fiction. In cases of marginal difference in proficiency and reputation, I have chosen the work of the partially successful experimentor over that of the competent journeyman. Among those who might have been included in the book except for various of the criteria above are: James Bacque, Henry Beissel, Ken Belford, Avi Boxer, Michael Charters, Fred Cogswell, R.G. Everson, Lawrence Garber, Eldon Grier, Don Gutteridge, David Helwig, Robert Hogg, Harry Howith, Patrick Lane, Steve McCaffery, Barry McKinnon, Stuart MacKinnon, Roy MacSkimming, Russell Marois, Tom Marshall, Seymour Mayne, John Metcalf, Susan Musgrave, Martin Myers, Chris Scott, Leo Simpson, David Solway, Peter Such, Scott Symons, Wilfred Watson, Tom Wayman, and Richard Wright. For access to information about these writers see Appendix A.

All the writers discussed are of either Canadian birth or residence. Among expatriate and immigrant writers I have excluded those whose work has been overwhelmingly about other-than-Canadian experience. Many recent immigrant writers — Jane Rule, Michael Bullock, Robin Skelton, Stanley Cooperman, J. Michael Yates — have continued to create work that is overtly a part of the literature and experiential worlds of their homelands. A few expatriates, notably Mavis Gallant, David Bromige, and Daryl Hine — have by choice entered fully into the literary traditions of other cultures. I have seen little point here in continuing the Canadian habit of indiscriminately claiming all writers of some Canadian residence as our own.

I have given considerable space in this volume to analysis and explanation of technique and form. I have done this in part because the period in Canadian writing being considered is one of continual search for new and more profound forms. In no way can much of this writing be opened even for thematic discussion without careful attention to the meaning of its techniques. I have also attempted by my attention to form to redress the tendency in recent Canadian criticism toward exclusively thematic interpretation. One must remember that it is by being encoded in the language and structure of literature that these 'themes' are transmitted from writer to reader. Ultimately, only the form of a writer's work speaks to us.

Numerous people assisted and encouraged me during the writing of this volume: my colleague, Clara Thomas, who wrote Volume I of Our Nature/Our Voices, Molly Blythe, Mary Ann Bricker, Margot Kent, and Jan Bartley, who performed most of the bibliographical research, George Bowering who contributed the fifteenth article, and my wife who assisted in the editing of the final manuscript. To all, my sincere thanks. I am also grateful to York University for grants toward bibliographical research and the acquisition of photographs.

Frank Davey
August, 1973

Introduction

Dominating all literary, cultural, and political developments of the past two decades in Canada has been the world-wide burgeoning of micro-electronic technology. We have become engulfed in a 'media' age in which the media themselves — radio, film, television, audio tape, video tape, microwave, xerox, microfiche, computer tape, etc. — have steadily increased in both power and number. Under the influence of technology, the information available to us has expanded even faster than the growing number of means we have to retrieve it. Together, the expansion of both information and media systems have effected radical changes on the relations between nation-states, on the distribution of power among states and individuals, and on the perceptual outlooks of artists and non-artists alike.

In contrast to the baleful predictions of Zamiatin and Huxley, the new technology has to date diversified and enriched man's perceptual world, disappointed rationalist views of reality, and decentralized rather than centralized political and cultural power. Man's amplified powers have discovered a vastness and complexity in the universe that appears to exceed infinitely his ability to understand and control it. In physics, astronomy, microbiology, and geology, almost every break-through experiment has delivered to the scientist problems even more baffling than the one he has just resolved. Man's attempts to rationalize his environment have increasingly backfired as he reaches the limits of his ability to predict all the effects of his environmental interventions. He has been forced to give up use of DDT to control insects, diethylstilbesterol to stimulate growth in cattle, lobotomy to cure schizophrenia, thalidomide to prevent nausea, phenacetin to treat headaches, phosphates and

11

enzymes to launder clothing. In man's political and cultural life, the new technology has revealed and stimulated unquenchable idiosyncrasies and irrationalities — Jesus Freaks, Hell's Angels, the Edmund Burke Society, the Hare Krishnas, Maharishi Mahesh Yogi, Leonard Cohen, Gay Liberation, the Beatles, the Vietnamese War — thus thoroughly discrediting the eighteenth-century dream of a spontaneously genteel brotherhood of 'reasonable' men.

Electronic technology altered history in numerous ways during the sixties and seventies. Television's graphic living-room views of the Vietnamese conflict not only made that war unfightable for America but made America itself repugnant to millions of Canadians. Computer technology, besides allowing man to walk on the moon, interwove the economies and currencies of western countries to such an extent that the economic woes of a single country could precipitate world-wide economic crisis. Computer technology was also partly responsible for the mitigating of the Cold War; early generation computers made nuclear war suicidally efficient, while the Soviet Union's need to buy fourth-generation technology from the U.S. became a significant factor in the establishing of the current detente.

In North America the combination of television and instantaneous microwave transmission made possible the overnight occurence of large-scale popular movements. The sixties became the period of the Civil Rights movement, Student Power, the F.L.Q., Black Power, the Black Panthers, Women's Liberation, Gay Liberation, as the television image of numerous single protest events flashed contagiously back and forth across the continent. The archetype for the university sit-in and student riot moved through electronic media from the University of Montreal to Berkeley, to Texas Southern, to Columbia, to Simon Fraser, to Sir George Williams, to San Francisco State. Television, radio, and the recording industry created the instant superstar: Janis Joplin, Bob Dylan, Frank Zappa, Joan Baez, Leonard Cohen — simultaneously making both gurus and millionaires of what would have otherwise been merely remarkable artists.

The media expansion kindled rapid interest in mixed-media experiences. "Light-shows" were featured at almost every rock concert at the height of the sixties. Collage and poetry, film and music, dance and photography, video tape and painting, were given almost every possible permutation during the decade. Poets like Canada's Michael Ondaatje became film-makers; painters like Greg Curnoe became poets and photographers. Toronto poet bpNichol performed sound poetry for music departments. Vancouver poet Bill Bissett produced books of a totally integrated graphic/linguistic experience. Mixed-media coincided with the search for mixed consciousness among drug experimentors. New combinations of human consciousness with marijuana, hashish, peyote, mescaline, amphetamines, LSD, became the inner equivalent of the mixed "psychedelic" experiences the new media provided. Drug and art worlds became inextricably combined, as artists reached for new visions through hallucinogenics and drug users attempted new combinations of media to give artistic form to their hallucinogenic experiences.

While increasing the power of governments, corporations, and institutions, the new media technology also radically enlarged the power of individual men. So great is this latter increase that the Soviet Union today will not permit its citizens to own photocopying equipment, tape recorders, offset printing presses, or mimeograph machines. Micro-technology has taken much of the control of television, book publishing, magazine publishing, and film producing out of the hands of large countries and industries. High quality films and books can be produced as easily in a small house in a small country as by a conglomerate institution in Hollywood or New York City. So dramatic has been technology's reduction of printing costs that distribution problems have occasionally been overcome by the simple expedient of giving the book or magazine away.

The revolution in printing costs spawned an international network of "correspondence" poetry in the sixties and "correspodence art" in recent years. Beginning in the fifties with Cid Corman's little magazine *Origin*, distributed free under the motto "to offer — to respond — to let be", a genre of cheaply printed magazines distributed free to those requesting or responding developed — *The Floating Bear* and *Wild Dog* in the U.S., *Tish* in Vancouver, *Tlaloc* in Wales, *Open Letter* in Victoria B.C., *grOnk* in Toronto. Most called themselves "newsletters", and printed not only experimental poetry in process but addresses of poets and magazines that the reader might wish to contact and news of poetry readings and publications from around the world. A later development has been "correspondence art" — an artform based on the sending of found or collaged visual materials through the mails — in magazines like *File* (Toronto), on postcards, or simply in envelopes.

In the cases of correspondence poetry and correpondence art, the new technology has helped create counter-movements which can exist side-by-side with the established forms which they reject. Before micro-technology, the old forms had to be overthrown and destroyed before the new could flourish; abstract impressionism replaced realism in painting, while modernism in poetry ended and discredited the Georgian lyric. In the past two decades, however, the decentralization made possible by portable, inexpensive, electric or electronic equipment has meant that a multiplicity of alternative aesthetic systems, or even value systems, can co-exist without any one of them needing to gain total domination to survive. The most striking examples of this have been the "youth culture" and the "counterculture". Across the western world during the sixties and seventies, people between the ages of twelve and twenty have been able to establish their own tastes in mores, clothing, music, and dialect. In the more significant counter-culture, even older people have been "dropping-out" or "opting out" of the dominant competitive and materialistic culture to attempt to establish non-competitive communal lifestyles around the activities they most enjoy. Unlike the youth culture, the counter-culture in some forms has tended to be self-sufficient not only in its tastes but in producing the objects of its world — food, clothing, books, pottery, furniture, magazines, etc.

The variety, inter-relatedness, and lack of central authority that have been characteristic of the new media culture have had some extraordinarily significant side-effects. One has been that the ecological crisis which has been facing the human race for more than a century has abruptly become so meaningful that a complete change in man's concept of himself seems likely to ensue. Ecologists had been talking of "field theory" — the concept of man as merely one more dependent element in a total environment — for decades. It was not until western culture, under the influence of microtechnology, abandoned monolithic centralization and became itself a "field" of co-existing equals, that man became capable of understanding the ecological trap. Suddenly the evidence faced him both in the ecologist's teaching and in the dancing electrons of the TV screen. In consequence, a major shift in man's sense of his relationship to the cosmos appears to be occuring: one as large and portentous as the shift from a god-centred to man-centred vision back in the seventeenth century.

Another large side-effect of man's new sense of the interdependence of things has been a resurgence and a humanizing of political consciousness. Like every other human activity in the age of micro-technology, politics cannot be compartmentalized. It is no longer the restricted province of the professional politician or the subject of only a special form of literary rhetoric. For the contemporary man, every action has its political dimension. Every poem, film or novel carries in its form political implications. The tightly controlled, formalistic, and elegant poem shares formal assumptions with a company directorship, while the loosely structured film or lifestyle shares assumptions with the commune. Politics and art have become interwoven as never before. Ronald Reagan moves from the controlled plots of the western movie to the Republican governorship of California. Marlon Brando, Geneviève Bujold, Paul Newman, Jane Fonda reach from more organically formed films to overt gestures of political concern. Allen Ginsberg, Pauline Julien, Joan Baez, Robert Charlebois, John Lennon, Jacques Ferron reach from similarly open and improvisational art to other defences of human individuality.

Amid this restructured world of diminished central authority and amplified individuals and counter-structures, Canada has struggled to become itself a significant counter-structure. Because of its proximity to the United States, Canada became a battlefield in the sixties between the centralized and incorporating power of traditional U.S. corporate capitalism and the decentralized and fragmentary forces of Canadian-operated micro-technology. Various large monolithic American corporations — Exxon, Texasgulf, Standard of New Jersey, Kraft Foods, IBM, McGraw-Hill, Rayonier, General Foods — fought to integrate the Canadian economy and culture totally into those of their own country. But for the efforts of individual Canadians to use micro-technology to begin new enterprises — building midget submarines in Vancouver, founding new publishing houses in Toronto — and to persuade reluctant governments to protect and aid these efforts, Canada's 'independence' could have been utterly subverted. Among the key events of this struggle were the publication of George Grant's *Lament for a Nation*, the founding of the Committee for an Independent Canada, the appointing of the Ontario Royal Commission on Book Publishing, the U.S. purchase of Ryerson Press, the attempted U.S. purchase of McClelland and Stewart and Labatt's Breweries, and the establishing of the Canadian Development Corporation.

Meanwhile, the superficial nationalism of the popular press flourished. In 1958, John Diefenbaker and the Conservative party were elected largely on the basis of anti-American and 'pro-Northern' feeling. The Pearson administration of the middle sixties gave Canada an illusory identity as the "honest broker" and peacekeeper for world society, and among its last actions gave the country its present flag. At the centennial, French president Charles de Gaulle's cry to a Montreal crowd of "Vive le Québec libre!" brought a groundswell of indignant nationalism across English Canada. Throughout the sixties, televised scenes from the Vietnamese war and from the numerous violent U.S. protests against it provided Canadian culture with a negative definition of unprecedented strength. The thousands of U.S. deserters and draft-resisters who abandoned their country for our own gave, in their direct assertion of

15

preference, proof that Canada was still in some important ways an 'un-American' place.

With the collapse of the Cold War and its divisions of world power into two centralized alliances, came new possibilities for Canadian foreign policy. Among the few new significant policies to result have been a reduction in NATO forces, continued diplomatic relations with Cuba, the claiming of control over the waters of the arctic archipelago, the claiming of pollution control and fishing rights in the Gulf of St. Lawrence and the inland waters of B.C., the diplomatic recognition of the People's Republic of China — in advance of the U.S. and most of its allies, and the refusal to agree to U.S. requests for a continental water policy or a continental energy policy. Although to many Canadian nationalists our foreign policy is still too close to being a pale shadow of that of the U.S., in the context of our history its vigour and independence exceed expectation.

Much stronger than the nationalism of the Canadian government has been that of Canadian publishers, editors, entertainers, and writers. Exploiting the micro-technology which makes alternatives to branch-plant culture possible, these people have founded a new recording industry, a film industry, and new publishing ventures such as House of Anansi, New Press, The Coach House Press, Peter Martin Associates, M.G. Hurtig, Alive Press, Talonbooks, Oberon Press, Press Porcépic, and James Lewis and Samuel, all of which have overtly or covertly worked to give greater definition and voice to the nation and to resist the invasion of Canada by monolithic U.S. corporations and values. Similar uses of the media have been made in French Canada, which have both increased the definition of Quebec culture and amplified separatist feeling. When we consider the implications of the 1970 'October Crisis' (the James Cross kidnapping and the Pierre Laporte kidnapping and murder), we should remember that the various technological developments that have amplified English-Canadian nationalism also amplify 'nationalistic' feelings within every region of the country. The replacing of strong central direction with a network of interacting and conflicting forces on a world scale, recurs at each level of social organization. The city decentralizes to become a 'field' of strong individuals and groups; the province decentralizes to accommodate the interacting assertions of its cities and municipalities; the nation-state decentralizes to accomodate the yearnings of its provinces. Technology's 'global village' has no dominant centre — neither in itself nor in its parts.

Throughout the past two decades Canada has constantly expanded and altered its institutional structures in order to keep pace with the rapid and geometric enlargement of knowledge and technology and their accompanying changes in social patterns. Canadian universities and colleges have increased from 28 in 1960 to over 93 in 1973. The Canada Council has grown from a small endowment-based foundation to a multi-million dollar patron of local artistic projects across the country. The Canadian Radio and Television Commission has declared stringent broadcast regulations which have prompted astonishing growth in both the recording industry and the music arts. Recent federal government initiatives have attempted to ensure that the manufacture and operation of giant computers will occur in this country, and that Canadians can thus be masters of their own information resources. Despite all these efforts, however, and the energies of such individual nationalists as Walter Gordon, Melville Watkins, Mel Hurtig, Dave Godfrey, and Robin Mathews, Canadian culture remains in state of siege.

In the shadow of U.S. centralized finance and industry, the world-wide media explosion has triggered an expansion throughout Canadian letters. New reprint series launched by McClelland & Stewart (New Canadian Library), Macmillan of Canada (Laurentian Library) and the University of Toronto Press have put more than one hundred and twenty titles back into print. A casebook series has been begun by Ryerson Press (Critical Views on Canadian Writers), and extensive monograph series begun by Copp Clark, McClelland & Stewart, and Forum House.

New economical printing techniques have also created an abundance of literary magazines: scholarly journals such as *The Malahat Review, Wascana Review, Mosaic,* and *The Journal of Canadian Fiction;* glossy independent journals such as *Prism International* and *Exile*; semi-professional magazines such as *Impulse, Quarry,* and *Northern Journey*; a book review tabloid, *Books in Canada*; and numerous little magazines: *Tish, Moment, Mountain, Intercourse, Blew Ointment, Up th Tube with One Eye Open, Yes, Island, Is, The Ant's Forefoot, grOnk, Cataract, Ganglia, Salt,* etc. The proliferation of the latter has been particularly important, since, as Louis Dudek has remarked, "the little magazine [is] where the real literary ferment is taking place."

Stimulated by both the amount of new writing in literary journals and by the availability of the compact, efficient technology of computer typesetting, the offset press, and xerox plate-making, Canadian literary book publishing has grown astronomically. In 1960 the scholarly journal *Canadian Literature* could locate only twenty-four volumes of poetry that had been published during the previous year, and was able to review each of them. By 1971 its editor, George Woodcock, was announcing the abandonment of "even the pretence of reviewing every book or pamphlet" by Canadian poets, and predicting that "250 or 300 titles" would be published in the current year. The change in fiction has been more qualitative than quantitative, as the growing number of independent Canadian publishers have offered the writer a wider spectrum of native editorial taste than ever before in Canadian history.

This expansion in Canadian publishing coincided with the expansion of Canadian universities and world-wide decentralization in cultural taste. The nationalistic spirit released by decentralization created both a significant commercial audience and a market within newly formed Canadian literature courses in high schools and universities. Poetry chapbooks which previously had been printed and sold in runs of under 250 copies began to sell rapidly in runs of 1000 to 5000 copies. Books by authors such as Leonard Cohen and Pierre Berton could record sales of more than 100,000 copies. Cohen and Berton, together with Al Purdy, Irving Layton, Earle Birney, Farley Mowat, Margaret Atwood, became the subject of newspaper articles, interviews in popular magazines, and radio and television programmes. The effect on Canadian writers was dramatic. For the first time an entire generation of writers remained in the country to write and publish. Expatriate writers such as Mordecai Richler returned. Under the complex impact of the micro-electronic age, the lure of Paris, London, and New York became no greater than that of Montreal, Toronto, and Vancouver; in addition, the latter were home.

Two Canadian critics provide the best introduction to the confusing and ostensibly conflicting changes which swept Canadian literature during this cataclysmic period: Marshall McLuhan and Eli Mandel. McLuhan, in his own impulsive and electric prose, managed throughout the sixties to report the information "explosion" and the electronic "revolution" almost as quickly as they happened. It was he who saw the "field" replacing the "channel" as the correct image for human relationships, who saw the retribalization of man as a consequence of the instantaneous electric media, who saw multiphasic, discontinuous, and inclusive reasoning replacing the sequential and categorizing logic man had inherited from Gutenberg and Plato, who wrote in the introduction to his landmark work, *Understanding Media*, "the mark of our time is its revulsion against imposed patterns." Mandel, a more conservative stylist and once known as a formalist poet, surprised Canadian letters in 1966 with the proposition that literature is "beyond system" and requires subjective and emotionally-engaged criticism rather than systematic analysis and explication. To Mandel, the new open forms of literature required open "irrational" response, a response "which does not attempt to impose on individual works or on art itself a structure of reason or indeed a pattern of any kind except that of perception."

What both men were announcing, and what much recent Canadian literature confirms, is the demise of the modernist period and the beginning of a decentralized, 'post-electric', post-modern, non-authoritarian age. McLuhan, however — despite his enthusiasm for the new world of "total electric drama" was still a modernist in seeking "controls ...[over] all the sensory thresholds of our being" and in preferring the early twentieth-century modernist artists who created controlled, multiply-centred forms — Joyce, Pound, Eliot, Yeats, Dos Passos, and the cubist painters. While McLuhan has been extremely conservative in his literary tastes, and has largely ignored contemporary and Canadian writers, Mandel extended McLuhan's theories to literature, finding in Canada a new writing that wanders "inconsistently and incoherently amidst the fragments of personality and history, mixing space and time ...."

Modernism had begun early in the twentieth century in the call of Ezra Pound for an "austere direct" poetry, and in T.S. Eliot's proselytizing, by essay and example, of a poetry of rigourously disciplined rhetoric, mythic and historical reference, rigidly sculptural structure, and totally impersonal and unemotional tone. The modernist sought, at the urging of Eliot, to link his artistic vision inseparably with some alleged central line of history, tradition, and orthodoxy in Western culture. He scorned the emerging twentieth-century phenomena of centralizing machinery, utilitarian values, mass culture, commercial art forms, and 'democratic' taste.

In fiction, modernism expressed itself variously in the complex and overtly structured novels of Joyce and Ford Madox Ford, in the detached matter-of-fact prose of Hemingway, and more recently in the mythologically ordered novels of John Updike or Canada's Sheila Watson. In criticism it gave rise to the New Criticism, which sought to replace the subjectivity of Edwardian and Georgian impressionist criticism with detached, impersonal analyses of language, form, and structure. The New Critics — Eliot, I.A. Richards, William Empson, John Crowe Ransom, Allen Tate, Cleanth Brooks — viewed the work of literature as a static, aesthetic object; they were interested not in its content but in the formal relations within it. In their polemic utterances they stood with Eliot in arguing that the function of art was to impose "a credible order on reality, to bring us to a condition of stillness and reconciliation, and then leave us ...to proceed toward a region where that guide can avail us no longer".

Modernism was essentially an elitist, formalistic, anti-democratic, and anti-terrestrial movement. Ultimately, as in the above quotation, it looked toward the complete abandonment of the material and processual worlds for a Platonic one of pure form and spiritual essence. Its rejection of the contemporary and the popular became a wishful rejection of materiality, biology, and mortality. In Canada, modernism seldom achieved the controlled discontinuities of a Joyce or Eliot; instead it was first represented in the cool, classical lyrics of A.J.M. Smith and the epigrammatic political poetry of F.R. Scott. In the forties and fifties, in the symbolist poetry of Robert Finch, in the linguistic inventions of James Reaney, and the discursive philosophic poetry of Ralph Gustafson and Eli Mandel, modernism became the dominant mode.

The theories and philosophies of modernism, however, became untenable in the new electronic environment. In the post-modern world of counterpointing influences, centres, and traditions, the claim that a single tradition can be central or orthodox has become meaningless. When micro-electronic technology offers new hope of resisting the centralizing forces of mechanical technology, utter rejection of the twentieth century becomes a less attractive option. When the very diversity and looseness of contemporary structures invite commitment and participation, the values of detachment and impersonality fade. The classical artistic concept of the totally integrated whole has no incarnation in a sensory reality that is everywhere fragmented, discontinuous, post logical. Contemporary man becomes suspicious of both the fabricated multiplex over-structures of Joyce and Eliot and of the centralized ones of institutional authority; the message of his electronically amplified senses is that his culture and the universe are randomly interacting cooperatives continually evolving new relationships and forms.

The modernist collapse is evident throughout contemporary Canadian writing. The modernists — Smith, Finch, Dudek, Webb — who recoiled from the popular mechanical world of homogenous culture and looked toward a largely mythical world of stability, religious devotion, and artistic splendour, are here noisily succeeded by the post-modernists — Nichol, Coleman, Gilbert, Marlatt, Godfrey, Thomas, Matt Cohen — who are equally revolted by the monolithic power-structure of early twentieth-century technology but who see in its electronic offspring new means of asserting human variety and significance. The modernists sought to control both their world and their art; the post-modernists seek to participate in anarchic cooperation with the elements of an environment in which no one element fully controls any other. The modernist yearned to replace a Newtonian universe of mechanical certainty with a Ptolemaic one of medieval diversity; the post-modernist believes that the Newtonian has already been neutralized in the relativity theory of

Einstein. To a modernist — like Margaret Atwood in her role as critic — lack of control over reality causes one to be a *victim*; to a post-modernist — like Gerry Gilbert — lack of control merely makes one a *participant*, the normal and desirable human condition. In all his writing, the post-modernist consciously or unconsciously works to assist the electronic media in the decentralization of human power, whether literary, political, or economic, and to make its already achieved decentralizations and anarchies visible and comprehensible to his fellow man in the forms and processes of art.

Most of the new Canadian writing of the sixties and seventies has taken process, discontinuity, and organic shape as its values rather than the humanistic ideal of the "well-wrought urn". The writers' goal in such work has been no longer to retreat from the experiential world but to embody — and thus make intelligible to his readers — its rapidly increasing variety, fragmentation, non-linearity, and unpredictability. Literary post-modernism has come alive in Canada in the chant-poems of Bill Bissett, in the competing Einsteinian realities of Dave Godfrey's *The New Ancestors*, in the fluid, multiphasic linguistic structures of Daphne Marlatt, in the elusive language realms of bpNichol, in the shifting perspectives of Matt Cohen's fiction, in the ambiguous plot of Robert Kroetsch's *Gone Indian*, or in the paranoid visions of John Newlove's *Black Night Window* and Margaret Atwood's *The Animals in that Country*. The attempt at the complete statement or 'masterwork' is abandoned; Michael Ondaatje's *The Collected Works of Billy the Kid* is an overt collection of forgeries; bpNichol's *The True Eventual Story of Billy the Kid* is a direct statement of the subjectivity of all views of reality: "there is no true eventual story but this one. had he told it to me i would have written a different one. i could not write the true one had he told it to me."

Throughout such writing we see the triumph of particularity over philosophy. Bare images and stimuli take precedence over ideas. Like the electronic media themselves, post-modern Canadian writing is phenomenological in content, presenting the unprocessed, pre-reflective phenomena of perception rather than 'rational' reflections of the modernist writer. The post-modern artist does not believe that he can absorb, structure, organize, and discourse definitively on the universe. The unorganized perceptual worlds of Nelson Ball, Margaret Atwood, George Bowering, bpNichol, provide a kinetic and participation-inviting contrast to the thoroughly digested and cerebral meditations of modernist poets such as Louis Dudek (*Atlantis*) and Ralph Gustafson (*Rocky Mountain Poems*). In much of the work there is a movement toward the placing of pure noun in kinetic context: found documents in such work as Bowering's *George, Van-*

couver, John Robert Colombo's *The Great San Francisco Earthquake and Fire,* Michael Ondaatje's *The Collected Works of Billy the Kid,* and Rudy Wiebe's *The Temptations of Big Bear* are presented without qualifications so that they can find their own weight and force within the overall book/reader field.

In this particularistic, phenomenological kind of writing the old Canadian modernist controversy between the "mythy" poets and the "Tarzanistic" realists is resolved. The post-modern particularist finds mythology innate within his environment. In the work of Gwendolyn MacEwen, Bill Bissett, Victor Coleman, Frank Davey, Robert Kroetsch, Adele Wiseman, the recent work of Eli Mandel, mythology blooms out of the mundane but effervescent realities of the everyday life. With mythology suddenly alive and contemporary (rather than imposed and artifactual), much of the pessimism which characterized earlier Canadian writing vanishes. For MacEwen, Nichol, George Elliott, Coleman, Marlatt, Kroetsch, our world is difficult but intensely rewarding. Even among such bleak visionaries as Atwood, Newlove, and Graeme Gibson, there is a strong sense of perverse excitement in the face of ominous objects and events.

No one style dominates the new writing. The writers acknowledge no central authorities other than the authorities who announce the end of authority: McLuhan, Charles Olson, Jack Spicer, Alfred North Whitehead. Vast varieties of style co-exist not only within the total literary scene but within individual groups of writers. Bill Bissett's mystical chants and chaotic visual poems are edited by stylistically conservative Dennis Lee and Margaret Atwood. Michael Ondaatje, a deliberate, craftly poet, makes a film about bpNichol, an exponent of spontaneous natural utterance. A group of surrealists in the European tradition — J. Michael Yates, Michael Bullock, and Andreas Schroeder — practices and publishes in Vancouver. Older modernist poets — Finch, Dudek, Souster, Smith, Page, Glassco, Webb — receive continued critical and classroom attention. In fiction, Matt Cohen's abruptly surprising tales counterpoint with Hugh Hood's casual realism, with Robert Kroetsch's boisterous quests for death, with Audrey Thomas's detailed portraits of the suffering consciousness.

Not unexpectedly, the critical reception of this writing has been mixed. The new writers whose work is most similar to traditional forms — Nowlan, Acorn, Atwood, MacEwen, Lee, Kroetsch, Newlove — have been most quickly accepted. Many critics have continued to judge by the control and logic-oriented criteria of modernism. The less traditional critics — perhaps influenced by the thematic bias of Northrop Frye — have been extremely slow to realize that the technical experiments of Nichol, Coleman, Marlatt, and Matt Cohen are ultimately more revolutionary than the nationalism of Lee and Atwood.

The burgeoning of a great disorder of new literary and intermedia forms, under the stimulus of an electronically decentralized and retribalized culture, is not likely to stop with the publication of this book. Technology continues to alter man's ways of viewing and dealing with his world — and, of course, to threaten to destroy it. The microfiche card, which can carry an 84 page book at the production cost of one dollar, may within a few years restructure once again man's publication patterns and reading habits. Typesetting computers able to read typescripts are today beginning to reduce Canadian printing costs and thus increase the viability of small presses. Within the century — providing the century's disorders prove commensurate with human survival — private homes may have computer terminals capable of delivering print-outs of both up-to-date information and world literature. The arts could be increasingly strong in Canada in an age in which everywhere a man stands is potentially, through technology, the centre of the field of human culture.

Atwood, Margaret. *Survival.* Toronto: House of Anansi, 1972. An idiosyncratic overview of Canadian literature, mostly since 1940.

Bowering, George. *Curious.* Toronto: The Coach House Press, 1973. A day-book of meditations on Canadian and some U.S. writers.

————. "Poets in their Twenties," *Canadian Literature* 20 (Spring 1964), 54-64.

Colombo, John Robert. "The Little Magazine as a Member of Society," *Continuous Learning* 5 (January-February 1966), 13-22.

————, ed. *Poetry/Poesie* 64, ed. John Robert Colombo and Jacques Godbout. Toronto: Ryerson Press, 1963. An anthology of poets newly emerged in 1963, including Atwood, Bowering, Davey, Kearns, MacEwen.

Dudek, Louis. "The Little Magazine," in John Glassco, ed., *English Poetry in Quebec* (Montreal: McGill University Press, 1965), pp.59-64.

————. "Nationalism in Canadian Poetry," *Queen's Quarterly* 75 (Spring 1968), 555-567.

————. "Poetry in English," *Canadian Literature* 41 (Summer 1969), 111-120. This issue was reprinted as the *The Sixties* (Vancouver: University of British Columbia Press, 1972).

Dudek, Louis, and Michael Gnarowski, ed. *The Making of Modern Poetry in Canada.* Toronto: Ryerson Press, 1967. An anthology of theoretical and polemical statements by Canadian poets and their editors since 1910.

Francis, Wynne. "The Expanding Spectrum: Little Magazines," *Canadian Literature* 57 (Summer 1973), 6-17.
_____ . "Literary Underground: Little Magazines in Canada," *Canadian Literature* 34 (Autumn 1967), 63-70.
Fulford, Robert, Dave Godfrey, and Abraham Rotstein, ed. *Read Canadian: a Book About Canadian Books*. Toronto: James Lewis and Samuel, 1971.
Geddes, Gary, and Phyllis Bruce, ed. *15 Canadian Poets*. Toronto: Oxford University Press, 1970. An anthology containing work by Atwood, Avison, Birney, Bowering, Cohen, Coleman, Jones, Layton, MacEwen, Mandel, Newlove, Nowlan, Ondaatje, Purdy, and Souster, with notes and bibliographies.
Gervais, C.H. "Vancouver's *Tish* Movement," *Alive* 26, pp.31-35.
Godfrey, Dave. "The Canadian Publishers," *Canadian Literature* 57 (Summer 1973), 65-82.
Godfrey, Dave, and Stan Bevington. Small Presses: an Interview," *Canadian Forum* 47 (August 1967), 107-109.
Grant, George. *Lament for a Nation*. Toronto: McClelland & Stewart, 1965. A historical analysis which argues that Canada has missed its major chance to achieve cultural identity.
Inkster, Tim. "The Coach House Press," *Alive* 28, pp. 13-18.
Klinck, Carl F., ed. *Literary History of Canada*. Toronto: University of Toronto Press, 1965.
McCutcheon, Sarah. "Little Presses in Canada," *Canadian Literature* 57 (Summer 1973), 88-97.
MacLennan, Hugh. "Reflections on Two Decades," *Canadian Literature* 41 (Summer 1969), 28-39. A personal and somewhat sociological retrospective. This issue reprinted as *The Sixties* (University of British Columbia Press, 1972).
McLuhan, Marshall. *The Gutenberg Galaxy: The Making of Typographic Man*. Toronto: University of Toronto Press, 1962.
_____ . *The Mechanical Bride. Folklore of Industrial Man*. New York: Vanguard, 1951.
_____ . *The Medium is the Massage: an Inventory of Effects*, with Quentin Fiore. New York: Random House, 1967.
_____ . *Understanding Media: the Extensions of Man*. New York: McGraw-Hill, 1964.
MacSkimming, Roy. "Questions of Cash," *Canadian Literature* 57 (Summer 1973), 83-87. An essay on the financial problems of independent Canadian publishers.
Mandel, Eli. *Criticism: the Silent-speaking Words*. Toronto: CBC Publications, 1966.
_____ , ed. *Poets of Contemporary Canada*. Toronto: McClelland & Stewart, 1972. An anthology containing work by

Acorn, Atwood, Bissett, Bowering, Cohen, MacEwen, Newlove, Ondaatje, Purdy, Rosenblatt.

———, ed. *Poetry 62*, ed. Eli Mandel and Jean-Guy Pilon. Toronto: Ryerson Press, 1961. An anthology of poets who emerged in the
late 1950's, including Cohen, Colombo, Jones, Nowlan, and Reaney.

New, W.H. *Articulating West*. Toronto: New Press, 1972. Essays on
myth and structure in modern Canadian literature.

Nichol, bp, ed. *The Cosmic Chef: an Evening of Concrete*. Ottawa:
Oberon Press, 1970. An anthology of Canadian visual poetry.

Olson, Charles. *Human Universe and Other Essays*. New York: Grove
Press, 1967. Theoretical essays on 'open field' composition of poetry.

Ondaatje, Michael, ed. *The Broken Ark: a Book of Beasts*. Ottawa:
Oberon Press, 1971. An anthology of recent Canadian poetry about
the beasts within.

———. "Little Magazines, Small Presses, 1969, "*Arts/Canada* 26
(August 1969), 17-18.

Purdy, Al, ed. *Storm Warning*. Toronto: McClelland & Stewart, 1971.
An anthology of poets newly emerged in 1970, including Bissett, Lee,
McFadden, Marty, Suknaski, Wayman, and Zieroth.

Ringrose, Christpher Xerxes. "Fiddlehead's Energy," *Canadian
Literature* 52 (Spring 1972), 87-90. An article on one of Canada's
oldest small magazines.

Smith, A.J.M. "Canadian Literature: the First Ten Years," *Canadian
Literature* 41 (Summer 1969), 97-103. This issue was reprinted as *The
Sixties* (University of British Columbia Press, 1972).

Souster, Raymond, ed. *New Wave Canada*. Toronto: Contact Press,
1966. An anthology of poets newly emerged in 1965, including
Coleman, Gilbert, Hogg, McFadden, Marlatt, Nichol, Ondaatje, Wah.

Woodcock, George. *Anarchism: a History of Libertarian Ideas and
Movements*. Cleveland: Meridian Books, 1962.

———. *Canada and the Canadians*. London: Faber and Faber,
1970.

———, Comp. "New Wave in Publishing," *Canadian Literature* 57
(Summer 1973), 50-64.

———. *Odysseus Ever Returning: Essays on Canadian Writers
and Writing*. Toronto: McClelland & Stewart, 1970.

———. "A Swarming of Poets," *Canadian Literature* 50 (Autumn
1971), 3-16.

Woodsworth, Anne. "Underground or Alternative," *Canadian
Literature* 57 (Summer 1973), 29-34.

Milton Acorn

(1923-   )

Born in Prince Edward Island, and working as a carpenter there and in Quebec and Ontario until the late 1950's, Milton Acorn has kept to an emphatically working-class lifestyle despite his various literary successes. Throughout most of his public years he has had self-declared communist leanings, and in recent times has announced sympathies for Maoist ideology.

Both Acorn's life and poetry have been characterized by considerable defiance and turbulence. Acorn has been consistently individualistic, unwilling to submit to the disciplines of political parties, to the orthodoxies of Canadian politics, or to any theories of literary form. This individualism, however, has led his own beliefs to be more confused than unique. His political poems and essays are a collage of personal grievances, working-class superstitions, and second-hand ideas from American and Chinese socialist writers. In the 1970's Acorn has added Canadian nationalism to these materials. His few efforts at literary criticism have been based largely on misunderstandings of contemporary literary movements and a misconstruing of influences and relationships.

Acorn's poetry encompasses a range from brilliant to mediocre. His best works, and there are many in this group, present his personal experiences at work, in love, out of work, out of love, in vivid images organic to the poem's subjects. Acorn is a superb carpenter of words and objects; his accounts of mining accidents, tavern brawls, adolescent prostitution, even of a horse walking, show him able to craft the particulars of common life into disturbing and evocative poetry.

Greatly contrasting in effectiveness are Acorn's large number of polemic poems. Here is the colonialist side of Milton Acorn, which repeats in poetry the clichés of American left-wing sociologists and political scientists and borrows the declamatory rhetoric of Ferlinghetti and the early Allen Ginsberg. Based on inaccurate and borrowed generalizations rather than personal experience, these poems are much less convincing, even in their political aspects, than Acorn's other work. Unfortunately, Acorn prefers this strident kind of poetry, as his book titles — *In Love and Anger* (1956), *Against a League of Liars* (1960), *The Brain's the Target* (1960), *Jawbreakers* (1963), *I've Tasted My Blood* (1969), and *More Poems for People* (1972) — suggest. Recently he has styled himself "the people's poet" and claimed to be writing exclusively for the working man.

Acorn's insistence on the importance of his polemic verse has undoubtedly impaired the appreciation of his poetry. His lyrics, his portraits of workers, and his various experiential poems (most of which have an indirect 'political' meaning more powerful than that of his overtly political work) have been overlooked by teachers and anthologists distracted by the public image he has created. His criticism and public statements have alienated a number of anthologists and fellow writers. Acorn's sense of mission has given to much of his work a seriousness that borders on fanaticism. Consequently, even readers in search of poetry specifically about the worker's world have tended to prefer the humane and humourous work of Acorn's friend and editor Al Purdy. Acorn is one of Canada's contemporary poets whose reputation will undoubtedly be enhanced by future editing and scholarship.

Acorn, Milton. *In Love and Anger*. Privately Printed, 1957.

. *The Brain's the Target*. Toronto: Ryerson Press, 1960.

. "Open Letter to a Demi-Senior Poet," *Moment* 4 (September 1960), repr. in Louis Dudek and Michael Gnarowski, ed., *The Making of Modern Poetry in Canada* (Toronto: Ryerson Press, 1967), pp.287-289.

. *Against a League of Liars*. Toronto: Hawkshead Press, 1961.

. "I was a Communist for my own Damn Satisfaction," *Evidence* 5 (1962), 32-38.

. *Jawbreakers*. Toronto: Contact Press, 1963.

. "58 Poems by Milton Acorn," *Fiddlehead* 56 (Spring 1963), 1-39.

. *I've Tasted my Blood, Poems 1956-1968*, selected by Al Purdy. Toronto: Ryerson Press, 1969.

. *I Shout Love, and On Shaving off his Beard*. Toronto: Village Book Store Press, 1971.

. "The Business of this Country is Selling Out," *This Magazine Is About Schools* V:1 (Winter 1971), 139-158.

. *More Poems for People.* Toronto: NC Press, 1972.

AGP (Alan Pickersgill?). "More Poems for the Bourgeoisie," *Alive* 26 (1973), 24.

Bowering, George. "Acorn Blood," *Canadian Literature* 42 (Autumn 1969), 84-86.

. "A Singing Hydrant Doesn't Slum," *The Globe and Mail Magazine,* June 14, 1969, p.20.

Gnarowski, Michael. "Milton Acorn: a Review in Retrospect," *Culture* 25 (June 1964), 119-129.

Livesay, Dorothy. "Search for a Style: the Poetry of Milton Acorn," *Canadian Literature* 40 (Spring 1969), 33-42.

Purdy, Al. "Burly Shoulders Among the Metric Nuances: Variety Amid the Sameness," *The Globe and Mail,* Dec. 30, 1972, p.29.

. "A Man of Stances," *Evidence* 8 (1964), 120-124.

. "To Share the World or Despair of It," *The Globe and Mail Magazine,* May 2, 1970, p.16.

Margaret Atwood

(1939-   )

Following a nervous debut to Canadian poetry readers in the early 1960's as M.E. Atwood, Margaret Atwood has enjoyed a spectacular climb to the summit of Canadian letters. The period 1966 to 1973 in Canadian literature has to a great extent been dominated by her. This period begins with her winning of the Governor-General's Award for her second book of poetry, *The Circle Game* — chosen over books by such old guard writers as F.R. Scott, Earle Birney, Miriam Waddington, and Robert Finch — and ends with her adulation in newspapers across the country for her layman's guide to Canadian literature, *Survival*. During this time she has published five books of poetry, many of such popularity as to warrant multiple printings, and one of such renown as to be republished in the U.S.; she has published two novels, both of which have met with considerable commercial and critical success; she has served as Writer-in-Residence at University of Toronto's Massey College, as a senior editor with House of Anansi, and as an organizer of the union of Canadian fiction writers.

Margaret Atwood's poetry is her most accomplished and important work. Her novels are auxilliary to the poetry, working out its themes in more explicit terms for the wider fiction audience. Her criticism, particularly the guidebook *Survival*, provides a further level of simplification, reducing the poetry and novels to straightforward theoretical statements.

In Atwood's poetry it is the consciousness of the writer or her persona which is the most important element, not any "information" about the poem's purported topic — love, pioneer life, animals, etc. She communicates the sense of what it is like to live her life with its

Double Persephone by Margaret Atwood. Hawkshead Press, 1961. Her first book.

particular fears, obsessions, and paranoias. *The Circle Game* (1966) sets the Atwoodian world of imminent and ubiquitous danger — lakes, trees, billboards, suitcases, other people, are all ominous and invading. Surfaces and boundaries are treacherously unstable; "centres" are illusory — the only functional centres "travel with us unseen." The "circle game", the self-deception most people practice to convince themselves there is stability and order, is ultimately for

Atwood the most insidious aspect of this environment, since rather than threatening her life it threatens her psyche. Wanting everything to appear predictable and orderly, the circle gamesters would invade anyone's mind in order to reduce its irrationality and eccentricity to

Margaret Atwood

the closed circle of orthodoxy.

The Animals in that Country (1968) and *Procedures for Underground* (1970) amplify this conception of a shifting and hostile post-modern world in which desperate and deluded pattern-makers still attempt to force a permanent form. Again the dangers Atwood sees are from two sources — from the fickleness of nature and from the arrogating and fascistic urges of man. In these poems physical, personal, and temporal space is constantly changing; meanwhile man confidently builds fences, relationships, contracts, and histories in the belief that he can fix them. Such men, failing to recognize the true anarchic of Heraclitean form of the universe, consequently bring about their own alienation from nature.

The poems of *The Journals of Susanna Moodie* (1970) and *Power Politics* (1971) differ from those of the preceding in being related by a persona and in constituting single narratives. The first is a reading of what the responses of the pioneer writer Susanna Moodie to the Canadian wilderness might have been had they not been filtered through various nineteenth-century literary and social conventions. These poems envisage a Moodie very much like Atwood, who sees the forests and streams as threatening shapes, who feels remote from her husband and fellow settlers, but who, in addition, cannot help trying to impose some order on the green chaos she senses around her. The persona of *Power Politics* is a contemporary young woman involved in a mutually sadistic love affair. Here we see two of the arrogant exploiters of the previous books intent on treating each other like "helpless" pieces of real estate.

The overall thematic range of Atwood's poetry is not large. This range is not expanded in the novels *The Edible Woman* (1967) and *Surfacing* (1972) but is rather elaborated and simplified. Once again the two central issues are man's attitude to an unstable and treacherous universe and man's tendency to apply his manipulative and exploitive treatment of that universe to his fellow man. The narrator of *The Edible Woman* is a naive college graduate who works for a consumer research agency, itself an exploiter of humanity. She becomes engaged to a lawyer who represents not only the legal world of codified regulation but, by being a rabbit hunter, the sportsman's world of arrogating masculinity. The unnamed narrator of *Surfacing* is a cold, manipulative and repressed young woman who is searching in Quebec bushland for her missing father and, by extension, for the reason for her unfulfilling life. Both novels detail their narrator's attempts to break free of self-restricting habits of mind and of an exploiting society.

These two books show Atwood to be a novelist brilliant at the verbal level of dialogue and epigram but methodical in her handling

33

of characterization and structure. Both novels have the same narrative pattern: a young woman of growing manipulativeness and cynicism finds that her body is rebelling and alienating her from the rationalist friends who have been killing her spirit; this rebellion ultimately saves her. Both novels have the same cast of characters: a sensitive young woman with a high potential for body rebellion plus variously grasping minor characters who have sold their souls to fashion and consumerism. Both works are clearly 'thesis novels' in which depth of characterization and credibility of action have been sacrificed to make vividly clear the danger and profound unnaturalness of disembodied rationalism and human exploitation.

Survival, Atwood's popular thematic guide to Canadian literature, has been useful in provoking interest in Canadian writing, but is of limited use to educators. The themes Atwood finds to dominate the literature — victimization and survival — are two main themes of her own work, and have been in no way as important to other Canadian writers. The case Atwood makes for their centrality to the literature is based on a very small portion of Canadian writing, largely books written in the last thirty years and, to a considerable extent, books published by Atwood's press, House of Anansi, which was founded in 1967. In looking for these themes, Atwood is often forced to use lesser writers — Graeme Gibson, Hugh Garner, Scott Symons — to document her case, and to ignore such accomplished ones as Robertson Davies, Hugh Hood, Henry Kreisel, bpNichol, Dorothy Livesay, and Robert Kroetsch.

Atwood, Margaret.   *Double Persephone.* Toronto: Hawkshead Press, 1961.

—. "War in the Bathroom" (story), *Alphabet* 8 (June 1964), 63-72.

—. "Superwoman Drawn and Quartered: the Early Forms of She," *Alphabet* 10 (July 1965), 65-82.

—. *The Circle Game.* Toronto: Contact Press, 1966.

—. *The Animals in that Country.* Toronto: Oxford University Press, 1968.

—. *The Edible Woman.* Toronto: McClelland & Stewart, 1969.

—. *The Journals of Susanna Moodie.* Toronto: Oxford University Press, 1970.

—. *Procedures for Underground.* Toronto: Oxford University Press, 1970.

—. "Polarities" (story), *Tamarack Review* 58 (winter 1971), 3-25.

—. *Power Politics.* Toronto: House of Anansi, 1971.

. "The Grave of the Famous Poet," in David Helwig and Joan Harcourt, ed. 72: New Canadian Stories (Ottawa: Oberon Press, 1972). pp.122-133.
. Surfacing. Toronto: McClelland & Stewart, 1972.
. Survival. Toronto: House of Anansi, 1972.
."Encounters with the Element Man," in Matt Cohen, ed., The Story So Far 2 (Toronto: The Coach House Press, 1973), pp.9-16.
. "Surviving the Critics," This Magazine VIII:1 (May-June 1973), 29-32.
. "Travels Back," Macleans 86 (January 1973), 28-31, 48.

Ayre, J. "Margaret Atwood and the End of Colonialism," Saturday Night 87 (November 1972), 23-26.
Bowering, George. "Get Used to It," Canadian Literature 52 (Spring 1972), 91-92.
Clery, Val. "A Plea for Victims," Books in Canada I:12 (November-December 1972), 45-46.
Cohen, Arnette. "Superably this side of Important" (rev. of The Edible Woman), The Globe and Mail Magazine, Oct. 11, 1969, p.18.
Davey, Frank. "Atwood Walking Backwards," Open Letter (second series) 5, Summer 1973, pp.74-84.
French, William. "Exhilarating: an All-Purpose Novel" (rev. of Surfacing), The Globe and Mail, Sept. 16, 1972, p.30.
. "Icon and Target: Atwood as Thing," The Globe and Mail, April 7, 1973, p.28.
Fulford, Robert. "A Clever and Effective Analysis of the Literature of Canada" (rev. of Survival), The Toronto Star, Nov. 4, 1972, p.79.
Geddes, Gary. "Poets in Residence" (rev. of Procedures for Underground), The Globe and Mail Magazine, Oct. 10, 1970, p.20.
Gibson, Graeme. Interview with Margaret Atwood, in his Eleven Canadian Novelists (Toronto: House of Anansi, 1973), pp.5-31.
Grosskurth, Phyllis. "Truth — and a Major Talent" (rev. of Survival), The Globe and Mail, Oct. 28, 1972, p.33.
. "Victimization or Survival," Canadian Literature 55 (Winter 1973), 108-110.
Gutteridge, Don. Review of Survival, Canadian Forum 53 (May 1973), 39-41.
Jackson, Marni. "A Poet and the Membrane of Mystery" (rev. of Procedures for Underground), The Toronto Star, Aug. 22, 1970, p.45.
Jonas, George. "A Choice of Predators," Tamarack Review 54 (Summer 1970), 75-77.
Mandel, Eli. "The Poet as Animal — of Sorts" (rev. of The Animals in that Country), The Globe and Mail Magazine, Oct. 12, 1968, p.17.
. Review of Double Persephone, Alphabet 4 (June 1962), 69-70.

Mathews, Robin. "Survival and Struggle in Canadian Literature," *This Magazine is About Schools* VI:4 (Winter 1972), 109-124.

McDonald, Marci. "A New Literary Star Emerges in Canadian Letters," *The Toronto Star,* Oct. 21, 1972, p.77.

Nichol, bp. "A Review," *Open Letter* (second series) 5, Summer 1973, pp.69-70.

Ondaatje, Michael. Review of *The Circle Game, Canadian Forum* 47 (April 1967), 22-23.

Pearson, Alan. "The Poetry of Margaret Atwood," *The Montreal Star,* Nov. 2, 1968, "Entertainments," p.8.

Purdy, A.W. "Atwood's Moodie," *Canadian Literature* 47 (Winter 1971), 80-84.

———. "Poet Beseiged," *Canadian Literature* 39 (winter 1969), 94-96.

Skelton, Robin. Review of *Procedures for Underground* and *The Journals of Susanna Moodie, The Malahat Review* 17 (January 1971), 133-134.

Stevens, Peter. "Deep Freezing a Love's Continual Small Atrocities" (rev. of *Power Politics*), *The Globe and Mail Magazine,* Apr. 24, 1971, p.16.

Webb, Phyllis. "Letters to Margaret Atwood," *Open Letter* (second series) 5, Summer 1973, pp.71-73.

Woodcock, George. "Are We All Emotional Cannibals?" (rev. of *The Edible Woman*), *The Toronto Star,* Sept. 13, 1969, p.13.

———. "Margaret Atwood," *The Literary Half-Yearly* XII:2, 233-242.

———. "The Symbolic Cannibals, " *Canadian Literature* 42 (Autumn 1969), 98-100.

Margaret Avison

(1918-   )

Although numerous poems by Margaret Avison appeared between 1943 and 1959 in poetry magazines and anthologies, not until 1960 did she publish a book-length collection. This work, *The Winter Sun* showed her to be a highly intellectual and deliberate writer.

The syntax of these poems is complex and extended, and their vocabulary intensely formal. Their allusions to mythology can be both obscure in substance and yet essential for even a superficial understanding of the the poem. Unlike much Canadian poetry of the 1960's, this work assumes that the pleasures of poetry are ones derived through analysis and reflection by a sophisticated, semi-scholarly reader. The affinities of this poetry are with the patterned, modernist work of A.J.M. Smith and Jay Macpherson.

Such stylistic conservatism is entirely congruent with the content of the poems of *The Winter Sun*. Most of them are poems of despair: despair about western humanism and its offspring — industrial urbanism in society and modernism in art — and despair about God's apparent withdrawal from the contemporary world. Men are seen as forced to rely wholly on their deficient intelligence. The savage Canadian winter becomes a major image here for both the frigid and sterile ethos of industrial economics and for the extreme remoteness of God's potentially warming love. God's presence is only a northern "winter sun", providing dim light without heat, faint hope without comfort and love.

Other imagery in *The Winter Sun* implies the fall of man from various states of grace. Rural peace has yielded to urban confusion. The reassuring Ptolemaic worldview has given way to the devastating relativism of the Copernican. Hope for salvation through

second series
: RESPONSE

featuring—

MARGARET
AVISON

JANUARY
1962

The 'Margaret Avison' issue of *Origin*, ed. Cid Corman, Kyoto, 1962.

Christ has given way to a resignation that the "Promised Land" is unattainable and that the only meaningful options for man are suicide or immersion in trivia ("The Mirrored Man"). Shadowing all the poems is the original Fall of Man which has so removed this world from God that he can be only a distant symbolic light ("The Fallen, Fallen World").

Miss Avison's prognosis for this condition is not overwhelmingly optimistic. She sees some hope in the suburbanite's misguided quest for a semi-rural life away form the inner city ("The World Still Needs"), and more hope in the apparent power of the cosmos to cancel the urban desecrations of man ("Prelude"). She proclaims, however, a need for man to be willing to take risks to escape a life of repetition and mediocrity ("The Swimmer's Moment"). The artist's role would appear to be essential to Avison here in showing us the way to "unbox ourselves" by "putting aside mudcakes, / the buying, selling, trucking .../ daring to gambol" so that there may be "an immense answering / of human skies" ("Intra-political").

The Dumbfounding (1966), Avison's second book, is as different from *The Winter Sun* as is the New Testament from the Old. The emphasis on original sin and on the remoteness of God is replaced by a fervent belief in His generosity and immanence. Toward her fellow man, Miss Avison herself is forgiving; instead of condemning the sordidness of the modern city, she here excuses it as being merely a manifestation of man's pathetic and mistaken attempts to participate in cosmic process. Even aircraft can suggest to her "a new leaf [that] is metal, torn out of that blue afloat in the dayshine" ("Black — White Under Green").

In *The Dumbfounding,* God's light has abandoned winter and, through Christ, "throbs" with "rivering fire". Man is no longer alienated, but clumsily participating. Avison's style has undergone a corresponding change. It is no longer synthetic and deliberate, but now moves in natural rhythms, colloquial syntax, and less formal diction. This relaxation in style gives to the poems a sense of emotional spontaneity that was entirely lacking in the calculated measures of the first book. Devotional poems such as "The Wood" and "The Dumbfounding" benefit particularly from this change since most of their force rests in the sincerity of testimony which they convey. In theological terms, Avison's stylistic shift is entirely consistent with a movement from a god-remote world, in which the individual must depend on the artificial forms fabricated by his intellect, to a world of immanent spirituality in which the artist can trust in forms available through divinely-guided instincts.

In recent poems Miss Avison has continued this kind of work in which the naturalness or authenticity of expression is a major ingredient — a naturalness which is antithetical to the sculptural, intellectual style in which she began but in keeping with a belief in an immanent divinity. Critics have associated her with United States post-modern exponents of organic form — Louis Zukofsky, Charles Olson, Robert Duncan, Robert Creeley, and Denise Levertov. It should be noted, however, that Margaret Avison's achievement is largely parallel to that of these poets, and certainly highly individual.

Avison, Margaret.   *The Winter Sun*. Toronto: University of Toronto Press, 1960.
        . 13 Poems; letter to Cid Corman. *Origin* (second series) 4, January 1962, pp.1-21.
        . *The Dumbfounding*. New York: Norton, 1966.

Bowering, George.   "Avison's Imitation of Christ the Artist," *Canadian Literature* 54 (Autumn 1972), 56-69.
House, Vernal.   "A Bow to Margaret Avison" (rev. of *The Winter Sun*), *The Globe and Mail,* July 30, 1960, "Review of Books" p.9.
Jones, Lawrence M.   "A Core of Brilliance, Margaret Avison's Achievement," *Canadian Literature* 38 (Autumn 1968), 50-57.
MacCallum, Hugh.   "Myth, Wit and Pop in Poems" (rev. of *The Dumbfounding*), *The Globe and Mail Magazine,* Jan . 7, 1967, p.13.
New, W.H.   "The Mind's Eyes (I's) (Ice): The Poetry of Margaret Avison," in his *Articulating West* (Toronto: New Press, 1972), pp.234-258.
Redekop, E.   *Margaret Avison*. Toronto: Copp Clark, 1971.
        . "The Only Political Duty: Margaret Avison's Translations of Hungarian Poems," *The Literary Half-Yearly* XIII:2, 157-170.
Smith, A.J.M.   "Critical Improvisations on Margaret Avison's 'Winter Sun'," *Tamarack Review* 18 (Winter 1961), 81-86.
        . "Margaret Avison's New Book," *Canadian Forum* 46 (September 1966), 132-134.
Wilson, Milton.   "The Poetry of Margaret Avison," *Canadian Literature* 2 (Autumn 1959), 47-58, repr. in George Woodcock, ed., *A Choice of Critics* (Toronto: Oxford University Press, 1966), pp.221-232.

Nelson Ball

(1942-   )

The unique contribution of Nelson Ball to contemporary Canadian poetry has been almost totally neglected. Ball is a poet of the minimal image; his poems, like the haiku, aim to combine the utmost economy with the sharpest possible visual clarity. They are brief, understated, and — on close scrutiny — explosive. They can also appear on superficial examination to be simplistic and trivial, and have consequently been dismissed or ignored amid the flood of new poetry experienced by Canda's critics during the last few years. Ball has published eight collections of poetry since 1966.

Ball is exclusively a poet of sensory perception; his subject is the phenomenal world — its patterns, textures, colours, spaces, noises, motions, interrelationships, and human gestures. The scale of work is consistently minute. Short poems composed of extremely short lines present tiny motions and subtle changes which humanity habitually overlooks or dismisses as insignificant — much the way Canadian criticism has regarded Ball's poems. Some poems attempt to deal with negative space — an old chair that is slowly being worn into air — or with negative light — snow so bright that one cannot perceive it.

Fundamental to Ball's poetry is an assumption that the smallest and most easily forgotten details can enshrine the deepest significances of the events in which they participate. In this view the cosmic lurks within the mundane, the epic within the minuscule, and wait only for the deft pen of the poet to release them. His poem "Epic" is composed of only eight one-syllable lines ("A / bird / eats / seeds / be- / neath / tall / grass") and manages successfully to convey the immense cosmic power which that fragile bird and its activity

41

represents and symbolizes.

number 10

Weed, ed. Nelson Ball, Kitchener, 1966-67

Many of Ball's poems have what he terms a "point of attention" at which its meaning becomes clear. Invariably this point involves a sensory image — the sound of glass breaking, the click of a door's lock. There is usually a force active here, a force which is primary to events much larger than those directly confronted in the poem. In one of Ball's poems, for example, the spinning wheel of an overturned and smashed car is made to testify to the power and brutality of the (undescribed) fatal collision which has just occurred. Others of Ball's poems centre on an insistence that the properties of an object have a significance quite apart form any possibility of human use.   Here the reader is encouraged to surrender any utilitarian attitudes to actuality, and even to believe that an object's properties most irrelevant to man can nevertheless be its most important.

42

In all of his work Ball withholds indications of his personal feelings in order to let small or easliy overlooked facts speak with their own power. In this and its other properties, his poetry is the only authentic descendant of that other stubborn and neglected Canadian imagist, W.W.E. Ross.

Nelson Ball has also been active as an editor and publisher, being founder of both *Weed* magazine and Weed/Flower Press. The latter has published books by the best new writers of the sixties, including George Bowering, Victor Coleman, bpNichol, John Robert Colombo, David McFadden, Gerry Gilbert, and John Newlove. The best examples of Nelson Ball's poetry can be found in *Beaufort's Scale* (1967) and *The Pre-Linguistic Heights* (1970).

Ball, Nelson.　*A Room of Clocks,* poems 1964-65. Kitchener, Ont.: Weed/Flower Press, 1965.

. *Beaufort's Scale.* Kitchener, Ont.: Weed/Flower Press, 1967.

. *Sparrows.* Toronto: Weed/Flower Press, 1968.

. *Force Movements 1966/69.* Toronto: Ganglia, 1969.

. *Waterpipes and Moonlight.* Toronto: Weed/Flower Press, 1969.

. *Points of Attention.* Toronto: Weed/Flower Press, 1971.

. *The Pre-Linguistic Heights.* Toronto: The Coach House Press, 1971.

. *Round Stone.* Toronto: Weed/Flower Press, 1972.

. *Dry Spell.* Toronto: Seripress, 1973.

. *Our Arms are Fetherless Wings.* Toronto: Seripress, 1973.

Barbour, Douglas.　"The Young Poets and Their Little Presses," *Dalhousie Review* L:1 (Spring 1969), p.116.

Fetherling, Doug.　Review of *Sparrows, The Canadian Forum* 49 (May 1969), 77.

Robinson, Brad.　Review of *Force Movements* and *Water Pipes and Moonlight, The Five Cent Review,* October, 1969.

Stevens, Peter.　Review of *Beaufort's Scale, The Canadian Forum* 48 (November 1968), 187.

Earle Birney

(1904-   )

Although Earle Birney began writing poetry in the late 1930's and won Governor-General's Awards for books published in 1942 and 1945, it is his work of the sixties and seventies that has had influence on his fellow writers. The reasons for this are numerous. One is that Birney was only a part-time poet before his retirement from the University of B.C. in 1965; most of his energy went to his teaching and to academic pursuits such as his editing of the manuscripts of the English novelist Malcolm Lowry. Another is that Birney's early poetry was stylistically conservative and offered little aid or leadership to other poets. Still another is Birney's participation in the popular causes and moods of each period. In the 1930's he was a Marxist and Trotskyist; in the Second World War a loyal volunteer to the Canadian army; in the politically and culturally stagnant late forties and fifties he was an academic Jack-of-all-trades, writing scholarly articles, popular articles, novels, and poems and editing manuscripts; in the Pearson years of Canadian internationalism he became a world traveller. Only in the middle sixties, when Canadian literary nationalism began to flourish, did Birney grow his now characteristic white beard and devote himself to the avant-garde of Canadian writing.

Birney was free to become an experimental poet late in life because he had never developed an idiosyncratic poetic. He has been a constant reviser both of individual poems and of his writing style. His early work shows formal borrowings from modernists such as Auden, Spender, and (in the case of "David") Archibald Macleish. His poems of the early sixties show influence by post-modernist American writers of free and projective verse. Much of his very recent

44

work (*Rag and Bone Shop,* 1970, and *What's So Big about Green,* 1973) participates in the international concrete poetry movement, which began in Europe in the 1950's. It is here that Birney expands most significantly poetry's technical resources.

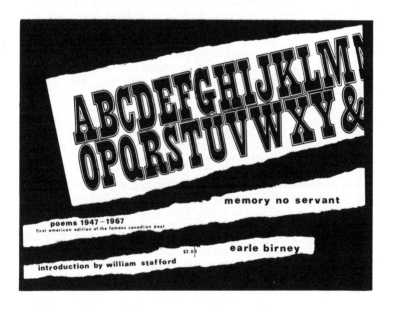

Memory No Servant by Earle Birney, New Books, 1968.

Throughout his career Birney has slowly moved from an adjective-dominated style (e.g. "Vancouver Lights") to a noun-dominated one ("The Mammoth Corridors"). This move has been related to another general shift in Birney from an argumentative thesis-oriented political poet, dependent on adjectives, to an apolitical, observing, and accepting one, reliant on facts and nouns. In general, his concerns have shifted between 1940 and 1970 from arguing what could be to celebrating what is. His worldview has moved from one of a potentially orderly man-centred universe to a post-modern one of fragmentary, colossally energetic, cosmic process uncaring of human life. His current interest in concrete poetry involves him in a poetry of random relationship and pure noun.

The most frequently taught Birney poem is still "David", first published in 1941. Weak in characterization but incredibly beautiful in its language and imagery, "David" is — despite its title — the story of its narrator Bobby, whose fall from a sentimental view of nature is precipitated by the fatal fall of David, his realistic companion and teacher, from a mountain peak they have climbed together. His travel poems, particularly those written in approximations of dialect, have also been extremely popular with Canadian educators. Free of the excessive didactism which marred Birney's early lyrics, these poems present in precise and exuberant language a delightfully positive attitude towards the riches of the trivial, mundane, and pathetic areas of human experience. Less well known, but equally deserving of classroom attention, are a number of recent and so far unanthologized narrative poems. "Charite, Esperance, et Foi" will undoubtedly become a classic of Canadian ironic verse. "Down Mammoth Corridors" is not only one of Birney's most interesting non-concrete formal experiments, but contains the most mature and satisfying view of man's relation to the cosmos that Birney has yet achieved.

Birney's prose is much less interesting than his poetry, and may ultimately be most important for having been one of the things which delayed his full commitment to poetry. *Turvey* (1949) is a comic war novel, much too long for the amount of humour and satire it possesses. *Down the Long Table* (1955), Birney's second novel, is a competent 1930's documentary which loses credibility in its last pages when Birney attempts to transform the central character from a weak into a strong man. *The Creative Writer* (1966) is a glib and condescending work of radio journalism in which Birney attempts a 'just folks' account of the writing life. His most recent prose publication, *The Cow Jumped over the Moon* (1972), is his best. This is an account of the writing of eleven of his poems, including "David". Birney has rarely been satisfied by the appraisals and interpretations of his critics; this book is filled not only with illuminating details about his approach to writing but with his own readings of many of his poems. Earle Birney is currently working on his autobiography, which one might reasonably expect to be a similarly entertaining and contentious book — one which assails his critics and argues his personal interpretations of his life and work.

Birney, Earle. *David and Other Poems.* Toronto: Ryerson Press, 1942.
    . *Now Is Time.* Toronto: Ryerson Press, 1945.
    . *The Strait of Anian.* Toronto: Ryerson Press, 1948.
    .*Turvey.* Toronto: McClelland & Stewart, 1949.
    . *Trial of a City and Other Verse.* Toronto: Ryerson Press, 1952.
    . *Down the Long Table.* Toronto: McClelland & Stewart, 1955.
    . *Ice Cod Bell or Stone.* Toronto: McClelland & Stewart, 1962.
    , ed. *Selected Poems of Malcolm Lowry.* San Francisco: City Lights, 1962.
    . *Near False Creek Mouth.* Toronto: McClelland & Stewart, 1964.
    . *The Creative Writer.* Toronto: CBC Publications, 1966.
    . *Selected Poems, 1940-1966.* Toronto: McClelland & Stewart, 1966.
    , ed. *Lunar Caustic,* by Malcolm Lowry. Joint editor with Margerie Lowry. London: Cape, 1968.
    . *Memory No Servant.* Trumansburg, N.Y.: New Books, 1968.
    . *Pnomes Jukollages and other Stunzas (Gronk* 3, series 4), Toronto, 1969.
    . *The Poems of Earle Birney.* Toronto: McClelland & Stewart, 1969. New Canadian Library Original no. 6.
    . *Rag and Bone Shop.* Toronto: McClelland & Stewart, 1971.
    . *Four Parts Sand,* with Bill Bissett, Judith Copithorne, and Andrew Suknaski. Ottawa: Oberon Press, 1972.
    . *The Cow Jumped Over the Moon:* the writing and reading of poetry. Toronto: Holt, Rinehart and Winston, 1972.
    . *What's So Big About Green.* Toronto: McClelland & Stewart, 1973.

Beattie, Munro. "Poetry (1935-1950)," in Carl F. Klinck, ed., *Literary History of Canada* (Toronto: University of Toronto Press, 1965), pp.761-765.
Colombo, John Robert. "Poetic Ambassador," *Canadian Literature* 24 (Spring 1965), 55-59.
Davey, Frank. *Earle Birney.* Toronto: Copp Clark, 1971.
Deacon, William Arthur. "Canadian Poet in Wartime" (rev of *David*), *The Globe and Mail,* Nov. 7, 1942, "Review of Books" p.10.
    . "Poet Judges Modern Man" (rev. of *Trial of a City*), *The*

Globe and Mail, Oct. 11, 1952, "Review of Books" p.23.

Fredeman, W.E.   "Earle Birney: Poet," *The British Columbia Library Quarterly* XXIII (1960), 8-15.

Geddes, Gary.   "A Passion Thrives Unsated" (rev. of *What's So Big About Green*), *The Globe and Mail,* Dec. 8, 1973. p.35.

O'Broin, Padraig.   "Birney Brings Cool Pity" (rev. of *Ice, Cod, Bell or Stone*), *The Globe and Mail,* June 2, 1962, "Review of Books" p.19.

New, W.H.   "Maker of Order, Prisoner of Dreams: The Poetry of Earle Birney," in his *Articulating West* (Toronto: New Press, 1972), pp.259-269.

Noel-Bentley, Peter C. and Earle Birney.   "Earle Birney: a Bibliography in Progression 1923-1969," *West Coast Review* V:2 (October 1970), 45-53.

Pacey, Desmond.   *Creative Writing in Canada.* Toronto: Ryerson Press, 1961, pp.150-153.

———. *Ten Canadian Poets.* Toronto: Ryerson Press, 1958, pp.293-326.

Robillard, Richard H.   *Earle Birney.* Toronto: McClelland & Stewart, 1971.

Smith, A.J.M.   "A Unified Personality," *Canadian Literature* 30 (Autumn 1966), 2-13.

Stevens, Peter.   "Offhand Dribbles or Wisdom's Joy?" (rev. of *Rag and Bone Shop*), *The Globe and Mail Magazine,* Jan. 23, 1971, p.7.

Waddington, Miriam.   "Poetry of a Frontier World" (rev. of *Selected Poems 1940-1966*), *The Globe and Mail Magazine,* May 21, 1966, p.13.

Watt, F.W.   "Barnstorming Poets Create in Solitude" (rev. of *Near False Creek Mouth*), *Globe and Mail Magazine, Dec. 19, 1964, p.20.*

Weaver, Robert.   "A Big Strong Book" (rev. of *Selected Poems 1940-1966*), *The Toronto Star,* June 4, 1966, p.17.

West, Paul.   "Earle Birney and the Compound Ghost," *Canadian Literature* 13 (Summer 1962), 5-14.

Wilson, Milton.   "Poet Without a Muse," *Canadian Literature* 30 (Autumn 1966), 14-20.

Woodcock, George.   "Two Looks at Birney," in his *Odysseus Ever Returning* (Toronto: McClelland & Stewart, 1970, New Canadian Library no. 71), pp.118-127.

Bill Bissett

(1939-)

For the past fifteen years Vancouver has contained the largest and most cohesive left-wing artistic subculture in Canada. Throughout all of these years Bill Bissett has been one of its most outspoken and iconoclastic poets. Bissett's rejection of the conventional or "straight" world has been vigourous — expressed not only in lifestyle but in ruthless alterations to conventional syntax and spelling. His contempt for orthodox society has caused him to be ejected from cross-Canada trains, evicted by countless landlords, beaten, harrassed by police, and arrested and sentenced to prison. His contempt for the orthodoxies of the printed word caused him for at least a decade to be regarded by the bourgeois world of literary criticism as little more than a wild man or a freak.

Bissett published more than fifteen books in the sixties, and so far in the seventies has published ten more. His first significant recognition outside of the underground literary world in which he works and lives, however, was the publication in 1972 by the House of Anansi Press of a selected Bissett, *Nobody Owns th Earth*. This was followed quickly by his inclusion in Eli Mandel's certifying anthology, *Poets of Contemporary Canada* (1972). Neither book, however, recognizes Bissett on his own anarchic terms. The Anansi selected poems, edited by Margaret Atwood and Dennis Lee, is a "Bissett methodized" — Bissett represented by his most tractable and accessible material. Much of the flavour of a real Bissett publication — that created by his use of smudged and broken typefaces, varying page sizes, one-of-a-kind crayon sketches and collages, and consciously obscure or sentimental material — is absent.

49

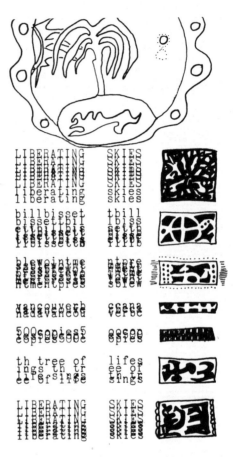

Liberating Skies by Bill Bissett. Blewointmentpress, 1969.

Bissett has been a one-man literary happening, almost impossible to contain in a single book. He is an exciting sound poet — particularly in his chants based on west coast Indian material; this part of his work can be sampled through his record *Awake in th Red Desert*. He is an innovator in concrete or visual poetry. His most interesting work here has been his use of the dimensions of the page as a principal element, and his occasional transformation of the page into a single alphabetic and orthographic tapestry. Bissett is also an accomplished graphic artist, with a recognizably unique style in both collage and pen-and-ink sketching. In addition, he has been an important west coast editor, working through his cavalierly named Blew Ointment Press and *Blew Ointment* magazine to preserve and advance the careers of numerous Vancouver writers including Judith Copithorne, Maxine Gadd, Gerry Gilbert, and Bertrand Lachance. In all of these activities, as well as in his day-to-day life, he has been politically active, attempting to disturb the complacent, enrage the dogmatic, and obstruct the mechanical and the unjust whether in literature or in the streets.

Informing all of Bissett's action has been a mystical and religious view of the world. Behind our own unreliable world of death, war, and persecution, Bissett sees a transcendent and immutable one in which pure joy, energy, and spontaneous form exclude the petty boundaries and restrictions of our philistine and puritanical culture. More Blakean than Emersonian, this other world of "th endless sun, the rose in th forhead", can become visible to us during incantation, prayer, or dream. At moments of extreme intensity — drug experience, sexual orgasm — a person can enter completely into this world of eternal condition. Many of Bissett's poems celebrate physical love in which the body becomes a "tempul burning" and opens the way to complete escape from materiality and temporality. Many other poems are religious chants — "holy day is due holy / day is due ..." — ostensibly designed to induce mystic feeling.

Because of the Platonic overtones of these poems, their diction superficially appears extremely limited. The dominant part of speech is the noun; most nouns are from a narrow elemental range — *tree, earth, fire, wind, water, sky, sun, moon, blood, heart* (in some books by Bissett such a list would comprise 80% of the nouns). They are nearly always unmodified. But these limitations are deliberately chosen by Bissett in his attempt to write of an unqualified, elemental, and pure visionary world — a world distinct from ours in its lack of categories, pluralities, divergencies, in its consisting only of elemental substance. Bissett's idiosyncratic quasi-phonetic spelling — *yu* for *you, th* for *the, tempul* for *temple* — is both a similar kind of simplification and a symbolic act of social rebellion. It is meant to indicate a sensibility that prefers cosmic clarity to the vagaries and stupidities of earthly convention, and is successful in doing this. To Bissett, the rules of grammar, church, academy, and state are all equally pernicious conspiracies to imprison the human spirit.

A major part of Bissett's work is his poetry of political and social castigation. This poetry is more accessible to the conventionally pragmatic reader than is the mystical verse, but most clearly has its origin in Bissett's mystic vision. The poet who yearns for heaven lives in hell — a hell not only of corporeality and plurality but of human deceit, brutality, exploitation, and petty distinction, a hell in which the poet must cynically inquire "were yu normal today did yu screw society". In these poems Bissett presents himself persecuted by police narcotic squads, incarcerated in a provincial prison, or mortally endangered by power-hungry doctors, psychiatrists, and

Bill Bissett

bureaucrats. All of such poems have the rare quality in contemporary poetry of total authenticity. Bissett is no detached middle-class social critic; he has lived and continues to live on the streets of hell, and has the artistic power to convey this experience in its fullness to the reader.

The two sides to Bissett's poetry cannot be fully understood in separation. One is the mystic's hope, the other is his horror at what still surrounds him. Together they make him one of the major voices in new Canadian writing. Despite the slowness of his recognition, it is clear that of all the new poets of the past two decades Bissett is definitely one of the most stubbornly and self-confidently unique talents. Although the idea must be repugnant to him, he has already assured himself an important place in Canada's literary history.

Bissett, Bill.   *Th Jinx Ship nd Othr Trips.* Vancouver: Very Stone House, 1966.
        . *We Sleep Inside Each Other All.* Toronto: Ganglia Press, 1966.
        . *Th Gossamer Bedpan.* Vancouver: Blewointment Press, 1967.
        . *Lebanon Voices.* Toronto: Weed/Flower Press, 1967.
        . *What Poetiks.* Vancouver: Blewointment Press, 1967.
        . *Where is Miss Florence Riddle.* Toronto: Fleye Press, 1967.
        . *Awake in th Red Desert* (book and stereo long-play record). Vancouver: Talonbooks and See/Hear Productions, 1968.
        . *Of th Land Divine Service.* Toronto: Weed/Flower Press, 1968.
        . *Liberating Skies.* Vancouver: Blewointment Press, 1969.
        . *Lost Angel Mining Company.* Vancouver: Blewointment Press, 1969.
        . *Sunday Work?* Vancouver: Blewointment Press, 1969.
        . *S th Story I to.* Vancouver: Blewointment Press, 1970.
        . *Blew Trewz.* Vancouver: Blewointment Press, 1971.
        . "Th Coor of Me Eyeees" and other poems, comprising all of *Air* 6 (Vancouver, 1971).
        . *Dragonfly.* Toronto: Weed/Flower Press, 1971.
        . *Drifting into War.* Vancouver: Talonbooks, 1971.
        . *I.B.M.* Vancouver: Blewointment Press, (1971?).
        . *Nobody Owns th Earth.* Toronto: House of Anansi, 1971.
        . *Rush.* Toronto: Gronk and Vancouver: Blewointment Press, 1971.
        . *Tuff Shit: Love Pomes.* Windsor: Bandit/Black Moss Press, 1971.

. *Four Parts Sand,* with Earle Birney, Judith Copithorne, and Andrew Suknaski. Ottawa: Oberon Press, 1972.

. *Th High Green Hill.* Vancouver: Blewointment Press, 1972.

. *Polar Bear Hunt.* Vancouver: Blewointment Press, 1972.

. *Pomes for Yoshi.* Vancouver: Blewointment Press, 1972.

. *Words in th Fire.* Vancouver: Blewointment Press, 1972.

. "Is it very Pig uv Writrs to Write abt othr Writrs," *Open Letter* (second series) 6, Fall 1973.

. *Pass th Food, Release th Spirit Book.* Vancouver: Talonbooks, 1973.

. *Th First Sufi Line.* Vancouver:Blewointment Press, 1973.

. *Air 10-11-12.* Vancouver: Air, 1973.

. *Living with th Vishyun.* Vancouver: New Star Books, 1974.

Barbour, Doug. "The young Poets and the Little Presses, 1969," *Dalhousie Review* 50 (Spring 1970), 116.

Davey, Frank. Review of *Nobody Owns th Earth, Canadian Forum* 52 (July-August 1972), 44-45.

Livesay, Dorothy. Review of *Th Jinx Ship nd Othr Trips, Fiddlehead* 72 (Spring 1967), 64-66.

Nichol, bp. "Deep Frieze" (rev. of *Nobody Owns th Earth*), *Books in Canada* I:4 (November 1971).

. "The Typogeography of Bill Bissett," afterword to Bissett's *We Sleep Inside Each Other All* (Toronto: Ganglia Press, 1966).

. "ZOUNDS! the Sounds of Bill Bissett," *Quarry* XVI:4 (Summer 1967), 43.

Perry, Sam. Introduction to *We Sleep Inside Each Other All* (Toronto: Ganglia Press, 1966).

Purdy, A.W. "Other Vancouverites," *Canadian Literature* 35 (Winter 1968), 83-85.

Scobie, Stephen. "A Dash for the Border," *Canadian Literature* 56 (Spring 1973), 89-92.

Stevens, Peter. "Creative Bonds in the Limbo of Narcissism" (rev. of *Nobody Owns th Earth*), *The Globe and Mail,* Dec. 4, 1971, p.33.

Clark Blaise

(1940-   )

In the stories of Clark Blaise, five of which are anthologized in *New Canadian Writing 1968* (1968) and ten of which are collected in *A North American Education* (1973), we find the strongest expression in recent fiction of the Canadian discomfort at having to share North America with her southern neighbour. The narrators of his stories and the style of the stories themselves all bear witness to the seductive and paralyzing strength of American culture.

Most of Clark Blaise's stories are narrated by a young man whose father, a Québecois, and mother, an English Canadian from Saskatchewan, moved to Florida at the close of World War II to search unsuccessfully for sudden wealth. The young man is variously named Paul Desjardins, Frankie Broussard, Franklin Thibidault; he is approximately seven years old when his parents reach Florida. His parents then move from business failure to business failure around the eastern and central U.S. — Florida, Georgia, New Jersey, Ohio, Kentucky. The boy possesses fragments of his father's Quebec francophone culture, fragments of his mother's British-oriented Saskatchewan heritage, fragments of various regional U.S. cultures, but is at home in none of these. When he finally chooses as a young college instructor to leave the U.S. and settle in Montreal, he is still without a culture — too intelligent and cosmopolitan to be comfortably American, too Anglicized to be a francophone, too Americanized to be English Canadian. Having grown up in a vortex of clashing ideals and traditions, "a North American education", he can accept and identify with none.

Other Blaise stories reveal their characters in similar dilemmas caused by conflicting cultures. A group entitled "The Montreal

55

Stories" concerns Norman Dyer, an American who has married a German wife and emigrated to Montreal where he teaches at an English-language university. Enchanted by French Canada, he refuses to live in Montreal's English-speaking western suburbs. He moves his family from section to section of the city, hoping to find a home in French, then in Greek, neighbourhoods, and meeting only with conflict, complication, and disillusionment. "Reality," he discovers, "hurts like nothing in this world." "The Keeler Stories" concern another emigré American, who teaches at a Montreal university and is married to an East Indian girl. On travelling with his wife to India, he is so affected by events on the Indian aircraft, by the oppressive Asian heat, and by the chattering, clamouring crowds, that his mind somewhat catatonically begins to believe he has entered Eliot's wasteland.

The form of most of Blaise's stories is casual, straightforward, factual narrative. There is very little reliance on symbolism or imagery; the only 'images' in the stories are the very ordinary physical objects encountered by the characters. In tone, the stories resemble the conversational, matter-of-fact prose of Hugh Hood. Structurally, nearly all of Blaise's stories work toward a disturbing or upsetting event — usually involving some devastating cultural collision — and terminate thereafter. This event usually is made all the more surprising by the low-key narrative which has preceded.

Blaise was born in Fargo, North Dakota, of French and English-Canadian parents, and lived as a child in Florida and Georgia. He appears to have suffered much the same "North American education" as that of his various characters, having attended, according to the dust-jacket of A North American Education, "twenty-five different schools before the ninth grade". He received an M.F.A. in Creative Writing from the University of Iowa and taught at the University of Wisconsin before choosing Montreal residence and Canadian citizenship in 1966. Individual Blaise stories can be found in the anthologies Great Canadian Short Stories (1971), The Narrative Voice (1972), and The Story So Far 1 (1970).

Blaise, Clark. New Canadian Writing, 1968. Stories by David Lewis Stein, Clark Blaise, and Dave Godfrey. Toronto: Clarke Irwin, 1968.
    . "Eyes" (story), Fiddlehead 91 (Fall 1971), 24-28.
    . "Is Oakland Drowning" (story), Journal of Canadian Fiction I:2 (Spring 1972), 25-26.
    . "The Voice of the Elephant" (story), Journal of Canadian Fiction I:2 (Spring 1972), 26-27.
    . A North American Education. New York: Doubleday, 1973.

Clery, Val.   "Surviving Ourselves," *Books in Canada* II:2 (April, May, June, 1973), 51-52.

Fulford, Robert.   "A Writer Brings a U.S. Viewpoint to Our Situation" (rev. of *A North American Education*), *The Toronto Star,* Feb. 3, 1973, p.85.

Legate, David M.   "Home Truths," *Montreal Star,* February 10, 1973, "Entertainments," p.3.

Marchand, Philip.   "In Search of a Place, In Search of a Self," *Saturday Night* 88 (May 1973), 35-39.

Rollins, Douglas.   "The Montreal Storytellers," *Journal of Canadian Fiction* I:2 (1971), 5-6.

George Bowering

(1936-   )

One of the major reasons for the prominence of Vancouver writers in the Canadian poetry scene today has been the work of George Bowering. Together with fellow poets Frank Davey, David Dawson, James Reid, and Fred Wah and critic Warren Tallman, he helped to found the poetry newsletter *Tish* in 1961 — a newsletter which proved to be one of the catalysts not only for a ten-year explosion of poetry in Vancouver but for what Raymond Souster has termed a "new wave" of poetry across the country. It is well known that Bowering and other *Tish* editors brought to the newsletter a decided admiration for various U.S. poets loosely termed "Black Mountain". It is less known that Bowering also brought to *Tish* a considerable knowledge of eastern-Canadian poetry including much respect for the work of Louis Dudek, Raymond Souster, and Irving Layton. Under Bowering's influence, Dudek's magazine *Delta* became one of the models for *Tish* and the brief amatory lyric — a form found in Dudek and Layton but not in the Black Mountain poets Olson and Duncan — one of its most frequent kinds of poems.

On leaving the newsletter in 1963 for a teaching career that would take him to Calgary, London, and Montreal before returning him to Vancouver, Bowering was a recognized Canadian poet, anthologized by John Robert Colombo in *Poetry 64* and Irving Layton in *Love Where the Nights Are Long,* and with his first collection of poems, *Points on the Grid,* pending from Contact Press. He has since become a major force in Canadian poetry, both as a writer and as a shaper of its future directions. He has published a novel, *Mirror on the Floor* (1967) — achieving here what George Woodcock terms a "humanization" of the French *choseiste* approach; a critical study of

Al Purdy (1969); an impressionistic autobiography (*Autobiology*, 1972); a day-book on contemporary Canadian and U.S. writers *(Curious,* 1973); and eleven additional books of poetry. He has founded and edited *Imago,* a magazine of the long poem — particularly important in Canadian poetry for its booklets by Victor Coleman, Frank Davey, Lionel Kearns, and David McFadden and for its astute selections of avant-garde British and U.S. writing — and the critical series Beaver-Kosmos Folios. He presently serves on the editorial boards of *Open Letter,* a Canadian tri-quarterly review of avant-garde writing, and of *the B.C. Monthly*, a counter-culture magazine of news and review.

Ever since 1961 Bowering has aspired to be a poet of accuracy and integrity. His poems have been attempts to present his experiences and perceptions with all their original power intact, to present the kinetics of perception unadorned with rhetoric or melodrama. For Bowering, art must aim to be life's twin, and thereby hope to isolate and highlight all those aspects of life which the cloyed and muffled senses of the non-artist fail to perceive.

In his early work — *Points on the Grid* (1963), and *The Man in the Yellow Boots* (1965) Bowering had difficulty in giving accurate renderings to other than intensely personal subjects. His love poems and travel poems here are authentic and moving, but his attempts to reach beyond the domestic into economics and politics are often contrived and rhetorical. In the latter he seems to have been drawn too often to popular left-wing generalizations and forgotten that the basis of his poetic is honestly observed particulars. This superficial political strain in Bowering's poetry persists as late as *Two Police Poems* (1969) and *Rocky Mountain Foot* (1969).

However, by the adoption of a skeptical and inquisitory point of view, Bowering has managed in a number of recent books to make the political personal. Always a measurer and investigator of intimate personal experience, he has become a measurer of the his-torical,cultural and political space which extends from his person. One such work is *George, Vancouver* (1970), subtitled "a discovery poem", in which Bowering presents his own consciousness as it in-quires into the discovery and charting of Burrard Inlet and Georgia Strait by Capt. George Vancouver in 1792. Another is *Sitting in Mexico* (1969) in which he presents his reactions to various scenes encountered in and around Mexico City — scenes with strong political implications.

In books like these Bowering proceeds from a minimum of pre-conceptions. His rhythms are short and definite, his syntax un-complicated, and his language precise and austere. He uses few ad-jectives, and advances with a deliberate care — naming objects and delineating feeling with the exactitude which noun and verb allow. His standards of precision are made clear in *Baseball* (1967) in which he praises Ted Williams for his batter's knowledge that a pitch "has to be perfect" and describes the exact choreography and throw necessary for a double play.

Baseball by George Bowering. The Coach House Press, 1967.

His most interesting and original poetry to date is *Genève*, a book based on the thirty-eight trump and court cards of the Geneva Tarot deck. Here, in a further step in his quest for personal and literary integrity, Bowering shuffles the cards into an order he will not know until the book has been written, and disciplines himself to record his spontaneous response to the upturned card before turning to its successor. So insistent is he on the poems being an authentic personal response that he deliberately avoids knowledge of the deck's history and symbolism. The method here is phenomenological — the examination of one's consciousness of events and opinions rather than the presentation of the events and opinions themselves. Such an examination, *Genève* suggests, can reveal more answers and ironies than the assertive intelligence can imagine. In this poetry truth is a constantly developing thing, an interaction between various phenomena including the poet.

George Bowering

He employs a similar phenomenological method of composition — "telling the story as it happens" — in two recent books of poems and prose poems, *Autobiology* and *Curious.* In the former Bowering dwells on powerful memories of his childhood, letting these spontaneously trigger rhymes, rhythms, and image patterns in the faith that these will lead him to new insights into his conscious and subconscious perceptions of himself. In *Curious* the 'subjects' are 48 Canadian and U.S. writers whom Bowering has known; again he uses the suggested associations of rhyme, pun, rhythm, and image as a way to the 'truth' of spontaneous perception. The resulting 'portraits' are not so much ones of the 48 writers as of the fields of reaction evoked in Bowering by the sound of their names.

Curious's method is one which Bowering has been moving toward throughout his career in his growing stress on integrity and his gradual loss of interest in polemic verse. The achievement of this method in *Genève, Autobiology,* and *Curious* has brought Bowering to maturity as a writer and provided one of the most significant milestones of post-modern Canadian poetry.

Bowering, George. *The Man in the Yellow Boots.* Mexico City: El Corno Emplumado, 1962.

. "Poets in their Twenties," *Canadian Literature* 20 (Spring 1962), 54-64.

. *Points on the Grid.* Toronto: Contact Press, 1964.

. "Poetry and the Language of Sound," *Evidence* 7 (ca. 1963), 19-26.

. *The Man in the Yellow Boots.* Mexico City: El Corno Emplumado, 1965.

. *The Silver Wire.* Kingston: The Quarry Press, 1966.

. *Baseball.* Toronto: The Coach House Press, 1967.

. *Mirror on the Floor.* Toronto: McClelland & Stewart, 1967.

. *Solitary Walk,* a book of longer poems by George Bowering and others. Toronto: Ryerson Press, 1968.

. *Rocky Mountain Foot.* Toronto: McClelland & Stewart, 1968.

. *The Gangs of Kosmos.* Toronto: House of Anansi, 1969.

. *How I Hear Howl.* Montreal: Beaver Kosmos Folios, 1969.

. *Sitting in Mexico (Imago* 12), 1969.

. *Two Police Poems.* Vancouver: Talonbooks, 1969.

. *George, Vancouver.* Toronto: Weed/Flower Press, 1970.

, ed. *Vibrations,* poems of youth. Toronto: Gage Educational Publishers, 1970.

. *Alfred Purdy.* Toronto: Copp Clark, 1971.

. *Genève.* Toronto: The Coach House Press, 1971.

, ed. *The Story So Far.* Toronto: The Coach House Press, 1971.

. *Touch: Selected Poems 1960-1970.* Toronto: McClelland & Stewart, 1971.

. *Autobiology.* Vancouver: Vancouver Community Press, 1972.

. "Confessions of a Failed American," *Maclean's* 86 (November 1972), 79-81.

. *The Sensible.* Toronto: Massasauga Editions, 1972.

, with Irving Layton, Hugh Hood, and Kerry Allard. "Conversation: Jewish Layton, Catholic Hood, Protestant Bowering," *Open Letter* (second series) 5, Summer 1973, pp.30-39.

. *Curious.* Toronto: The Coach House Press, 1973.

. *Layers.* Toronto: Weed/Flower Press, 1973.

. *In the Flesh.* Toronto: McClelland & Stewart, 1974.

. *Flycatcher* (stories). Ottawa: Oberon Press, 1974.

Cameron, Donald. "The Test of Real is the Language" (interview), in his *Conversations with Canadian Novelists* (Toronto: Macmillan of Canada, 1973), pp.3- 16.

Coleman, Victor. Review of *Autobiology, Open Letter* (second series) 2, Summer 1972, pp.80-82.

Davey, Frank. "The Message of George Bowering," *U.B.C. Alumni Chronicle* 24 (Summer 1970), 13-15.

. "A Note on Bowering's *Genève,*" *Open Letter* (second series) 1, Winter 1971-72, pp. 42-44.

Garnet, Eldon. "Two Bowerings Embrace Past, Present, Future," *Saturday Night* 86 (November 1971), 49.

Godfrey, Dave. "Andrea or Andre," *Canadian Forum* 47 (May 1967), 45-46.

Grosskurth, Phyllis. "New Canadian Novels," *Saturday Night* 82 (May 1967), 39, 41.

Kearns, Lionel. "Recycled Self," *The B.C. Monthly* I:2 (November 1972), 84-85.

Scobie, Stephen. "You Gotta Have Heart," *Books in Canada* I:11 (October 1972), 31-32.

Sowton, Ian. "Moving from Word to Word," *Edge* 3 (Autumn 1964), 119-122.

Stevens, Peter. "Creative Bonds in the Limbo of Narcissism" (rev. of *Genève*), *The Globe and Mail,* Dec. 4, 1971, p.33.

. "Essence and Breath and a Sign of Life" (rev of *Touch*), *The Globe and Mail Magazine,* Aug. 28, 1971, p.17.

Weaver, Robert. Review of *Rocky Mountain Foot, The Toronto Star,* March 29, 1969, p.19.

Woodcock, George. "Mod Murders," *Canadian Literature* 36 (Spring 1968), 74-75.

Juan Butler

(1942-   )

Both of Juan Butler's novels, *Cabbagetown Diary* (1970) and *The Garbageman* (1972), are first-person narrations by excessively violent young men. In both novels all the major incidents are graphically described acts of sickening brutality.

Cabbagetown Diary is the two-month diary of Michael Taylor, a young man who has grown up in Cabbagetown, Toronto's downtown slums. Although Taylor sees himself as superbly masculine, level-headed, and capable, he is confused and self-contradictory figure. Part of him despises the filth, duplicity, and stupidity of his fellow Cabbagetown residents; another part is fascinated to witness — as close up as possible — this brutality and depravity. Still another part has no compunction about committing any act of viciousness, including murder, so long as it proves unpunishable and ostensibly in his own self-interest. From his childhood experiences Taylor has learned the same cynicism most Cabbagetowners learn; his only distinction is the extent to which his calculating intelligence can modify the consequences of cynicism.

It requires a reading of *The Garbageman* to make the entire significance of *Cabbagetown Diary* come clear. The narrator of this novel is a middle-class youth and would-be novelist, whose father is a brutal alcoholic and brother a self-lobotomized speed freak. Like Taylor, he has witnessed the world to be an arena of aimless, absurd, and irrational violence. He has confirmation of this in the writings of the French poet Andre Breton, and subsequently chosen a life of deliberate surrealistic violence as the only valid and pleasurable response to a similarly violent world. His world view is thus a consciously chosen and philosophically analyzed equivalent to that

63

embraced unconsciously by *Cabbagetown Diary's* Michael Taylor. His recognition that he can enjoy torturing, mutilating, and executing his fellow man would have been possible to Michael Taylor had not his love-hate relationship with Cabbagetown constantly confused and limited his thinking.

Butler presents his vision of a disgusting and disturbing world, randomly violent and irrationally cruel, with the same directness and brutality as his characters find in the world confronting them. His diction is blunt and uncompromising, his descriptions of scenes of mutilation and torture are extraordinarily detailed. His choice of first-person narrators who are unconscious or conscious sadists places the reader in intimate face-to-face contact with the novels' horrors. These methods are impressively successful, especially in *The Garbageman.*

Butler, Juan. *Cabbagetown Diary: a Documentary.* Toronto: Peter Martin Associates, 1970.
. *The Garbageman.* Toronto: Peter Martin Associates, 1972.

Christy, Jim. "Laying Waste the Wasteland," *Books in Canada* I:10 (August 1972) 9
Edwards, Mary Jane. "Two Torontos," *Canadian Literature* 51 (Winter 1972), 91-92.
Fetherling, Doug. "Madness Beyond Fashion: Fresh, Shocking, Masterfully Done" (rev. of *The Garbageman*), *The Globe and Mail,* June 10, 1972, p.32.
. "Social Stereotypes Slumming Predictably" (rev. of *Cabbagetown Diary*), *The Globe and Mail Magazine,* Mar. 14, 1970, p.16.
Taylor, Charles. "Writer's Plight: Slim Pickings from Publishers' Bonanza," *The Globe and Mail,* Apr. 7, 1973, p.23.
Woodcock, George. "Boredom, Distaste, Admiration," *Journal of Canadian Fiction* I:4 (1972), 94.

Austin Clarke

(1932-   )

Of the many writers who have emigrated to Canada in the last twenty years — Jane Rule, Audrey Thomas, Doug Fetherling, J. Michael Yates, George Amabile, George Jonas, Mike Doyle, Robin Skelton, Stanley Cooperman, Robin Blaser — Austin Clarke is one of the few who have sought to give literary form to the experiences of his adopted country. Clarke was born in Barbados, and educated there and at the University of Toronto. After teaching for a short while in Barbados, he emigrated to Canada in 1956.

His first two novels, *Survivors of the Crossing* (1964) and *Among Thistles and Thorns* (1965) are set in Barbados, and present poignant views of the struggles of illiterate but cheerful blacks to subsist in an economy brutally manipulated to favour white interests. Canada plays a part in *Survivors of the Crossing*, and though it is an indirect part, it is of considerable significance. Exaggerated accounts of Canadian life and Canadian labour conditions contained in a letter to home by a Barbadian cane-field worker who has emigrated to Canada prompt his friends back in the cane-fields to attempt a strike against their employers. As is usual in Clarke's novels, the Canadian influence on the Barbadians is disruptive and disillusioning; despite the immediate comic overtones of the strike, its result is increased poverty, community disintegration, and for its leaders, long prison terms.

In his subsequent works Clarke has concentrated on exploring this collision between white Canadian and black Barbadian cultures. Both *The Meeting Point* (1967) and *Storm of Fortune* (1973) — which form the first two parts of a trilogy — as well as most of the stories collected in *When he was Free and Young and Used to Wear Silks*

65

(1971) are set in Toronto and centre on the difficulties and indignities encountered there by Barbadian immigrants. Clarke displays remarkable insight into the psychologies of both the black and white characters of these novels. His treatment of inter-racial conflict is consistently even-handed; ignorance, carelessness, and confusion affect the behaviour of all characters, and give to all their tragedies distinctly comic overtones. Clarke employs a detached and ironic viewpoint throughout to prevent his reader from identifying strongly with any of them.

In fictional technique Clarke is quite conventional. All of his novels are told from a single and consistent point of view and move steadily forward in time. Clarke's strengths are in the wit and authenticity of

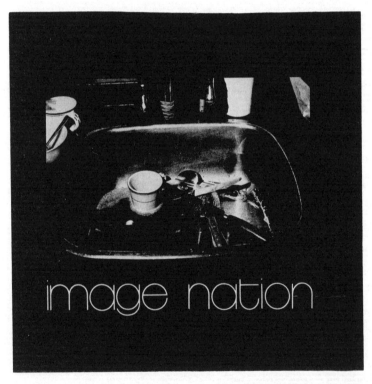

Image Nation 12, 1973.
A photography magazine ed. David Hlynsky.

his dialogue and in his skillful development of dramatic situations. His characterizations are noticeably shallow and undifferentiated — even from novel to novel. In his Toronto novels he tends to portray a group of similar black individuals encountering the dominant white culture, rather than the interacting of well-defined individuals from both cultures.

Clarke, Austin.   The Survivors of the Crossing. Toronto: McClelland & Stewart, 1964.
_____. Amongst Thistles and Thorns. Toronto: McClelland & Stewart, 1965.
_____. The Meeting Point. Toronto: Macmillan of Canada, 1967.
_____. "Stokely Carmichael," Montrealer 41 (November 1967), 45-49.
_____. When he was Free and Young and He Used to Wear Silks, Toronto: House of Anansi, 1971.
_____. Storm of Fortune. Boston: Little, Brown, 1973.

Bannerman, James.   "A Black Child Views White Truth," Maclean's 78 (October 16, 1965),68.
Boxill, A.   "The Novels of Austin C. Clarke," Fiddlehead 76 (Spring 1968), 69-72.
Brown, L.W.   "Austin Clarke in Canadian Reviews," Canadian Literature 38 (Autumn 1968), 101-104.
Dobbs, Kildare.   "Austin Clarke: a Hot New Novelist to Watch" (rev. of Storm of Fortune), The Toronto Star, June 9, 1973, p.75.
_____. "Caribbean Renaissance," Saturday Night 80 (November 1965), 59-60.
Gibson, Graeme.   Interview with Austin Clarke, in his Eleven Canadian Novelists (Toronto: House of Anansi, 1973), pp.37-54.
Hammond, Arthur.   "Unblinkered by Bitterness" (rev. of Amongst Thistles and Thorns), The Globe and Mail Magazine, Oct. 2, 1965, p.16.
Hanlon, Michael.   "Dialect Overloads Novel" (rev. of The Survivors of the Crossing), The Globe and Mail Magazine, Dec. 5, 1964, p.28.
Marshall, Tom.   "Rum Mixes," Books in Canada I:4 (November 1971), 21.
Richler, Mordecai.   "If Austin C. Clarke Doesn't Appear on Front Page Challenge Does this Prove Prejudice?" Saturday Night 83 (November 1968), 68, 70.
Scott, Chris.   "Plain Black on White Background," Books in Canada II:2 (April, May, June 1973), 38.
Simpson, Leo.   "Burst Innocence in Crystal Fragments" (rev. of When He Was Free and Young and He Used to Wear Silks), The Globe and

Mail Magazine, Oct. 21, 1971, p.8.

Tyrwhitt, Janice. "Clarke Closes In," Tamarack Review 38 (Winter 1966), 89-91.

Waddington, Miriam. "No Meeting Points," Canadian Literature 35 (Winter 1968), 74-78.

Wald, George. "Sword and Ploughshares" (interview with Austin Clarke), phonotape. C.B.C. Learning Systems, 1970.

Watmough, David. "Humour in Affliction," Canadian Literature 23 (Winter 1965), 74-76.

Wolfe, Morris. "What is Was Like to Grow Up in Barbados," Saturday Night 86 (October 1971), 33-34.

Leonard Cohen (1934-   )

The only major Canadian poet of the sixties to follow the lead of A. J.M. Smith and Robert Finch in taking a Platonist rather than Herclitean view toward reality was Leonard Cohen. All of Cohen's writing has argued for the importance of reducing life to ceremony, and transmuting its treacherous actualities into the trustworthy simplicities of mythology and art. Like Smith, he has celebrated escape into stasis, and frequently defined this stasis in imagery of jewels and minerals. Like Smith and Finch, he has been in poetic technique a pattern-maker, preferring to build geometric stanza forms and elaborate webs of imagery rather than write a poetry that deals directly with experience.

Cohen was born in Montreal where his family lived in its affluent Westmount district. He published his first book of poetry, Let Us Compare Mythologies (1956), shortly after graduating from McGill University. He spent the next few years attempting graduate study at Columbia University, working in his family's clothing business, and writing an unpublished novel, Ballet of Lepers. In 1961, he published his second book of poetry, Spice Box of Earth, and in 1963 a novel, The Favorite Game. During the next ten years his principal residence was the Greek island of Hydra, from which he commuted to New York and Montreal. In this period he published Flowers for Hitler (1964), Parasites of Heaven (1966), a second novel, Beautiful Losers (1966), Selected Poems (1968), and began a much publicized career as a composer-singer. In 1972 he returned to Montreal and, shortly after the publication of the poetry collection Energy of Slaves (1972), announced his retirement as a popular entertainer. Cohen's record albums include Songs of Leonard Cohen, Songs from a Room, and

Songs of Love and Hate.

His songs can be divided into two groups: a larger one concerned with a man's behaviour within love, and a lesser one concerned with a wide range of social issues including love. Both groups present an alienated protagonist, confused and disappointed by the world's values and often ready to welcome his own annihilation. Cohen's vision here is of a society in imminent collapse because of the greed and lust of its members. He would escape a world unfeelingly ordered by "hunters", "highways", and "blueprints", even if through a "slaughter house" where he would "wait ... with the lamb". Similarly, the lover's goals cannot be satisfied within the material universe. To Cohen, lovers are involved in impossible quests for perfection and purity; to imagine this quest ever fulfilled would be to sell out to society and embrace domesticity, mediocrity, and anonymity, to emulate not Christ but "just some Joseph looking for a manger".

Most of Cohen's poems and songs have a mildly nostalgic quality, similar to the elegiac tone of Finch, but closest to the fin de siècle romanticism of early Yeats. Their language is highly decorative, and their imagery of the imprecise but suggestive kind that can be easily projected into by the subjective reader. Their prosody has been markedly conservative, conservatism which has contributed to their evocation of nostalgia. The recognizably "poetic" qualities of this prosody plus the vague and ornate romanticism of the imagery account for much of Cohen's popularity with young readers.

Another popular aspect of Cohen's work has been his theme of moral non-responsibility. To Cohen, the artist is free of any obligation toward a corrupt social world and an unsatisfying physical environment, and all people are at some time potential artists. In fact, as "I" learns in Cohen's novel *Beautiful Losers,* the free man's obligation is to achieve martyrdom by ignoring physical reality, its particularity, and its 'common sense' restrictions. Like Finch, Cohen distrusts particularity and singularity, and prefers to see men live toward eternity rather than work for the here and now. The ultimate goal for Cohen is to annihilate one's own identity and gain the anonymity of sainthood.

The ornamentalism of his poetry as a worldly object has continually contradicted his claim to regard the things of the material world as worthless vanities. Much of the time Cohen has exploited his rejection of materiality by arbitrarily manipulating its words and images into fanciful but meaningless constructs. Such egotistic delight in linguistic beauty would appear to be more the way of decadence than of martyrdom. Cohen's latest steps toward self-

69

The Spice Box of Earth by Leonard Cohen.
McClelland & Stewart, 1961.

abnegation, however, do attempt a more likely saint's language of monastic simplicity, restraint, and silence. These are contained in *The Energy of Slaves* (1972) — a collection of poetic fragments, failed-poems, and anti-poems. Here the poetic craftsman of his earlier work becomes another "beautiful loser", ridiculing his abilities and mocking his past accomplishments. It is a more intriguing and surprising book than any by Smith or Finch, and more consistent with Cohen's praise of martyrdom than any of his other collections. Its closest parallel in Canadian poetry is the terse and grudging fragments of Phyllis Webb's *Naked Poems* — which have been followed by more than seven years silence. *The Energy of Slaves* marks the first time Cohen has emulated Miss Webb in disdaining the beauties of language along with the rest of the vanities and absurdities he believes the material world to be.

Cohen has shown only occasional interest in formal experimentation — in poetry chiefly in the broken forms of *The Energy of Slaves* and in fiction in the outrageous rhetoric of *Beautiful Losers*. The latter is constructed around two extraordinary characters who narrate the book in idiosyncratic styles which play a major role in their characterization. In terms of the norms of society, both are madmen. "I" is self-obsessed, highly distractible, physically and mentally constipated, and addicted to fanatsy and voyeurism; his writing is halting, disjointed, repetitive, self-indulgent, confused. "F" is a fanatic and a sensualist; his writing is a torrent of brilliant images, epigrams, absurd generalizations, and seductive logic, which becomes even more fluid and structureless when he becomes deranged by syphilis. *Beautiful Losers* is essentially a novel of style; its plot is completed and revealed in its opening pages. Michael Ondaatje, in his ingenious analysis of the novel, terms it "the work of a stylistic exhibitionist". Under close scrutiny like that of Ondaatje, the novel can be found in almost every sentence to contain purpose and meaning; unfortunately, its excesses of style distract most readers from its matter and discourage them from the attentive reading it deserves.

Cohen, Leonard. *Let Us Compare Mythologies.* Montreal: McGill Poetry Series, 1956. Repr. Toronto: McLelland & Stewart, 1966.
    . *The Spice Box of Earth.* Toronto: McClelland & Stewart, 1961.
    . *The Favorite Game.* London: Secker and Warburg.
    . *Flowers for Hitler.* Toronto: McClelland & Stewart, 1964.
    . *Beautiful Losers.* Toronto: McClelland & Stewart, 1966.
    . *Parasites of Heaven.* Toronto: McClelland & Stewart, 1966.

. *Selected Poems, 1956-68.* McClelland & Stewart, 1968.
. *The Energy of Slaves.* Toronto: McClelland & Stewart,
1972.

Bannerman, James.   "Is Bathroom Scribbling Necessary," *Maclean's*
79 (May 14, 1966), 46.
Bissett, Bill.   "!!!!!!", *Alphabet* 13 (June 1967), 94-95.
Bowering, George.   "Inside Leonard Cohen," *Canadian Literature* 33
(Summer 1967), 71-72.
Bromige, David.   "The Lean and the Luscious," *Canadian Literature*
10 (Autumn 1961), 87-88.
Buitenhuis, Peter.   "Two Solitudes Revisited: Hugh MacLennan and
Leonard Cohen," *Literary Half-Yearly VIII:2, 19-32.*
Colombo, John Robert.   *"Cohen: The Operative I"(rev. of Parasites of
Heaven),* The Globe and Mail Magazine, Dec. 10, 1966, p.22.
Djwa, Sandra.   "Leonard Cohen: Black Romantic," *Canadian
Literature* 34 (Autumn 1967), 32-42.
Dudek, Louis.   "Three Major Canadian Poets—Three Major Forms
of Archaism," *Delta* 16 (November 1961), 24.
Duffy, Dennis.   "Beautiful Beginners," *Tamarack Review* 40 (Summer
1966), 75-79.
Edinborough, Arnold.   "Elegant Forms," *Saturday Night* 76 (October
14, 1961), 45.
Gibson, Graeme.   "Two Troubled Young Men," *Saturday Night* 78
(November 1963), 41.
Gose, E.B.   "Of Beauty and Unmeaning," *Canadian Literature* 29
(Summer 1966), 61-63.
Jackson, Marni.   "Leonard Cohen: he's Bored, Bitter, and Out of
Love" (rev. of *The Energy of Slaves*), *The Toronto Star,* Nov. 25, 1972,
p.64.
Kleiman, Ed.   "Blossom Show," *Alphabet* 9 (November 1964), 78.
Lamb, Sidney.   " 'Libalobaglobawoganummynummy' or 'The Lusts
that Bleat or Low': Sidney Lamb reviews Leonard Cohen," *Mon-
trealer* 40 (June 1966), 35-36.
Morley, Patricia A.   *The Immoral Moralists: Hugh MacLennan and
Leonard Cohen.* Toronto: Clarke, Irwin, 1972.
Ondaatje, Michael.   *Leonard Cohen.* Toronto: McClelland & Stewart,
1970.
Pacey, Desmond.   "The Phenomenon of Leonard Cohen," *Canadian
Literature* 34 (Autumn 1967) 5-23.
Purdy, A.W.   "Leonard Cohen: a Personal Look," *Canadian Literature*
23 (Winter 1965), 7-16.
Waddington, Miriam.   "Bankrupt Ideas and Chaotic Style" (rev. of
Beautiful Losers), *The Globe and Mail Magazine*, Apr. 30, 1966, p. 17.

. "A Snowman in his Image's Grip" (rev. of *Selected Poems*), *The Globe and Mail Magazine*, July 27, 1968, p. 13.

Woodcock, George. "The Song of the Sirens — Reflections on Leonard Cohen," in his *Odysseus Ever Returning* (Toronto: McClelland & Stewart, 1970, New Canadian Library no. 71), pp. 92-110.

Matt Cohen (1943-   )

Matt Cohen's fiction has been characterized by elaborate and usually successful experimentation with narrative technique. Cohen is not often content with the single point of view of most fiction writers. Instead Cohen wants to show two or more perspectives on the same event, or to show how even personal events can recur and by time alone fall into new perspectives.

In *Korsoniloff* (1969), Cohen's first novel, the viewpoint divides through the mild schizophrenia of the title character. Andre Korsoniloff is a young professor of philosophy who respects neither his intellectual role nor the impulses of his body. He finds the former routine and sterile, and the latter, because of a traumatic childhood experience, frightening and alien. The novel is his journal, and he can write or speak in the first person only of the half-hearted scholar, the listless lover that his day-to-day self has become. The impulsive self — one that insults his students, vigorously possesses his women, and seeks to assault if not kill his enemies — he can speak of only in the third person, as "Korsoniloff". He is a trapped man — disliking the only self he can accept, and estranged from the only self which is emotionally real.

Most of Cohen's writing explores this relationship between actuality and the kinds of selfhood which a character potentially can direct on that actuality. Korsoniloff can deal with actuality through the unexacting closed-system approach of the rationalist, and possesses as a remote potential the ability to deal with it through the open-ended approach of the free man who is instinctively confident of his own identity. In the next novel, *Johnny Crackle Sings* (1971), similar choices exist for young Johnny Harper, and once again they help determine the narrative structure.

The narrative range of *Johnny Crackle Sings* is broader than that of *Korsoniloff;* it is not circumscribed by the mind of one character. Cohen here has stepped back from the narrative action so that the writing can consist of omniscient reporting, newspaper clippings, interviews, personal letters between minor characters, Johnny Harper's fantasies, and long passages of externally unidentified dialogue among the central characters. Many of these stylistic variations reflect shallow, limited, and false possibilities for Johnny Harper's life. They also show the reader how complex Cohen believes experience to be. No one technique can relate Johnny Harper/Johnny Crackle's story; no one stylistic section of the novel can contain the "truth" about it. It cannot be contained *in* words. Instead it exists *between* words, in the relationships between sections of the novel, where its dimensions are open, unspecified.

Like Andre Korsoniloff, Johnny Harper is torn between some kind of 'formula' existence and the life that is a natural extension of his being. He has run away from a mother who wishes "he'd settle down and have children" and a school system that aims its graduates toward "Successland in grade thirteen or university or knocking up the store keeper's daughter". He has temporarily found some self-realization in working on a farm and in playing a guitar. But the latter activity prompts his girlfriend's father to attempt to remake him into "Johnny Crackle", an international rock musician. Once again Johnny must flee if he is to prevent having himself rigidly defined and circumscribed.

To Cohen human freedom subsists in freeing oneself from all habits, customs, roles, and expectations which would limit one's possible avenues of self-development. Korsoniloff seeks to avoid both "overly composed people" and "orderly preparation for an orderly future" but is imprisoned by his fear of spontaneous action. Johnny Harper aims for "condition Zero" — a relaxed catatonic condition in which all surrounding phenomena are observed and yet blend "so perfectly that they all cancel out". Johnny does not want to be circumscribed even by expectation: "There's no point in hoping for anything anyway. If I did it just might happen and then where would I be?".

Cohen's most recent novel, *The Disinherited* (1974), examines four generations of an eastern Ontario farming family. All three men who have owned the farm have found their lives restricted by its ownership, and their relationships with women complicated and embittered. Second-generation Simon Thomas even surrendered the farm to his son, Richard, in order to live with a common-law wife in town. The novel centres on his grandson, Eric Thomas, who must decide, while his father lies dying in hospital, whether to accept the farm, to take up an academic career in Edmonton, or leave himself open to some unknown third possibility. Eric is the only one who ever has this third, anarchic or "condition zero" possibility entirely open to him, and he discovers it only at the very end of the book.

Although the novel is constructed in a relatively conventional manner, Cohen again uses the shifting point of view to make clear certain aspects of his narrative. Most of the chapters are interior monologues by Eric or his father Richard; we are led to see parallel features in their lives: their choice of women as lovers, their attraction to orthodox middle-class women for wives, their being required to choose at one point in their lives between academic careers and possession of the Thomas farm. Helping to bind the various chapters together is an important sub-theme: that the land cannot be "possessed", that it will inevitably assert its own authentic "condition zero" selfhood and return to wilderness, thus "disinheriting" its exploiters. To think otherwise was the mistake of the farm's founder and a mistake which each of his descendants has had to "inherit" in turn.

Too Bad Galahad by Matt Cohen. The Coach House Press, 1972.

Most of the characters of Cohen's short stories, collected in *Columbus and the Fat Lady* (1972), are prisoners of their circumstances. Because they have never been able to discover their selfhood through free action, they have not been able to establish other than superficial relationships with others. They can lead solitary lives in the midst of companionship. They hear each other's dialogue without understanding.

"Tell me about yourself," Barbara said. "What do you do?"

"Nothing much."

"How exciting. You should move to the country. Everyone is moving to the country these days."

They cannot empathize with each other nor comprehend the events that have trapped them. In "The Watchmaker" a jeweller continually agonizes about his parents' decision to sacrifice themselves to save him from a Nazi deathcamp. In "Spadina Time" the same events, written in identical prose passages, keep returning on the thoroughly dwarfed characters. Many of Cohen's characters flee into fantasy ("The Nurse that Came from Outer Space", "The Toy Pilgrim") — fantasy which becomes often a more real part of their lives than phenomenal event.

The prose of these stories is as complex as that of the novels. Passages of fantasy blend into passages of literal accounting. Dialogue takes frequent, unexpected, and non-rational turns. The stories' sequences, disruptions, and events break and repeat to document the relativity of time to the perceiving consciousness.

Cohen, Matt.   "Nihilism or Insanity: the Strange Life of Ichabod Oise," *This Magazine is About Schools* I:4 (Autumn 1967), 49-56.

. *Korsoniloff*. Toronto: House of Anansi, 1969.

. *Johnny Crackle Sings*. Toronto: McClelland & Stewart, 1971.

. *Columbus and the Fat Lady and other Stories*. Toronto: House of Anansi, 1972.

. *Too Bad Galahad*. Toronto: The Coach House Press, 1972.

. "The Buck Stops Here," *Open Letter* (second series) 4, Spring 1973, pp.24-28.

, ed. *The Story So Far #2*. Toronto: The Coach House Press, 1973.

The Disinherited. Toronto: McClelland & Stewart, 1974.

Atherton, Stan.   "Snap Crackle Pop," *Journal of Canadian Fiction* I:1 (1971), 87-88.

Barbour, Douglas.   Review of *Johnny Crackle Sings, Canadian*

Forum LI (January, February 1972), 80.

Batten, Jack.   "Real Chips off the Rock" (rev. of *Johnny Crackle Sings*), *The Globe and Mail Magazine,* Oct. 9, 1971, p.19.

French, William.   "Five of a Kind in a Fair Gamble" (rev. of *Korsoniloff*), *The Globe and Mail Magazine,* Sept. 27, 1969, p.17.

Gairdner, William.   Review of *Columbus and the Fat Lady, Open Letter* (second series) 5, Summer 1973, pp.91-92.

Gibson, Graeme.   Interview with Matt Cohen, in his *Eleven Canadian Novelists* (Toronto: House of Anansi, 1973), pp.59-84.

Nichol, bp.   "Zip Crackle Pop," *Books in Canada* I:4 (November 1971), 11-12.

Strenski, Ellen.   Review of *Columbus and the Fat Lady, Open Letter* (second series) 5, Summer 1973, pp.86-90.

Woodcock, George.   "Five New Novelists Enter the Literary Lottery" (rev. of *Korsoniloff*), *The Toronto Star,* Oct. 11, 1969, p.25.

Victor Coleman

(1944-   )

In the movement of Canadian poetry toward increasingly open and anarchic forms, Victor Coleman has been undoubtedly a leading figure — providing not only the example of his own poetry but also his enormously productive talents as an editor. Largely self-educated, he married and entered the book trade as a production assistant for Oxford University Press in Toronto shortly after dropping out of high school. In 1965, he founded *Island* magazine and Island Press, publishing ventures which served to move the avant-garde centre in Canadian poetry from Vancouver and the fading poetry newsletter *Tish*, to Toronto. Most of the original *Tish* editors were contributors to *Island*, and one, Fred Wah, had his first book published by Island Press. Behind the Canadian publishing scenes, Coleman was almost equally busy, lobbying successfully for Contact Press's publication of *Bridge Force* by *Tish* editor Frank Davey and heavily influencing the shape of Raymond Souster's anthology *New Wave Canada*.

Coleman joined The Coach House Press as "linotype operator and delivery boy" in 1967. Finding here an outlet for his editorial ambitions, he discontinued *Island* and Island Press, and founded the Coach House literary magazine *Is*. The major Coach House editor since 1969, he has built the press into the home of such new Canadian writers as George Bowering, Michael Ondaatje, bpNichol, Frank Davey, and David McFadden, and the guest press of such U.S. writers as Robert Creeley and Allen Ginsberg.

To most readers Coleman's poetry is a difficult and challenging experience. It is highly allusive, reflecting the poet's immense knowledge of oriental and western philosophy and of contemporary international art, writing, and music. It is also formally unlike any poetry written in Canada before 1960. Coleman not only recognizes no need for formally shaped verse but no need for even the rudiments of beginning, middle, or end or a hint of the epigrammatic line. His poems are relaxed meditations that record and testify to his reflections on friends, journeys, landscapes, politics, and art. There is little intensity of emotion. Curiously, few of the poems attempt to record in detail events external to Coleman's consciousness; any narrative line is invariably interior.

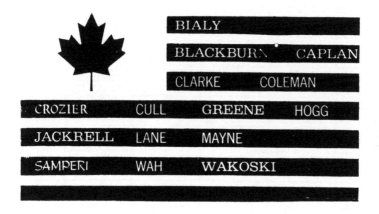

Island, ed. Victor Coleman, 1964-66.

Coleman employs the present tense to describe nearly all the actions in the poems. Thus political events, statements of philosophers, movements of characters all occur contemporaneously with the meditations they enter. This technique gives many of his poems the flavour of stage direction, as if Coleman were invoking the late twentieth-century world rather than reporting it. Such a flavour is a

79

natural extension of Coleman's belief that the artist creates his reader's view of reality, in fact that only the artist's imagination can give a portarit of reality that approaches accuracy. Coleman overtly uses the dramatic mode in one of the most readable and entertaining of all his books, *Some Plays: On Words* (1971).

Throughout Coleman's work is expressed the conviction that ordered and logical statements and artforms can do no more than travesty the cosmos of which they attempt to speak. Even song and the unfettered present-tense meditations of the poet can at best provide approximations and intimations of the "seraphic reflections", the "continents of speech", the "delight in sun" that constitute man's cosmic context. Thus Coleman deliberately accentuates the

Light Verse by Victor Coleman, The Coach House Press, 1967.
One of 26 copies.

desultory, fragmentary, ikonic, and private aspects of his work. He estimates that a good reader might understand 10% of most of his books, but that if he wrote to give more comprehension the accuracy of the work would be impaired. His preoccupation with perception of cosmic order and the impairment of this perception is indicated in the puns of some of his book titles — One/Eye/Love (1967), and Light Verse (1969).

As these titles also suggest, Coleman will often attempt to use the linguistic features of his writing as guideposts to meaning. Puns and near-puns can redirect both the poet's thought and the poem. Rhymes, especially within the lines, are similarly explored to illuminate the significance of events or statements. Even assonance and consonance can lead Coleman to what he believes are glimpses into the orders of a magical universe.

Coleman, Victor.   From Erik Satie's Notes to the Music. Toronto: Island Press, 1965.
          . "History is Happening — Right Now!" (rev. of W.C. Williams, In The American Grain), The Toronto Star, Apr. 1, 1967, p. 36.
          . One/Eye/Love. Toronto: The Coach House Press, 1967.
          . Light Verse. Toronto: The Coach House Press, 1969.
          . Back East. (Imago 15) Vancouver, 1971.
          . Old Friends' Ghosts: poems 1963-68, Toronto: Weed/Flower Press, 1971.
          . Some Plays: On Words. Buffalo, N.Y.: Intrepid Press, 1971.
          . America. Toronto: The Coach House Press, 1972.
          . Parking Lots. Vancouver: Talonbooks, 1972.
          . Strange Love. Toronto: privately printed, 1974.
          . Speech Sucks. Vancouver, Talonbooks, 1974.
          . Stranger. Toronto: The Coach House Press, 1974.

Bates, Pat Martin.   "Two 'lautgedichte' Singers: Victor Coleman and bpNichol," Arts Canada 27 (April 1970), 64.
Davey, Frank.   Review of Some Plays: On Words. Open Letter (second series) 3, Fall 1963, pp.90-91.
Flowers, Slim (Gerry Gilbert).   "Canada's Top Poet" (conversation between Coleman and Gilbert), The B.C. Monthly I:2 (November 1972), 86-87.
MacSkimming, Roy.   "Subversive Light," Canadian Literature 37 (Summer 1968), 88-90.
Stevens, Peter.   "So-so. Even With Pictures" (rev. of Parking Lots), The Globe and Mail, Sept. 23, 1972, p.33.

John Robert Colombo

(1940-   )

The principle aim of John Robert Colombo's poetry has been to resuscitate and reappraise the past. His methods have been preponderantly documentary and artifactual, with special dependence on the art of the found object.

Colombo's greatest talents are those of a skilled editor. This is the career he has followed all of his adult life, editing *The Varsity Chapbook* (1959) while attending the University of Toronto, the English-language section of the Ryerson Press anthology of new poetry *Poetry 64* (1963), an anthology of Canadian poets' favourite poems, *How Do I Love Thee* (1970), a companion anthology *Rhymes and Reasons* (1971), and an anthology of Canadian visual poetry *New Direction in Canadian Poetry* (1971) — as well as serving throughout the sixties as managing editor of *The Tamarack Review*. Three of Colombo's volumes of poetry are found poems taken — or edited — from the prose of single writers: *The Mackenzie Poems* (1966) from that of William Lyon Mackenzie; *John Toronto* (1969) from that of Bishop John Strachan; and *Leonardo's Lists* (1972) from that of Leonardo da Vinci. *The Great San Francisco Earthquake and Fire* (1971) consists of found poems edited from the relevant newspaper stories. *The Great Wall of China* (1966) is largely a collage of historical and scholarly documents on the ten thousand *li* wall.

The variety of editing tasks he has undertaken, especially those for *The Tamarack Review,* have given Colombo a firm place in the Toronto literary establishment — so firm that many of the city's avant-garde community regard him with some distrust. Most of Colombo's poetry, however, has been decidely experimental, and

82

has earned him respect among the international avant-garde descendants of Dada and concrete poetry. A further complication in Colombo's reputation is that a number of these experiments, including the various lists of *Neo Poems* (1970), have been severely criticized by Canadian academicians and counter-culture writers alike.

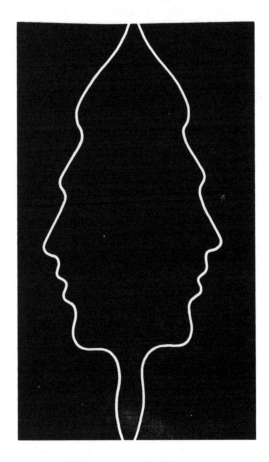

Miraculous Montages by John Robert Colombo.
Heinrich Heine Press, 1966.

One factor in Colombo's reputation has been his failure to create a sense of personal involvement, sincerity, or passion in even his created work rather than his found work. Instead he allows a tone of urbane detachment to pervade throughout. His own poetic idiom, as represented in *The Varsity Chapbook* and *Abacadabra* (1967), is extremely discursive and descriptive; in *Neo Poems* it is deliberately disengaged, witty, and superficial. In all these cases the thematic weight of the poems tends towards inconsequentiality and banality. In *The Great Wall of China* his own links and commentaries are more prosaic than most of the book's found prose, and tend to reduce the found passages to simplistic and obvious interpretations.

The only stylistic centre Colombo has demonstrated in his writing has been in his work as an editor and collagist of found materials. The best of these works is *The Great San Francisco Earthquake and Fire* which consists entirely of juxtaposed sections taken from eyewitness and journalist accounts of that disaster. Nearly as impressive is *The Great Wall of China* — except for Colombo's attempts to philosophize on the wall and link its building to Quebec separatism. Both works are outstanding examples of documentary poetry, examples which explore convincingly the ability of fact and document to work unassisted in a poem with every bit as much evocative power as the finely turned image or the inspired metaphor.

All of Colombo's work, of whatever style, is concerned with some aspect of the past. The largest single group of personal poems in *Abacadabra* are commentaries on Western paintings. His documentary and found poems focus on personages from Toronto history, the San Francisco earthquake, the African trader Alfred Aloysius Horn, Louis Riel, and Ancient China. In both kinds of poems Colombo attempts to find beauty in the horrors of the past, in disaster, cruelty, barbarism, even in the legends of Dracula. The found poems work to give a new experience from old information. They dislocate the reader's sense of the past, and yet at the same time, by their preserving of the past's words, remind him of his old sense of the past and of the ironic space between that past and the poet's new world.

Colombo, John Robert.   *Fragments*. Privately printed, 1957.
      . *This Citadel in Time*. Toronto: Hawkshead Press, 1958.
      . *This Studied Self*. Toronto: Hawkshead Press, 1958.
      . *Two Poems*. Toronto: Hawkshead Press, 1958.
      . *Variations*. Toronto: Hawkshead Press, 1958.
      . *Fire Escapes*. Toronto: Hawkshead Press, 1959.
      . *The Impression of Beauty*. Toronto: Hawkshead Press, 1959.
      . *In the Streets*. Toronto: Hawkshead Press, 1959.

                . *Poems and other Poems.* Toronto: Hawkshead Press, 1959.

                . *Poems to be Sold for Bread.* Toronto: Hawkshead Press, 1959.

                . *This is the Work Entitled Canada.* Toronto: Purple Partridge, 1959.

                . *Three Poems in Two Colours.* Toronto: Hawkshead Press, 1959.

                . *Towards a Definition of Love.* Toronto: Hawkshead Press, 1959.

                , ed. *The Varsity Chapbook.* Toronto: Ryerson Press, 1959.

                . *Lines for the Last Day.* Toronto: Hawkshead Press, 1960.

                . *Millenium.* Toronto: Hawkshead Press, 1960.

                . *They!* Toronto: Hawkshead Press, 1960.

                ,ed. *Poetry/Poesie 64,* ed. John Robert Colombo and Jacques Godbout.   Toronto: Ryerson Press and Montreal: Editions du Jour, 1963.

                . *The Great Wall of China.* Toronto: Delta Canada, 1966.

                . *The Mackenzie Poems.* Toronto: Swan Publishing Co., 1966.

                . *Miraculous Montages.* Don Mills, Ont.: Heinrich Heine Press, 1966.

                . *Abacadabra.* Toronto: McClelland & Stewart, 1967.

                . *John Toronto.* Ottawa: Oberon Press, 1969.

                , ed. *How Do I Love Thee.* Edmonton: M.G. Hurtig, 1970.

                . *Neo Poems.* Vancouver: Sono Nis Press, 1970.

                . *The Great San Francisco Earthquake and Fire.* Fredericton, N.B.: Fiddlehead Poetry Books, 1971.

                , ed. *New Directions in Canadian Poetry.* Toronto: Holt, Rinehart, and Winston, 1971.

                , ed. *Rhymes and Reasons.* Toronto: Holt, Rinehart and Winston, 1971.

                . *Leonardo's Lists.* Toronto: Weed/Flower Press, 1972.

                . *Praise Poems.* Toronto: Weed/Flower Press, 1972.

Christy, Jim.   "Ornaments and Embellishments," *Canadian Literature* 50 (Autumn 1971), 84-85.

Francis, Wynne.   "Found Poetry," *Montreal Star,* May 13, 1967, "Entertainments", p.7.

Geddes, Gary.   "Poets in Residence" (rev. of *Neo Poems*), *The Globe and Mail Magazine,* Oct. 10, 1970, p.20.

Gibson, Kenneth.   "The Curate's Egg," *Alphabet* 17 (December 1969), 66.

Gustafson, Ralph. "Mighty Nothing Called a Wall," *Canadian Literature* 34 (Autumn 1967), 90-91.

Jackson, Marni. "The Poet Who Will Not Be Pigeonholed" (rev. of *Neo Poems*), *The Toronto Star*, Aug. 29, 1970, p.53.

Purdy, Al. "Old Rhetoric in a Poetic Setting" (rev. of *The Mackenzie Poems*), *The Globe and Mail Magazine,* June 4, 1966, p.16.

Stevens, Peter. "The Gospel According to Pop," *Canadian Literature* 34 (Autumn 1967), 91-93.

Weaver, Robert. "A Revealing Introduction to Poetry" (rev. of *How Do I Love Thee?*), *The Toronto Star*, Oct. 31, 1970, p.53.

Frank Davey   by George Bowering   (1940-   )

Frank Davey was founding & managing editor of *Tish*, so in the first issue, Sept. 1961, when he was himself a stripling, he wrote: "There is no such thing as an isolated image; poetry being sensation, image is omnipresent in a poem. A successful poem is one into which the poet has put the most possible of his body. Not just used his intelligence, not just his sense of rhythm, not just his ocular powers, but used a combination of the maximum of all his faculties."

It seems to me that that is a good description of jazz, the art of this continent, for which the practitioner must work to become a master, then give himself over to the source of improvisation. The master of us all said: "The breath whose might I have invoked in song / Descends on me; my spirit's bark is driven, / Far from the shore."

Davey's talk about the body was not a call for gut & thigh poetry. He has served the intellect well, having been in school continuously since grade one, a PhD now, & a most perceptive & unusually candid critic of writing & ideas. The key word in that early statement may have been "faculties." Davey would argue that the poet's measure appertains equally & synthetically to his world, his mind-body, & his poem. The foot in the poem's passage is stept from the end of his own leg, a dance on the distances of his place, successively Vancouver, Los Angeles, Victoria, Montreal, Toronto, memory, arcana, & marriage.

A difference over the past decade, however is apparent: though Davey has not abandoned his proper sense, he has matured, that is he is no longer hard, he is fully coloured; one no longer meets his poem, one enters & on entering discovers a person wholly confessed. It is not, I say though, like the experience of the poems

86

spit out by the "Confessional" poets, & it is not like the poems of his contemporaries, Margaret Atwood & John Newlove, who never relinquish the hold of personality over the message.

That may be because Davey works in the tradition of Charles Olson, who said: "Art does not seek to describe but to enact," & Robert Duncan, who said: "We recognize an image in the process of the poem not because of some device of speech, not as a descriptive arrangement of words or a striking word, but because we see as we write."

So Frank's writing is notable for its candour, but it is a candour that has been earned & protected by diligent study of language, of rime, of meaning made thru gesture, not forwarded by thesis. It is only natural, then, that the poetry should have become richer over the years — the poet is student at his craft's own board, & the achievements lead to further probings & understandings by the poet, simultaneously of the self & the means of showing the self. "The self" describes not a thing but process.

Thus the earlier poems work at enacting a discovery of place in the geographical & historical senses. In a booklength poem called *The Scarred Hull* (1966), we hear stories of the sailing ships that sank in the waters below Vancouver Island, & of the retarded kids in then Mrs. Davey's "special" school. It was a kind of obvious *juxtaposition*, but it is a long poem that works as such. Davey, probing always, nearly always works in sequentials, often in his version of the serial poem, an invention of the San Francisco poets, Duncan, Jack Spicer, Robin Blaser, *etc.* The serial poem is not simply a long poem in numbered cantos — it insists that all sections be discrete though symbiotic, that the sequence & indeed the body of the poem be "dictated", & that any poet's "control" of his materials will ruin the poem. It calls for, then, what Garcia Lorca called the *duende,* what Zen artists refer to as *yugen*, the experience the downhill skier has when he does what he has to do a split-second before he knows he has done it. With its semi-ordained structure *The Scarred Hull* is no serial poem, but later sequences such as *Weeds,* Davey's best poem so far, move in that Coltrane-like music. What is required is not the pulse of soul, but the flight of spirit. It is the difference between James Brown & Marion Brown.

& yet, one portion of Davey's authenticity is his scholarly curiosity & the candour that clinches it. This is most obvious in his seeing into the works of Charles Olson & Margaret Atwood, but it also animates much of the verse. Its only real enemy is not the reluctance of scholarly research to be lyrical, but Davey's weakness for wit. His is not the Victor Coleman wit that is at the nexus of all that poet's versification, but a kind of riming bravado that pretends to en-

A POETRY NEWSLETTER - VANCOUVER   January 13
                                                      1962

TISH 5

                    Editor   Frank Davey

Contributing Editors   James Reid   Fredric Wah
                        George Bowering   David Dawson

Distributed by mailing list.   Address all correspondence to TISH,
                                3591 W. 11th Ave., Vancouver 8, B.C.

EDITORIAL

TISH is now a poetry newsletter, an organ designed to tell its readers WHAT'S GOING ON in Vancouver. That is, we seek to define the scene as completely as possible. We have discarded the format of a magazine of poetry because we find it too narrow (or too broad) a framework for what we have in mind.

After four issues we now know what we want to do. We have reached the stage where we can say NO; we can reject a good poem if it does not interest us. The fact that it may be good does not alter the fact that it may not work the way we feel a poem should work. We print poems which conform to our taste, poems which move somewhat in the same direction as our own. This is true, not only of poems submitted by the readers, but of the poems submitted by the various co-editors as well. The desired result is a selection of poetry which indicates our poetic stance, which defines our scene.

In the last issue we printed our first review, WHY DOESN'T SOMEBODY TELL THE TRUTH? We will continue this policy of accepting and rejecting literary works in order both to solidify our tastes and to convey them to our readers. Likewise, the essays on poetry and poetics will continue. Contributions from our readers are welcome in both areas.

In order to fulfill its purpose, and at the same time survive, TISH does require participation by the readers. Poems, essays, criticisms—anything of relevance will be gratefully received. If submitting prose, please keep the length within reasonable bounds (2 Gestet. pages). And, if you are so inclined, SEND MONEY. The cost per issue is getting too high for just a few of our supporters to cover. Please, send money (or 2¢ stamps).

Notice also our guest page. Henceforth, a minimum of one page per issue will be devoted to guest poets—any poets who submit material which reflects a purpose and technique somewhat similar to our own. So please, keep the poems and letters (and financial contributions, if possible) coming.

                                                    david dawson

Tish: a Poetry Newsletter, 1961-1969.

joy the groans it elicits. Happily, it has just about disappeared in the latest works, such as "A Light Poem", in which the puns are discovery themselves, the old poets' archetypes (WCW's "Make Light of It")

It is curious that as poet (eleven books of verse by 1973), critic, & editor, Davey has been at the nose of the *avant-garde* for a dozen years, but the image-makers of Ottawa & Toronto know little of him. That is largely because till this time at least, he has been a determined mover in the little-press world, Coach House Press, Talonbooks, *etc.* His body of work, though, & its forsheeting sincerity, will ensure him his influence on our art as it enters further into the post-lyric stage.

The influence will be, perhaps, something like that of Raymond Souster for the period between 1945 & the recent past. Not that Davey's concerns are Souster's — they are more properly those that may operate as a result of Souster's work in clearing the way for the Canadian lyric in the fifties & early sixties. Like his predecessor (who championed the influence of Olson twenty years ago), Davey is as an editor, critic & proselytizer, more interested in battling for the craft than in making literary friends of connections, & as a result the latter arrive. He has a history of confrontations with poets & critics over poetics & *belief.* In the great majority of cases his stand is better-researcht & more sensitive in the area of language, where literature lives. Poetry, as Dante attested, thrives on contention, & the serious poet is prepared to defend his beliefs, believing that his argument is a defense of poetry. So Davey's arguments during the *Tish* days were solid arguments for a poet in his early twenties. Today his writings in *Open Letter*, & his editing of that only Canadian journal of serious literary contention, carry a good deal more responsibility than they should have to in a community that produces so much poetry & fiction.

But even were Davey not to leave his name on a large & inventive body of criticism & theory, his poems, in their very particulars of rime, notation, rhythm, image, tone, would sound as the nicest music heard in the post-Layton period. Listen to the melody that sounds even from this second stanza of a "history" poem called "The Caughnawaga Bell", written during the winter of 1969-70:

> The year is 1701,
> the bell, cast in France,
> weighs 800 lb.,
> the ship that brings the bell
> is captured by the British,
> brought to Salem; the bell
> sold by auction to a New England meeting hall.
> But these Iroquois

on the night of another winter in 1704
accompanied by French soldiers,
raid the town cut down their bell
& carry it, carry it on their shoulders
for what was likely 200 miles
to the shores of Lake Champlain.

Davey, Frank.   "Anything But Reluctant: Canada's Little Magazines,"
    Canadian Literature 13 (Summer 1962), 39-44. Reprinted in Louis
    Dudek and Michael Gnarowski, ed., *The Making of Modern Poetry in
    Canada* (Toronto: Ryerson Press, 1967), pp.222-227.
        . *D-Day and After.* Vancouver: Tishbooks, 1962.
        . *City of the Gulls and Sea.* Victoria: privately printed,
1964.
        . "Black Days on Black Mountain," *Tamarack Review* 35
(Spring 1965), 62-71.
        . *Bridge Force.* Toronto: Contact Press, 1965.
        . "Rime: a Scholarly Piece," *Evidence* 9 (*ca.* Winter 1965),
98-103. Reprinted in Louis Dudek and Michael Gnarowski, ed., *The
Making of Modern Poetry in Canada* (Toronto: Ryerson Press, 1967),
pp.295-300.
        . *The Scarred Hull.* (*Imago* 6) Calgary, 1966.
        . "More Heat on Daedalus," *Open Letter* 8 (November
1968), 26-27.
        . *Five Readings of Olson's 'Maximus'.* Montreal: Beaver
Kosmos Folios, 1970.
        . *Four Myths for Sam Perry.* Vancouver: Talonbooks, 1970.
        . *Earle Birney.* Toronto: Copp Clark, 1971.
        . *Weeds.* Toronto: The Coach House Press, 1971.
        . *Griffon.* Toronto: Massasauga Editions, 1972.
        . *King of Swords.* Vancouver: Talonbooks, 1972.
        . *l'an trentième: selected poems 1961-70.* Vancouver: Van-
couver Community Press, 1972.
        . *Arcana.* Toronto: The Coach House Press, 1973.
        . *The Clallam.* Vancouver: Talonbooks, 1973.

André, Michael.   Review of *Arcana, Queen's Quarterly* 80 (Winter
    1973), 658-659.
Bailey, Don.   "A Quiet Human Voice," *Books in Canada* II:3 (July-
    September, 1973), 33-34.
Barbour, Douglas.   Review of *Arcana* and *King of Swords, Canadian
    Forum* 53 (September 1973), 42-43.
Bowering, George.   "The Canadian Poetry Underground," *Canadian
    Literature* 13 (Summer 1962), 65-67.

. Review of *City of the Gulls and Sea, Canadian Author and Bookman* 41 (Autumn 1965), inside back cover.

Coleman, Victor. "Now We Are Six," *Canadian Forum* 45 (March 1966), 283-284.

Dudek, Louis. "Trouncing the Younger Poets," *Canadian Literature* 34 (Autumn 1967), 83-84.

Garnet, Eldon. Review of *Weeds* and *Four Myths for Sam Perry, Saturday Night* 87 (June 1972), 41-42.

Mays, John Bentley. "About Frank Davey," *A-Space Magazine* 2 (1974).

Purdy, A.W. "Levels of Excitement," *Canadian Literature* 29 (Summer 1966), 70-71.

Scobie, Stephen. "Tragedy Revisited" (rev. of *The Clallam*), *The Edmonton Journal,* Feb. 16, 1974.

Sowton, Ian. Review of *D-Day and After, Queen's Quarterly* 69 (Winter 1963), 645-646.

Stevens, Peter. "Facts, to be Dealt With," *Canadian Forum* 47 (September 1967), 139.

Tallman, Warren. "Poet in Progress," *Canadian Literature* 24 (Spring 1965), 23-27.

Whittaker, Ted. "West Coast Myth and Marriage Mapped," *The Varsity* XCI:62 (March 19, 1971), 12.

Louis Dudek

(1918-   )

The explosion in Canadian little magazine and small press publishing in the 1960's was the extension of a very young tradition. This tradition was established in the 1940's and 1950's, considerably before the generosities of the Canada Council, by the energies and financial sacrifices of a number of men, among them F.R. Scott, Patrick Anderson, John Sutherland, Raymond Souster, Peter Miller, and Louis Dudek.

Dudek had published some social protest verse in *The McGill Daily* while attending McGill University during 1936-40, but first became involved in Canadian publishing and the Canadian poetry scene in 1943 when, together with Irving Layton, he joined John Sutherland in the editing of *First Statement,* founded by Sutherland in 1942. Although graduate study at Columbia University took Dudek from Montreal to New York later that year, he continued to contribute to *First Statement* and to its successor, *Northern Review,* during his eight year absence. In New York he came in contact with Paul Blackburn, Cid Corman, Herbert Gold, and, by letter, with Ezra Pound.

Dudek returned to Montreal and McGill University as a teacher in 1951, and almost immediately devoted his energies to reviving the experimental kind of alternate publishing that had been begun a few years before by Sutherland's *First Statement* and First Statement Press. His knowledge of the U.S. avant-garde and of its dependence on the editorial aggressions of such men as Pound and Corman, had convinced him that the survival of a serious and creative Canadian poetry required that the poets have access to an alternate means of publication to that of the commercial publishers. He encouraged and advised Raymond Souster in his editing of the little magazine *Contact* (1952-54), and, with Irving Layton, unofficially directed the editorial policies of Aileen Collins' magazine *CIV/n* 1953-54). One of his most important acts occurred in 1952 when, with Layton and Souster, he founded Contact Press. Dudek and Souster remained with this press throughout its life, 1952-1967, and took major editorial roles. A list of the poets published by the press during these years constitutes a history of the new Canadian poetry of the period — Dudek, Souster, Layton, Phyllis Webb, Eli Mandel, D.G. Jones, W.W.E. Ross, Alden Nowlan, Al Purdy, Milton Acorn, Gwendolyn MacEwen, George Bowering, Frank Davey, John Newlove, and Margaret Atwood.

Finding even the Contact Press structure too inflexible for many of his ambitions for poetry, Dudek undertook two concurrent publishing ventures. One was the McGill Poetry Series, entirely operated and financed by Dudek, which introduced Canadians to the work of Daryl Hine and Leonard Cohen. Another was *Delta,* a personal literary magazine in which he attempted to keep Canadian writing within the international avant-garde community and encourage the socially-aware, realistic kind of writing he had always favoured. On the termination of Contact Press in 1967, he transformed *Delta* into another small press, Delta Canada, which has published books by John Robert Colombo, Glen Siebrasse, and Ron Everson, as well as Dudek's *Collected Poetry.* Dudek's most recent press is 'D.C.', founded to allow Glen Siebrasse total control of Delta Canada.

Dudek has been an active poet, having published nine volumes since 1946. Throughout his career he has aimed for a realistic, experiential verse, a verse that arises from the facts of actuality rather than from any preconceptions brought to actuality by the poet. In his criticism he has been extremely harsh on those he terms the "mythy" and "academic" poets, the former whom he accuses of applying to actuality overstructures borrowed from the work of the mythopoeic critic, Northrop Frye, and the latter whom he accuses of preferring "word-patterns" to experience. In recent statements he has asserted the "hard" austere values of the modernist tradition against the post-modern fragment-structures of such writers as George Bowering and bpNichol. His own early poetry consists almost entirely of short lyrics that derive a concluding insight or philosophical observation from the description of a particular scene or event. They contain little metaphor or literary image, depending instead on the evocative power that is innate within the names and qualities of physical phenomena.

In his later work — *Europe* (1955), *En Mexico* (1958) and *Atlantis*

20 CENTS A COPY

FIRST
STATEMENT

IN THIS ISSUE—

JOYCE AND MANN— JOHN B. SQUIRE

STORIES JOHN SUTHERLAND, J. S. GLASSCO

POEMS MIRIAM WADDINGTON, RAYMOND SOUSTER, IRVING LAYTON.

DOROTHY LIVESAY'S POEMS— F. R. SCOTT

ARTICLES CRITICISM & REVIEWS

DECEMBER, 44 & JANUARY, 45. VOL.2, NO.10

CANADIAN PROSE & POETRY

First Statement, ed. John Sutherland, 1943-45.

(1967) — Dudek concentrates on the book-length meditative poem, something of an innovation in a Canadian poetry that had for decades consisted either of book-length narratives or collections of incidentally-related lyrics. In these, however, a moralizing tendency leads Dudek away from his earlier reliance on experienced particulars, and creates the appearance of reliance on overstructure: specifically, the overstructure of moral preconception. There are still numerous passages of objective description, but these often seem more the illustrations for a sermon than particulars from which the poem's generalizations have proceeded.

Here Dudek is an anti-humanist, who celebrates the power of the cosmos while lamenting the folly, vanity, and weakness of man. Many of his early poems had explored the shabby beauty of working-class life, and argued for Marxism not as a panacea but merely as the way of making life most endurable. His later poems are similarly pessimistic. They catalogue the appalling gap between church wealth and peasant poverty in Mexico, and the astonishing discrepancy between the great works of European culture and the ignorance and vulgarity which Dudek believes to have always been its essential and dominant reality. Over all the men of Dudek's work tower the inhuman palaces of lost Atlantis — North Atlantic icebergs that promise only an "infinite night".

Louis Dudek has had the most influence on subsequent generations of Canadian poetry of any poet in Canadian literary history. His lyrics, that build from anecdote or observation to a punchline of humour or philosophy, have provided one of the commonest structures in recent Canadian verse, being evident in the work of Al Purdy, George Bowering, Seymour Mayne, Michael Ondaatje, Lionel Kearns, Alden Nowlan, John Newlove, to name only a few. His work with the structure of the long meditational poem has marked the beginning of a period in which widespread experiment in this form has been one of the unique characteristics of Canadian poetry. Notable among those following Dudek's lead here, although usually without his didacticism, have been Bowering, Victor Coleman, Daphne Marlatt, Frank Davey, bpNichol, and Dennis Lee.

Dudek, Louis. *Unit of Five.* Poems by Louis Dudek, Ronald Hambleton, P.K. Page, Raymond Souster, James Wreford, edited by Ronald Hambleton (Toronto: Ryerson Press, 1944), pp.3-18.
———. *East of the City.* Toronto: Ryerson Press, 1946.
———, ed. *Canadian Poems 1850-1952,* edited by Louis Dudek and Irving Layton. Toronto: Contact Press, 1952.
———. *Cerberus.* Poems by Louis Dudek, Irving Layton, Raymond Souster. Toronto: Contact Press, 1952.

. *The Searching Image*. Toronto: Ryerson Press, 1952.
. *Twenty-four Poems*. Toronto: Contact Press, 1952.
. *Europe*. Toronto: Laocoon (Contact) Press, 1954.
. *The Transparent Sea*. Toronto: Contact Press, 1956.
. *En Mexico*. Toronto: Contact Press, 1958.
. *Laughing Stalks*. Toronto: Contact Press, 1958.
. *Literature and the Press*. Toronto: Ryerson Press, 1960.
. *Montreal: Paris of America*, by Louis Dudek and Michel Regnier. Toronto: Ryerson Press and Montreal: Editions du Jour, 1961.
. "Northrop Frye's Untenable Position," *Delta* 22 (October 1963). 23-27.
, ed. *Poetry of Our Time*. Toronto: Macmillan of Canada, 1965.
. *Atlantis*. Montreal: Delta Canada, 1967.
. *The First Person in Literature*. Toronto: CBC Publications, 1967.
, ed. *The Making of Modern Poetry in Canada:* Essential Articles on Contemporary Canadian Poetry in English, ed. Louis Dudek and Michael Gnarowski. Toronto: Ryerson Press, 1970.
. *Collected Poetry*. Montreal: Delta Canada, 1971.
. "The Misuses of Imagination," *Tamarack Review* 60 (1973), 51-67.

Barbour, Douglas. "Poet as Philosopher, " *Canadian Literature* 53 (Summer 1972), 18-29.
Cogswell, Fred. "Wisdom and Beauty in Dudek's Poem," *Montreal Star*, March 2, 1968, "Entertainments", p.7.
Francis, Wynne. "A Critic of Life: Louis Dudek as a Man of Letters," *Canadian Literature* 22 (Autumn 1964), 5-23.
Frye, Northrop. Review of *En Mexico* and *Laughing Stalks, University of Toronto Quarterly* 28 (July 1959), 354-356.
Gnarowski, Michael. "Louis Dudek: a Note," *Yes* 14 (September 1965), 4-6.
Hull, Geoffrey. "A Perennial and Prolific Poet" (rev. of *Collected Poetry*), *The Toronto Star*, July 24, 1971, p.55.
Lee, Dennis. "Poetic Gravity," *Books in Canada* I:3 (1971), 14, 19-20.
Livesay, Dorothy. "The Sculpture of Poetry," *Canadian Literature* 30 (Autumn 1966), 26-35.
Stevens, Peter. "Essence and Breath as a Sign of Life" (rev. of *Collected Poetry*), *The Globe and Mail Magazine*, Aug. 28, 1971, p.17.
Watt, F.W. Review of *Collected Poetry, Canadian Forum* 51 (January, February 1972), 82-83.
Weaver, Robert. "A Puritan Dudek, an Efficient Webb," *Saturday*

Night 86 (November 1971), 50, 52.

Wilson, Milton.   Review of Europe, Canadian Forum 35 (October 1955), 162-163.

           ,et al. "Correspondence (concerning Dudek's Europe)," Canadian Forum 35 (November 1955), 182-184.

George Elliott

(1923-   )

George Elliott's single work of fiction, The Kissing Man (1962), concerns a perennial subject in Canadian literature, the small town. In a number of ways The Kissing Man invites comparison with the classic of Canadian small-town fiction, Stephen Leacock's Sunshine Sketches. Both are set in rural Ontario in the early part of this century. Both are collections of stories which are arranged to form a whole which is arguably a novel.

The tone and theme of The Kissing Man, however, are vastly different from those of the Leacock work. Elliott treats his characters with gentleness and sympathy; his stories speak poignantly of the limited successes these characters find in seeking the love and understanding of their fellow townsmen. The theme of The Kissing Man is that man should act affirmatively toward life — should view life as an active and joyous process rather than as a waiting for death. Many of the people in the town "have given up living in order to die", or have lost sight of life in the drudgery of "monthly reports" and "balance sheets". Over the remainder hangs the shadow of the Orange Lodge which demands the paralysis of total social conformity. Elliott's stories centre on the few characters who have worked to create love and joy — "the kissing man", "the man who lived out loud", Allison Kennedy who designed and built a ballroom "for love".

His prose, despite occasional awkwardnesses, especially in the opening story, is extremely delicate in texture. A tendency to withhold all but the most essential details gives the stories an air of insubstantiality close to that of fantasy or dream. The stories are thus as liberated from the uninspired materiality of daily life as Elliott would have his characters be.

Elliott, George.   *The Kissing Man*. Toronto: Macmillan of Canada, 1962.

Harlow, Robert.   "Other Sides of the Moons," *Canadian Literature* 14 (Autumn 1962), 72-73.

Kirkup, Hilda.   Review of *The Kissing Man, Canadian Forum* 42 (May 1962), 45.

Stafford, Ellen.   "Toronto Author Conjures a Magic Book of Dreams" (rev. of *The Kissing Man*), *The Globe and Mail,* Mar. 10, 1962, "Review of Books" p.19.

Marian Engel

(1933-   )

Marian Engel's three novels are all interior monologues by southern-Ontario women, lucidly written in a conventional and non-demanding stream of consciousness style. Engel was born in Toronto, and although educated at McMaster University in Hamilton and McGill University in Montreal, has returned to Toronto to live. Like a number of her Toronto contemporaries, her principle concern appears to be "the heathen blanket of southern Ontario guilt" she sees around her. All of her protagonists are prisoners of this guilt. It accuses them from the sordidness of the slum housing they have left middle-class homes to inhabit. In the first two novels it lurks in the symbolic heaviness of both women's bodies — Sarah Porlock of *No Clouds of Glory* (1968) is letharagically overweight and heavy-boned; Mim Burge of *The Honeyman Festival* (1970) is burdened by the flesh of an immense and overdue foetus.

Sarah Porlock is a thirty-year old English literature Ph.D., the youngest and only one unmarried of her four Toronto sisters. She has tried to escape her shrewish Methodist mother, who yearns only for "respectability", by fleeing to Europe; for "Yurp" is to Methodists a place from which come "Commies, evolution, Catholicism and sex." In Europe she has two affairs, the most intense being with her youngest sister's Italian husband. But the guilt follows her. The affairs lead not to freedom but to an unsettling abortion, her retreat to Toronto, and her unhappy constriction in a University of Toronto teaching post.

The career of Mim Burge is remarkably similar. Born in Godwin, a bitter and life-thwarting Ontario town, and educated at the University of Toronto, Mim also seeks her freedom in Europe. Her five-year affair, however, with a second-rate American movie producer, ends not in abortion but her abandonment. She then drifts into a spiritless marriage, the imprisoning motherhood of four children, and custody of a cockroach-infested, mid-Victorian Toronto house.

In both books the male characters are hollow and ineffectual. Both girl's fathers live in their wives' aggressive shadows and die defeated. Mim's grandfather was the builder of "meanly designed and meanly-executed" cement block buildings; her lover Honeyman is the talented but ambitionless producer of commercially-successful formula movies. Sarah's Italian lover turns out to be even more enslaved to the work ethic than the proverbial Protestant, and uses his globe-circling engineering career to avoid other than superficial relationships with women.

The world of these novels is ruled by bitch-goddesses who accuse everyone of "disgrace, indiscretion, inconsideration", who believe that coloured towels "are vulgar and their purpose is to disguise dirt". Even in Italy they rule the Roman Catholic family of Sarah's lover. They willfully destroy the innate joyfulness of their daughters and castrate the wills of their sons. Marian Engel would persude us that both "heroines" have some chance of escaping this world. In the final pages of *No Clouds of Glory* Sarah is suddenly about to find salvation in un-Protestant Montreal, and in those of *The Honeyman Festival* Mim is about to benefit from some new insights into herself gained during an unpremeditated attack on that Protestant authority-figure, a policeman. But neither ending is particularly strong or convincing.

In her third novel, *Monodromos* (1973) Engel avoids an improbably hopeful conclusion but, perhaps as a result, creates a desultory and inclusive story. The protagonist, Audrey Moore, a 36-year old woman from a Lake Ontario village, has been seeking freedom and purpose in Europe ever since her abortive marriage to a homosexual pianist a decade before. Like Engel's other heroines, she experiences a conflict between her puritannical heritage and the relaxed sensuality of the Mediterranean. This conflict prevents most of the elements of her life — her Canadian past, her curiousity about Cypriot history, the death of her English lover, the charm of her Cypriot lover, the self-destructiveness of her estranged husband — from taking on meaning to her. Unfortunately, the chaotic life of Audrey Moore is not lifted by Engel to any level of fictional perspective or poetic insight, but allowed to entangle the novel itself in Audrey's directionlessness.

The one constituent which dominates all of Engel's fiction is the morally and sexually confused heroine. As portrayed, these women

VOLUME 6 NO. 4   FIFTY CENTS

Northern Review

of Writing and the Arts in Canada

- **THE SPOOR OF AN ANGEL:**
  ROY CAMPBELL

- **BABBITT JUNIOR:**
  PETER VIERECK

- **WILFRED OWEN:**
  POETRY, PITY AND PROPHECY:
  DENNIS S. R. WELLAND

  OTHER CONTRIBUTORS:
  DELMAS W. ABBOTT, L. A. MacKAY,
  NICHOLAS JOOST, DESMOND PACEY,
  JOHN SUTHERLAND, THOMAS I. COOK

OCTOBER—NOVEMBER, 1953   MONTREAL, CANADA

Northern Review, ed. John Sutherland, 1946-56.

are exceedingly unlikely to change and enrich their lives or to find meaning within their personal chaos. So far Engel as a novelist has had a similar problem — an inability to find meaning in artistic chaos; in three novels she has either made unconvincing claims for her protagonist's potential or left her in unenlightening confusion. It may be that Engel will have to solve the post-modern problem of finding meaning within chaos before her fiction can move past the obsessive desolation of Sarah's, Mim's, and Audrey's lives.

Engel, Marian.   *No Clouds of Glory.* Toronto: Longman, 1968.
    . *The Honeyman Festival.* Toronto: House of Anansi, 1970.
    . *Monodromos.* Toronto: House of Anansi, 1973.

Buitenhuis, Peter.   "Brilliant Pastiches in Search of a Meaning," *The Globe and Mail,* Saturday, Nov. 10, 1973, p.32.
Cecil, C.D.   "Marian Engel's Tidy, Economical First Novel," *Montreal Star,* June 1, 1968, "Entertainments", p.7.
Gibson, Graeme.   Interview with Marian Engel, in his *Eleven Canadian Novelists* (Toronto: House of Anansi, 1973), pp.89-114.
Grosskurth, Phyllis.   "A Hip, Hip and a ... Wait, Whoa" (rev. of *No Clouds of Glory*), *The Globe and Mail Magazine,* Feb. 17, 1968, p.18.
    . "Trapped in a Biological Bathtub" (rev. of *The Honeyman Festival*), *The Globe and Mail Magazine,* Dec. 5, 1970, p.20.
Lee, Hope Arnott.   Review of *No Clouds of Glory, Canadian Forum* 48 (July 1968), 94.
Wainwright, Andy.   "Beyond Women's Lib," *Saturday Night* 85 (October 1970), 34-35.

Robert Finch

The poetry of Robert Finch has invariably raised strong feelings among both its admirers and detractors. Two of his books, *Poems* (1946) and *Acis in Oxford* (1961), have been honoured with Governor-General's Awards. The former was also the object of a vicious book review by John Sutherland which caused seven of the editors of Sutherland's magazine, *Northern Review,* to resign. Among recent reviewers, George Woodcock has found Finch's poetry to be "of craftsmanship and fine sensibility" while Peter Stevens has called it "dull", "flabby", "pointless", "limp", and "paltry".

Although Finch published his first poem in 1929 and his first book in 1946, three of his five books have been publications of the sixties: *Dover Beach Revisited* (1961), *Acis in Oxford,* and *Silverthorn Bush* (1966). Finch's influence on recent poetry has been for the most part confined to the unwitting encouragement of poets of antithetical persuasion; most new poets who are aware of Finch regard his work as the epitome of the controlled, self-conscious artistry that they seek to avoid. The only poets publishing today in modes similar to Finch have been his contemporaries, A.J.M. Smith and Jay Macpherson, and among younger writers the Anglo-Canadian David Wevill, the expatriate Daryl Hine, and Leonard Cohen.

The essential element in Finch's poetry is its rejection of the physical world — either as valuable in itself or as a Yeatsian way to a spiritual world beyond. To Finch, a professor of French at the University of Toronto, man's physical world of process and energy is vulgar, treacherous, noisome, and ephemeral. His favourite scenes within it display either some permanence-suggesting geometric or jewel-like qualities or else a remarkable freedom from life's colours — being "blanched", "pallid", "grey", "fading", "gelid", or "pellucid". He is thus in complete opposition to the dominant Heracliteans of Canadian poetry — Purdy, Birney, Layton, Coleman, Nichol, Atwood, Bissett, and Souster. Finch often seeks to have the pale, deathly light of eternity shine through his poems by means of transparence-evoking imagery. He seeks "the hush between gale and gale", "rest / from heat and hail", "silence, before a silent tree." Believing himself in this world to be "lost at the center of change", he would remove himself to a place where "time is no object", where "time marks time" and adopt for himself a "livery of grey".

To a large extent this timeless world becomes the world of his poetry. Most of his poems are rooted in no time or place. In style, the poems possess a pervasive sameness of image, rhythm, point-of-view, and mood. Their objects are symbolic, ornamental, or evocative. These are seldom allowed to display any idiosyncrasies derived from their histories or from the moment in which they presently exist. The settings of the poems are vague; a beach or a room could be almost any beach or room. The people are of indeterminate age, sex, appearance, and personality. They are generic characters — the foreman, the leader, the explorer — representative of classes of mankind without having any of the specificity from which Finch apparently recoils.

Finch is essentially an elegiac poet, lamenting the loss of the childhood sense of timelessness, the loss of the comparative peacefulness of pre-industrial society, and mankind's loss of Eden. He takes a condescending and patrician point-of-view toward his reader. This is particularly noticeable in poems which satirize the petty joys of the bourgeois or which assume the 'royal we' in a presumptuous attempt to generalize for all men. He views the poet as the voice of wisdom and intelligence — as a teacher who delivers carefully formulated statements to an elite of humanity.

The major flaw in Finch's poetry is its failure to communicate any trace of involvement or emotion. His poems are too carefully tailored, too elegantly phrased, to appear as anything more than a combination of metrical exercise and neo-Platonic philosophy. Even in the dramatic monologues of *Dover Beach Revisited,* in which Finch attempts to make the characters of Matthew Arnold's elegiac poem speak again, his calculated diction and mechanically iambic rhythms prevent any suggestion of authentic feeling.

Throughout most of his early work Finch was a Canadian Housman, working a narrow range of nostalgic and time-fearing subjects in a similarly narrow range of metrical forms and a similar tone of stoic dispassion. Although in the sixties he has added some heavily iambic 'free verse' to his staple of quatrains and sonnets, this addition did not alter any of the other limiting characteristics of his writing.

Finch, Robert.   *New Provinces.* Poems of Several Authors (edited by F.R. Scott). Toronto: Macmillan of Canada, 1936, pp.1-11.
            . *Poems.* Toronto: Oxford University Press, 1946.
            . *The Strength of the Hills.* Toronto: McClelland & Stewart, 1948.
            . *A Century Has Roots.* A Masque Performed at Hart House Theatre to Commemorate the One Hundredth Anniversary of the Founding of University College, Toronto, 1853. Toronto: University of Toronto Press, 1953.
            . *Acis in Oxford.* Toronto: University of Toronto Press, 1961.
            . *Dover Beach Revisited.* Toronto: Macmillan of Canada, 1961.
            . *Silverthorn Bush.* Toronto: Macmillan of Canada, 1966.
            . *The Sixth Sense.* Individualism in French Poetry. Toronto: University of Toronto Press, 1966.
            . *French Individualist Poetry 1686-1760: an Anthology,* ed. Robert Finch and Eugene Joliat. Toronto: University of Toronto Press, 1971.

Birney, Earle.   "Important Poems of Robert Finch" (rev. of *Poems*), *The Globe and Mail,* April 5, 1947, "Review of Books" p.7.
Bedingfield, Dolores.   "Reticent Poet Remains Aloof" (rev. of *Acis in Oxford* and *Dover Beach Revisited*), *The Globe and Mail,* Dec. 30, 1961, "Review of Books" p.17.
Daniells, Roy.   "Earle Birney et Robert Finch," *Gants du Ciel* 11 (Printemps 1946), 83-96.
Mathers, Kay.   "The Triumvirate of Robert Finch as Poet, Painter, and Pianist," *Saturday Night* 63 (September 20, 1947), 16.
Peter, John.   "No True Life," *Canadian Literature* 12 (Spring 1962), 72-74.
Stevens, Peter.   "On the Edge, on the Surface," *Canadian Literature* 32 (Spring 1967), 72.
Woodcock, George.   "The Virtues of Urbanity," *Canadian Literature* 13 (Summer 1962), 71-72.

Northrop Frye

(1912-   )

For two decades Northrop Frye has been not only the foremost literary critic in Canada but one of the most influential theoretical critics in the English-speaking world. His central work, *Anatomy of Criticism* (1957), brought him international acclaim as a credible successor to the New Critics, and made him a mandatory inclusion in studies of twentieth-century critical theory. In Canada he became a myth in his own right, giving authoritative direction to Canadian poetry from 1950-59 through his annual book reviews in the *University of Toronto Quarterly*'s "letters in Canada" issues, attracting would-be disciples among both critics and poets, and unwittingly creating antagonists among many writers and critics who misunderstood his writings or feared his influence and power.

Frye was born in Sherbrooke, Que., and educated at Moncton, N.B., and at Victoria College and Emmanuel College of the University of Toronto. In 1936 he was ordained as a United Church minister, but shortly after resumed graduate study at Oxford University. He joined the English Department of Victoria College in Toronto in 1939, served as chairman of the department from 1952-1959, and as principal of the college from 1959 to the present. In 1947 and 1957 respectively, he published his two masterworks, *A Fearful Symmetry: a Study of William Blake* and *Anatomy of Criticism*. Since then he has published numerous collections of essays and lectures which consolidate and illustrate various of the principles proposed in the first two books. These collections include: *The Well-Tempered Critic* (1963), *The Educated Imagination* (1963), *T.S. Eliot* (1963), *Fables of Identity* (1963), *A Natural Perspective: Essays on the Development of Shakespearean Comedy and Romance* (1965), *The Return of Eden:*

Four Essays on Milton's Epics (1965), *Fools of Time: Studies in Shakespearean Tragedy* (1967), *The Modern Century (1967)*, *A Study of English Romanticism* (1968), *The Stubborn Structure* (1970), and *The Bush Garden: Essays on the Canadian Imagination* (1971).

Anatomy of Criticism stands as one of the most monumental yet elusive works in the history of literary criticism. It departs radically from the New Criticism and traditional Aristotelian criticism in asserting the primacy of imagination over mimesis in literary art. To Frye, man is essentially a dreamer and a visionary; poetry constitutes a verbal universe which transmutes and transcends material creation and imitates only "the total dream of man". The *Anatomy* is divided into four essays, "Historical Criticism: Theory of Modes," "Ethical Criticism: Theory of Symbols," "Archetypal Criticism: Theory of Myths," and "Rhetorical Criticism: Theory of Genres." The first essay proposes a classification of literature into myth, romance, high mimesis, low mimesis, and irony according to the relationship between the hero and both his fellow man and environment. The second proposes the classification of writing as literal, descriptive, formal, mythical, and anagogic and argues that "literature" comes into being as writing moves from the "discursive" or "literal" phase toward the anagogic and thus becomes increasingly indirect in its signification. The third essay suggests the continuing presence of myths and archetypes in literature of all modes and genres through the process of "displacement", and the consequent presence of Classical and Biblical myth within all western literature. The fourth essay attempts to distinguish between literary forms largely on the basis of rhythm; the rhythm of *epos* is recurrent, of prose-fiction continous, of drama decorous, of lyric associative, and of non-literary prose logical. It is impossible to provide more than this partial skeleton of the *Anatomy* here; it must be stressed that almost every major proposal in the book receives extensive expansion, subdivision, and qualification. It must also be stressed that Frye's introduction to the *Anatomy* insists that the work is a hypothetical and schematic structure and not, as it has often been considered, a systematic and dogmatic one.

Certain provocative critical principles stand out in Frye's work. Perhaps the best-known is his mistrust of value-judgements. He tells us that "the sense of value is an individual, unpredictable variable, incommunicable, undemonstrable, and mainly intuitive reaction to knowledge." Literary value judgements are extensions of social acceptability and convention; "criticism becomes more sensible when it realizes that it has nothing to do with rejection, only with recognition." Frye himself tends to present his value-judgements as factual nomenclature and employs terms such as "naive allegory", "discursive writing", "superficial convention", "popular literature", "conventionalized literature", and "doggerel" as if they were absolute terms free of perjorative connotation. Another controversial Frygian principle is that there is only one mythic pattern behind all literature: the Biblical one of the quest to regain the lost garden. This pattern and its "displacing" variants so direct man from within his own dreams "that there is really no such thing as self-expression in literature".

Frye's work as a critic of Canadian literature has been extensive, but is nevertheless disappointing in terms of the searching brilliance of his central works. His 1943 essay "Canada and its Poetry" is notable for introducing to Canadian poetry an unfortunately conceived dichotomy between "Tarzanism" — poetry based on "the primitive and direct" and a poetry (here preferred by Frye) of the "consciously literary". Such a dichotomy is far removed from the powerful (and primitivist) central argument of the *Anatomy* which rejects "aesthetic idolatry" and writing that is "an act of conscious will" and which claims instead that art is based on "mystery and magic" and that the writer is moved unconsciously by mythology and language to act as "a mid-wife" to the poem. Two later essays, "The Narrative Tradition in English-Canadian Poetry" (1946) and "Preface to an Uncollected Anthology" (1956), explore the mythic connotations of an immense, bleak, and hostile Canadian landscape and its influence on the "desolation and loneliness" of much Canadian literature. His "Conclusion" to the *Literary History of Canada* (1965, gen. ed. Carl F. Klinck) enlarges on these essays, adding observations on the isolation of "frontier" communities, the consequent "garrison mentality" of both the society and its literature, and the frequency in Canadian literature of the "pastoral myth" — both the 'Golden Age' myth of a nostalgically-perceived past and the myth of man's kinship to nature and animals.

Except for this last observation, Frye has done very little to apply the principles of the *Anatomy* to Canadian literature. One wishes particularily that he would apply to it his Theory of Modes, since the literature appears not to conform to his general principle that literature descends from the romantic, through the high mimetic and low mimetic, to the ironic. Canadian literature is one which lacks a high mimetic period, having begun in the low mimetic and moved in this century to the ironic. Curiously, numerous Canadian writers have attempted to construct the missing high-mimetic: Pratt in *Toward the Last Spike*, Birney in *David*, Leonard Cohen in *Beautiful Losers*, Newlove in "The Pride", Gutteridge in *Riel*, MacEwen in *King of Egypt, King of Dreams*, Wiebe in *The Temptations of Big Bear*.

Frye's most significant effect to date on Canadian literature has been by means of the many misunderstandings his work has suffered among students, book reviewers, and writers. The most serious has been the misconception of Frye as an apologist for poetry of the

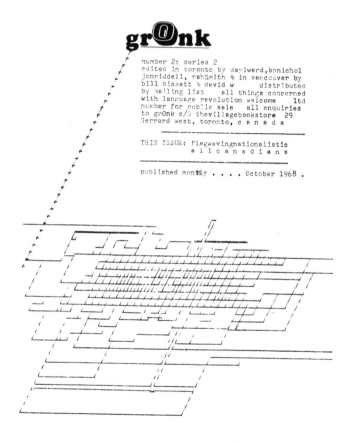

grOnk, ed. bpNichol, David Aylward et al., 1967-   .

symbolist and Gnostic traditions. This misconception has its origin in his opposition to the New Criticism's emphasis on common-sense everyday reality, in his proposing a "numinous" world of the over-leaping imagination that transcends the New Criticism's reason-bound materiality. Close reading of Frye, however, reveals that he has little in common with the symbolist desire (seen in Canadian poetry in Smith, Finch, Cohen, and Webb) to renounce one's material being and become an angel rather than a man. Far from preaching escape from materiality, Frye calls for an eschatalogical return to wholeness — a wholeness in which the dream transforms and humanizes the actual, in which the material is transfused with a Blakean light. Thus for Frye literature is educative — enlarging both the reader's tolerence for his fellow man and his understanding of life.

A similar misconception has been the view of Frye as a Platonist. Again this seems to have been based on the apparent "otherworldliness" of his theory of literature as a combination of dream and mythology, as well as on the preference for "consciously literary" writing he expressed in the 1943 essay. This misconception unfairly links Frye with an aestheticist and formalist tradition in Canadian poetry which includes not only Smith and Finch but Gus-tafson, LePan, Macpherson, Reaney, and early Eli Mandel. Interest-ingly enough, Frye makes in the *Anatomy* a specific condemnation of aestheticism as a pursuit which leads to "an exaggerated cult of style, a techique of making everything in a work of art, even a drama, sound all alike ... like the author at his most impressive." Elsewhere in the *Anatomy* his senses of nature as "an infinite and eternal living body", of life as "a vast mass potential literary forms", of the universe as essentially "creative", mark him as much more of a Heraclitean than a Platonist. The remarkable fluidity of his critical schema, his refusal to allow this schema to be considered as anything more than working hypothesis, and his profound suspicion of value-judgement are all noticeably consistent with a Heraclitean position.

A third misconception about Frye is that his theories of poetry require a conscious effort by the contemporary poet to incorporate mythology into his writing. This idea has led to the so-called "mythopoeic" or "Frygian" school of Canadian poetry and to such ill-conceived works as Reaney's *A Suit of Nettles* and Macpherson's *The Boatman*. Rather than being Frygian, this school constitutes a betrayal of Frye's ideas. To Frye the significance of the mythological patterns evident in literature resides in their having arisen spon-taneously and unselfconsciously from human life and in their thus reflecting desires and urges completely innate within man. Archetypes, he tells us, "are most easily studied in highly conventionalized literature: that is, for the most part, naive, primitive, and popular literature." To deliberately impose myth on literature as an act of "conscious will" is to circumvent, if not disrupt, the natural process by which man continues in Frye's view to build "his cities out of the Milky Way".

Far from resembling the conscious myth-usage of the "Frygians" or the craftly practices of Smith, Finch, and Wilfrid Watson, Frye's theory of composition — based on Blake's dictum, "the authors are in eternity" — resembles that of such contemporary pre-reflective writers as Gerry Gilbert, Daphne Marlatt, George Bowering, Victor Coleman, bpNichol, and Bill Bissett. These are the only group of Canadian writers who share Frye's belief that a conscious search for pure form implies that "the vanity of the ego has replaced the honest pride of the craftsman". They are the only writers who have shown faith in the ability of the universe to direct composition through open, random, or multiphasic forms, or a belief that the "craft" of writing involves a listening to "Mother Nature". Frye's comments on composition resemble a summary of the salient points of many of their manifestos:

... as long as the father of the poem is assumed to be the poet himself, we have once again failed to distinguish literature from discursive verbal structures. The discursive writer writes as an act of conscious will, and that conscious will, along with the symbolic system he employs for it, is set over against the body of things he is describing. But the poet, who writes creatively rather than deliberately, is not the father of his poem; he is at best a mid-wife, or, more accurately still, the womb of Mother Nature herself: her privates, so to speak.

He is responsible for delivering it in as uninjured state as possible, and if the poem is alive, it is equally anxious to be rid of him, and screams to be cut loose from all the navel-strings and feeding tubes of his ego. (*AC* 98)

Frye, Northrop. *Fearful Symmetry. A Study of William Blake.* Princeton: Princeton University Press, 1947, Paperback ed., Boston: Beacon Press, 1962.

, ed. *Selected Poetry and Prose of William Blake.* New York: The Modern Library, 1953.

. *Anatomy of Criticism: Four Essays.* Princeton: Princeton University Press, 1957. Paperback ed., New York: Athenaeum Press, 1966.

, ed. *Sound and Poetry.* New York: Columbia University

Press, 1957.

_____, ed. *The Collected Poems of E.J. Pratt* (second edition). Toronto: Macmillan, 1958.

_____. *Fables of Identity.* New York: Harcourt Brace and World, 1963.

_____. *The Educated Imagination.* Toronto: CBC Publications, 1963. Reprinted, Bloomington: Indiana University Press, 1964.

_____, ed. *Romanticism Reconsidered.* New York: Columbia University Press, 1963.

_____. *T.S. Eliot.* Edinburgh: Oliver and Boyd, 1963.

_____. *The Well-Tempered Critic.* Bloomington: Indiana University Press, 1963.

_____. *A Natural Perspective: Essays on the Development of Shakespearean Comedy and Romance.* New York: Columbia University Press, 1965.

_____. *The Return to Eden: Five Essays on Milton's Epics.* Toronto: University of Toronto Press, 1965.

_____, ed. *Blake: A Collection of Critical Essays.* Englewood Cliffs, N.J.: Prentice-Hall Inc., 1966.

_____. *Fools of Time: Studies in Shakespearean Tragedy.* Toronto: University of Toronto Press, 1967.

_____. *The Modern Century.* Toronto: Oxford University Press, 1967.

_____. *A Study of English Romanticism.* New York: Random House, 1968.

_____. *The Stubborn Structure.* London: Methuen & Co. Ltd., 1970, Ithaca: Cornell University Press, 1970.

_____. *The Bush Garden: Essays on the Canadian Imagination.* Toronto: House of Anansi Press, 1971.

Bates, Ronald. *Northrop Frye.* Toronto: McClelland & Stewart, 1971. New Canadian Library, Canadian Writers 10.

Krieger, Murray, ed. *Northrop Frye in Modern Criticism.* New York: Columbia University Press, 1966. English Institute Essays.

Hugh Garner

(1913-   )

In recent years Hugh Garner's short stories have been regularly included in both academic and popular anthologies, while his novels
have enjoyed continued paperback popularity. Garner's subject in
nearly all his books has been working-class Ontario. In his public
declarations he has cast himself as the voice of the workers, the
unemployed, the pensioners, and the other "little" people of this
region.

He has published four volumes of short stories, *The Yellow
Sweater* (1952), *Men and Women* (1966), *The Violation of the Virgins*
(1971), and the selected *Hugh Garner's Best Stories* (1963). These
stories tend to be lacking in subtlety and in depth of characterization.
Most of them present personality types rather than firmly drawn
idiosyncratic characters. The situations in which the characters find
themselves are usually more interesting than the characters
themselves. Although the world-view of these stories is simplistic
and often banal, most of them can provide an enjoyable and
provocative reading experience at the secondary school level.

Of Garner's seven novels, the best-known are *Storm Below*
(1949) and *Cabbagetown* (1950, rev. 1968). The former is the account
of a typical voyage of a Canadian corvette in World War II. The
documentary aspect of the novel is very strong, but its characters are
stereotyped and its attitudes toward the characters coloured by sen-
timentality. Garner's overt display of his personal feelings toward the
events he describes works to undermine much of the effectiveness of
the factual material. *Cabbagetown* tells the stories of a number of
families who live in Toronto's impoverished "Cabbagetown" area
during the great depression. This is a more skilfully written work than

113

Storm below; Garner restrains himself from intrusive commentary and allows the facts of the stories to generate their own response in the reader. Once again, however, the characterizations are slight, and greatly overshadowed by the power of the plot and of the documentary aspects of the setting.

A unique combination of naturalistic and working-class attitudes pervades Hugh Garner's fiction. His work suggests a belief that individual men are relatively powerless in the face of the large social and political events which swirl around them. His characters are usually prisoners of circumstance — trapped by education, family, world history, and fate into prostitution in Cabbagetown or death in the fiery North Atlantic. Although naturalism and complex characterization are not antithetical, this belief may well have led Garner to neglect individual portrayals. Such a belief is very similar to the working-class conviction of its being a victim of a class-struggle — a frequent theme in Garner's work. It is accompanied by a large number of working-class attitudes and superstitions. Young women, in Garner, are deflowered usually as a result of rape or of their own drunkenness. Middle-aged white-collar workers are usually crass, sexually frustrated, and ineffectual. Business executives and small businessmen are only one failure away from a life of alcoholism and relentless decline. Paradoxically, the declared attitudes in Garner's fiction are liberal and humane; however, the covert ones contained in characterization and event tend to dominate.

Recent novels by Hugh Garner include *A Nice Place to Visit* (1970) — a work, apparently based on the Stephen Truscott trial, which once again unites documentary and naturalism — and the detective novel *The Sin Sniper* (1970).

Garner, Hugh. *Storm Below*. Toronto: William Collins & Sons, 1949. Reprinted Toronto: Ryerson Press, 1968 and Richmond Hill: Simon & Schuster, 1971.

    . *Cabbagetown*. Toronto: William Collins & Sons, 1950. Revised edition Toronto: Ryerson Press, 1968, reprinted Richmond Hill: Simon & Schuster, 1971.

    . *Waste No Tears* (pseud. Jarvis Warwick). New Toronto: News Stand Library, 1950.

    . *Present Reckoning*. Toronto: William Collins & Sons, 1951.

    . *The Yellow Sweater and Other Stories*. Toronto: William Collins & Sons, 1952.

    . *The Silence on the Shore*. Toronto: McClelland & Stewart, 1962. Reprinted Toronto: Ryerson Press, 1968 and

Richmond Hill: Simon & Schuster, 1971.
. *Hugh Garner's Best Stories.* Toronto: Ryerson Press,
1963. Reprinted Toronto: Ryerson Press, 1968 and Richmond Hill:
Simon & Schuster, 1971.
. *Author, Author!* Toronto: Ryerson Press, 1964.
. *Men and Women.* Toronto: Ryerson Press, 1966.
. *A Nice Place to Visit.* Toronto: Ryerson, 1970. Reprinted
Richmond Hill: Simon & Schuster, 1971.
. *The Sin Sniper.* Richmond Hill: Simon & Schuster, 1970.
. *Violation of the Virgins.* Toronto: McGraw-Hill Ryerson,
1971.
. *Some Are So Lucky; The Magnet; a Trip for Mrs. Taylor.*
Toronto: Simon & Pierre, 1972.
. *One Damn Thing After Another.* Toronto: McGraw-Hill
Ryerson, 1973.

Anderson, Allan. "An Interview with Hugh Garner," *Tamarack
Review* 52 (Third Quarter, 1969), 19-24.
Dobbs, Kildare. "The Garnering of Garner," *Saturday Night* 79 (May
1964), 27-28.
Fetherling, Doug. *Hugh Garner.* Toronto: Forum House, 1972.
Fulford, Robert. "Hugh Garner: He's Worth Cherishing" (rev. of
Violation of the Virgins), *The Toronto Star,* Nov. 6, 1971, p.49.
. "Hugh Garner Stikes Out at Publishers" (rev. of *One
Damn Thing After Another*), *The Toronto Star,* Sept. 29, 1973, p.G5.
. "On Hugh Garner: Everyone Loses Everything. Nobody
Knows Anybody," *Maclean's* 76 (November 2, 1963), 73-74.
Hall, William F. "New Interest in Reality," *Canadian Literature* 40
(Spring 1969), 66-68.
. "Without Confidence," *Canadian Literature* 19 (Winter
1964), 55-57.
Irwin, Joan. "Garner the Pro," *Tamarack Review* 31 (Spring 1964), 98.
McPherson, Hugo. "Men and Women — Red All Over," *Canadian
Literature* 31 (Winter 1967), 59-61.
Moss, John G. "A Conversation with Hugh Garner," *Journal of
Canadian Fiction* I:2 (1971), 50-55.
Pacey, Desmond. Review of *Men and Women, Canadian Forum* 47
(July 1967), 91-92.
Parr, Jack. "Who's Hugh in Canadian Fiction," *Journal of Canadian
Fiction* I:1 (1971), 85-86.
Ross, Mary Lowry. "Human Paradox," *Saturday Night* 78 (March
1963), 29-30.
Spettigue, D.O. "The Hugh Garner Papers at Queen's," *Douglas
Library Notes,* Queen's University, Vol. XIII, No. 4, Summer 1969.

Sypnowich, Peter. "Hugh Garner's New Hero — an Outsider who Wants In" (rev. of *A Nice Place to Visit*), *The Toronto Star,* Sept. 19, 1970, p.73.

Waddington, Miriam. "Garner's Good Ear," *Canadian Literature* 50 (Autumn 1971), 72-75.

Watmough, David. "The Observing Lens," *Canadian Literature* 17 (Summer 1963), 68-70.

Woodcock, George. "A Writer's Authentic Look at Toronto's Underside" (rev. of *The Sin Sniper*), *The Toronto Star,* Aug. 1, 1970, p.47.

Graeme Gibson

(1934-   )

Graeme Gibson is one of a number of Toronto writers for whom the restricting spirit of the old Orange and Presbyterian Ontario is still alive to be attacked. The characters of his novels are all faced with one choice: surrender to the conventional marriages, dehumanizing careers, and materialistic values upon which the culture of the province is alleged to insist or take flight to another country — preferably in the company of an unconventional woman. These novels, particularly *Five Legs* (1969), suggest a number of oversimplifications: that Canadian academic careers are dull and corrupt, that marriage is entered into only by materialistic and frigid women, and that rebellious and meaningful lives are possible only in Europe or the U.S.

In his writing techniques Gibson is himself attempting to rebel against conventional narrative structures and unimaginative character portrayals. Unfortunately, the rebellion appears to be without significant artistic objective. In *Five Legs* Gibson's rendering of his character's thoughts in awkwardly broken sentences ("Don't know them and what's more. don't. want to. them or him.") creates for the reader more confusion than verisimilitude. In fact, the painfully "experimental" prose distances the reader from the characters so that the latter can never come alive as powerful and experienceable figures. In both *Five Legs* and *Communion* (1971) Gibson also uses rapidly shifting points of view, which again serve mostly to obscure the plot and distance the characters.

Gibson does have a strong claim to speak of Protestant Ontario in the 1950's and 1960's. He was born in London, Ontario, attended Upper Canada College, Trinity College School, College Militaire

Royal de St. Jean, and the University of Western Ontario, where he failed to complete an M.A., and has taught in Toronto at Ryerson Polytechnical Institute. *Five Legs* is set in London, Ontario, where its central character, Lucan Crackell, is a professor of English, and *Communion* is set in Toronto where its central character, Felix Oswald, is a failed M.A. student employed in a pet store.

Marriage is the central issue of *Five Legs*. Lucan Crackell has chosen to marry the self-absorbed and middle-class Rose rather than travel aimlessly with his free-thinking and pregnant girlfriend. He has thus submitted himself to a 'closed' and predictable life-pattern — institutionalized marriage, an acquisitive lifestyle, and a routine and intimidating academic position, complete with pension, life insurance, and tenure. It is a life circumscribed by bureaucratic planning and ruled by public standards of respectability. The other two important men in the book are faced with parallel decisions. Martin Baillie must choose between 'irresponsible' elopement with his beloved bohemian girlfriend or a 'settled' marriage with the tiresome but respectable Susan. When he chooses Susan, and the conventional academic career necessary to support her, the conventional world immediately runs him down and kills him by means of a hit-and-run automobile. Gibson's message — conventionality kills — is so taken to heart by the third character, Felix Oswald, that he shuns sexual intercourse in fear of a compromising entanglement.

In *Communion* the virgin Felix has fled London, fled women, and fled the university, and is living a narrow and routinized existence of his own in Toronto. Ironically, his fear of entrapment has driven him into an equally dehumanized condition. He travels punctually each day between his basement room, his job, and the stone cemetery statues with whom he has fallen in love. He imagines that freedom may await him in the forests of the Ontario north, but when he goes there he finds that they offer him only an allegory of his own victimization. He later tries to hitch-hike to the U.S., only to encounter a sadistic truckdriver, cynical immigration officials, and the extraordinary violence of a Detroit night. The conclusion, in which Felix is unfelicitously dumped into the middle of a ghetto streetfight, while thematically satisfactory is artistically most unsatisfactory. Felix's arrival here is totally improbable and contrived.

Neither of Gibson's novels are particularly readable, the elaborate narrative methods are annoyingly pretentious in that they suggest a profundity that they do not deliver. The characters are tedious and unimaginative people for whose fates it is difficult for a reader to feel concern. Both are strangely contrived and overwritten for novels which set out to attack an allegedly contrived and over-systemized society.

Gibson, Graeme.   *Five Legs.* Toronto: House of Anansi, 1969.
        . *Communion.* Toronto House of Anansi, 1971.
        . *Eleven Canadian Novelists* (interviews). Toronto: House
of Anansi, 1973.

Bacchus, Ataur.   "Out of a Somewhat," *Alphabet* 17 (December
    1969), 91-92.
Bickerstaff, Isaac.   "Rear View," *Books in Canada* I:7 (January 1972),
    9.
Coles, Don.   "Subliminal Flickers from a Fiery Despair" (rev. of *Com-
    munion*), *The Globe and Mail,* Nov. 6, 1971, p.31.
French, William.   "A Glowing Anti-Puritanism, in Sorrow" (rev. of *Five
    Legs*), *The Globe and Mail Magazine,* Apr. 19, 1969, p.19.
Geddes, Gary.   "The Muse Acclimatized," *Canadian Literature* 42
    (Autumn 1969), 93-96.
Symons, Scott.   Review of *Five Legs, Saturday Night* 84 (May 1969),
    46, 48-49.

Gerry Gilbert

(1936-   )

The most extreme (and therefore least publicly known) example of the movement of Canadian writing to mutiphasic, relativistic, and phenomenological forms has been the work of "Canada's National Magazine", Gerry Gilbert. Gilbert chooses the most recalcitrant of subjects: the ordinary breakfast-to-bedtime experiences local to his own life. He presents these in their random sequence because it is exactly this sequence that he wishes to make substantial to his readers. He avoids even the minimal amount of 'packaging' that gives shape to a George Bowering or Daphne Marlatt lyric; neatness, conciseness, or rhetorical form would directly betray the randomness of reality he seeks to evoke, and merely duplicate the various institutional and political structures which he believes to distort life and oppress men.

Gilbert's experiential world is that of most men alive in these decades, mundane, trivial, thoroughly non-spectacular — enriched only by the easily missed miracles of animals, plants, the weather,or intimate human gesture. He presents this world in the way in which it impinges on him: a puzzlingly discontinuous flow of broken images. "AND", the title of one of his books, is the usual Gilbert conjunction, since it implies no logical structure or relationship. To Gilbert, experience is endless *non sequitur.*

His background as a television cameraman is reflected in the fact that most of his perceptions of experience manifest themselves as visual images in motion. Familiar objects, sounds, activities of the poet's day juxtapose or fade erratically together in the manner of the cinematic collage. "Why doncha watch the scenery", Gilbert suggests in one poem; in another "everything is on the screen". The space between lines is often enlarged in his work so that it suggests a blank spot somewhere between the resolution and perception of sensory stimuli.

Phone Book by Gerry Gilbert.
Weed/Flower Press and Ganglia Press, 1969.

Gilbert describes his poems as "ghosts of old blues I knew". Although this implies a subjective element, very little of Gilbert's own reflections enter into his poetry. Most of the work draws on his pre-reflective consciousness — on conversations he overhears, people, billboards, insects he sees. The few reflective passages are playful rather than analytical — a toying with etymology or rhyme — and reveal a mind more devoted to the surfaces of coincidence and wit than to the extraction of meaning. In fact, the term 'meaning' implies far more structure than Gilbert believes to exist in experience. To pursue such meaning, his poetry suggests, is to go beyond the properties of actuality — hence to create illusion, falsehood.

Gerry Gilbert has remained faithful to his concepts of experience and art since he emerged as a writer in Vancouver in the early sixties. Among Canadian writers, he has been a genuine rebel, totally unwilling to seek the attention of readers or the praise of critics by the sacrifice of principle or style. Rather than being affronted by the fact that none of his nine books of poetry have yet been reviewed by Canada's national magazine of literature, *Canadian Literature,* he has founded and edited his own magazine of review and political commentary, *The B.C. Monthly.* Here the strong political implications of Gilbert's poetic — that any 'overstructure' or 'packaging' is an authoritarian imposition on the individual lives of men — are openly expressed in numerous essays by other members of the Vancouver correspondence-art and writing community.

Gilbert, Gerry.   *White Lunch.* Vancouver: Periwinkle Press, 1964.

———. "1000 Words on Lee-Nova," Arts/*Canada* 26 (April 1969), 15.

———. *Phone Book.* Toronto: Ganglia Press and Weed/Flower Press, 1969.

———. *Quote (New York, July 1965).* Toronto: Ganglia Press, 1969.

———. *Money.* Vancouver: Georgia Straight Writing Series, 1971.

———. "Sixteen Cedar Laminates," (illustrated), Arts/*Canada* 28 (August-September 1971), 60-61.

———. *And.* Vancouver: Blewointment Press, 1971.

———. *Apr. 35, 1978.* Vancouver: I.B. HeShe&ItWorks, 1971.

———. *Lease.* Toronto: The Coach House Press, 1972.

———. *Skies.* Vancouver: Talonbooks, 1973.

Bowering, George.   "Gerry Gilbert," *Open Letter* (second series) 4, Spring 1973, p.57.

Coleman, Victor.   Review of *Money, Open Letter* (second series) 1

(Winter 1971-72), 76-80.

Dudek, Louis. "The New Vancouver Poetry," *Culture* 25 (December 1964), 324-326.

Flowers, Slim (Gerry Gilbert). "Canada's Top Poet" (interview with Victor Coleman), *The B.C. Monthly* I:2 (November 1972), 86-87.

Purdy, A.W. "Who's Got the Emphasis?", *Canadian Forum* 44 (September 1964), 142-143.

John Glassco

(1910-   )

All of John Glassco's works have been eccentric achievements, more attached to the values and fashions of the past than to those of post-war Canada. Since 1958 he has published five books: three of poetry (*The Deficit Made Flesh*, 1958; *A Point of Sky*, 1964; and *Selected Poems*, 1971) an edition and completion of Aubrey Beardsley's erotic prose romance *Under the Hill* (1959), and *Memoirs of Montparnasse* (1970). Each one invokes some portion of the past: the poetry comprises an elegy to courageous but futile actions by both the poet and by settlers and farmers in the Quebec Eastern Townships; the additions to *Under the Hill* recreate the language and sensibility of the English Decadent period; *Memoirs of Montparnasse* offer intense glimpses of literary Paris of 1928-29.

Behind much of Glassco's backward-looking vision is a conviction that man and all his creations are "destined for slaughter in the course of things." In Glassco's poetry man is born into a world of "endless horror" and "entrapment". His ultimate destiny is a "shape of blackness", the "gape of all and the loss of the person". Although this pessimism is superficially similar to that of Ralph Gustafson, Phyllis Webb, Eli Mandel, or John Newlove, Glassco's response most certainly is not. Directly and indirectly his poems encourage the perception of beauty within cruelty and ruin. His reflections on failed settlers and their despoiled farmsteads present a sensibility which finds a melancholy delight in the defeats of others. His explicit philosophical comments suggest that the pain of life can be made endurable by being transformed into art — an idea reminiscent of the "Life imitates Art" dictum of Oscar Wilde. Life is a "melancholy art" Glassco advises; and joy is an "ecstatic suffering".

UNDER THE HILL

by Aubrey Beardsley
and John Glassco

Under the Hill by Aubrey Beardsley
and John Glassco. Grove Press, 1967.

The transformation of pain into pleasure and life into art forms the basis of Glassco's writing technique. Glassco is a consummate stylist, and writes a poetry of delicate phrasing and of extended, precisely qualifying, syntax. Much of his poetry converts human tragedy and failure into elegant poetic reflection — reflection that both conveys cerebral pleasure in the poet and evokes it in the reader. Abandoned buildings become "ruins wreathed in grace"; they "wear ... the final grace of rotting and attrition like a crown." To paraphrase a Glassco title, the "deficit" in mankind's lot is redeemed in the "flesh" of exquisite language and form.

The metamorphosis of life into "pure form" and of sexuality into ritually stylized forms is the essential task undertaken by Glassco in his completion of *Under the Hill*. In Beardsley's imagination the central characters, Tannhauser and Venus, engage in delicately choreographed social and sexual pleasures; flesh is reduced to "succulent limbs," an "instrument" of music, an "aperitif". Glassco extends and amplifies this world; in his second chapter he creates a glittering, visually textured scene of the "art" of flagellation. The young male victims strike "an exquisite pose", their female torturers whip them in "chromatic progression" to the accompaniment of "fresh music", "piercing cries", and "antiphonal rhetoric". Both Beardsley's language and that of Glassco succeed in forging from emotionally-charged and thoroughly fleshly phenomena a cold, impersonal, sculpture of graceful metaphor and geometric, dehumanizing image.

Glassco's *Memoirs of Montparnasse* are the earliest of his writings, although not published until 1970. Begun in Paris in 1928 when Glassco was an 18-year-old seeking the magic of Montparnasse, and completed in a Montreal hospital in 1932-33, they exhibit the gay hedonism of youth rather than the bittersweet vision of his later work. The book is an intriguing visual document of the Paris of Joyce, Hemingway, Fitzgerald, Callaghan, Andre Breton, Robert Desnos, Ford Maddox Ford, and Gertrude Stein, and a rich work of apprenticeship literature. As a characterization, the young John Glassco takes form as one of the most engagingly insouciant and pretentious figures in our literature. The quality of the writing is again superb; the prose is direct, witty, and filled with sparklingly vivid sketches of once-romantic places and soon-to-be-famous men.

Glassco, John.   *The Deficit Made Flesh*. Toronto: McClelland & Stewart, 1958.
        . *Under the Hill*. by Aubrey Beardsley and John Glassco. New York: Grove Press, 1967 (c. 1959).
        . *Under the Birch:* the Story of an English Governess, by

Miles Underwood (pseud.). Paris: Ophelia Press, 1965. First published in 1960 with title *The English Governess.*

. *A Point of Sky.* Toronto: Oxford University Press, 1964.

,ed. *English Poetry in Quebec.* Montreal: McGill University Press, 1965.

. "The Art of Pornography," *Edge* 9 (Summer 1969), 101-113.

Memoirs of Montparnasse. Toronto: Oxford University Press, 1970.

, ed. *The Poetry of French Canada in Translation.* Toronto: Oxford University Press, 1970.

. *Selected Poems.* Toronto: Oxford University Press, 1971.

. "Countess Isobel and the Torturer," *Jewish Dial-og,* Summer 1972, p.33.

. "Pigtail Man," *Jewish Dial-og,* Hanukah 1973, pp.47-48.

Bessai, Diane E. "Eclectic Craftsman," *Canadian Forum* 45 (July 1965), 94-95.

Colombo, John Robert. "Three Poetic Images, One Success" (rev. of *A Point of Sky*), *The Globe and Mail Magazine,* May 1, 1965, p.16.

French, William. "Pursuing a Dream in Paris Remembered" (rev. of *Memoirs of Montparnasse*), *The Globe and Mail Magazine,* Mar. 7, 1970, p.16.

Laurence, Margaret. "Roses and Yew," *Tamarack Review* 54 (1970), 77-80.

Mandel, E.W. "A Special Adequacy," *Canadian Literature* 26 (Autumn 1965), 71-72.

Mandel, Eli. "To Understand, Risking Poetry's Betrayal" (rev. of *The Poetry of French Canada in Translation*), *The Globe and Mail Magazine,* June 20, 1970, p.15.

Skelton, Robin. Review of Selected Poems, *The Malahat Review* 23, pp.5-7.

Waddington, Miriam. "But How Does Glassco Feel about Montreal?" (rev. of *Montreal*), *The Globe and Mail,* Nov. 17, 1973, p.34.

Woodcock, George. "Literary Worlds and their Denizens," *Canadian Literature* 44 (Spring 1970), 67-68.

Dave
Godfrey (1938-   )

Dave Godfrey has been among the most energetic of the new wave of Canadian literary and economic nationalists in the 1960's and 1970's. Recognizing that those who control a country's media also control its culture, he began working toward the wresting of a significant portion of the country's book publishing industry from foreign control. He helped to found three of the period's new nationalistic commercial publishing houses, House of Anansi, New Press, and Press Porcépic. He became one of the principal initiators of the Independent Publishers Association, an association of Canadian-owned presses which have bonded together to form a political lobby and to attempt to solve common distribution problems. His conviction that a country's literary independence is tied to its degree of economic independence is reflected in his being not only a co-editor of *Read Canadian: a book about Canadian books* (1971) but also co-editor, with nationalist economist Mel Watkins, of *Gordon to Watkins to You* (1970).

As a fiction writer, Godfrey is the most accomplished of the nationalistic wave. As in the best traditions of fiction, Godfrey's emphases always fall strongly on character, situation, and language, and on the implications these project, and very lightly on the purely polemic or 'thesis' elements to which committed activists frequently yield their art. Characteristically, nationalist Godfrey sets very few of his writings in Canada; most are set in the United States, the source of our culture's greatest danger, or in Africa, where other small cultures struggle against the large. Also characteristically, Godfrey emphasizes the effects of cultural imperialism not on major political events but on the individual's private life. His narrative methods are

126

usually oblique. He allows the necessary facts of his tales to unfold slowly and irregularly, similarly to the way they unfold in actuality. Often a reader will have little idea what the central experience of a Godfrey short story is until the final few lines. Godfrey's favourite structuring technique is juxtaposition. The significance of a story will lie in the relationship between the frame narrative and an interior narrative ("The Winter Stiffs") or between two apparently unrelated narratives ("The Hard-Headed Collector").

His collection of short stories, *Death Goes Better with Coca-Cola* (1967) presents a series of tales linking the cynical beholding and causing of death with the Coca-Cola world's American dream. The jaded killers and near-killers of this book are all either Americans or Americanized citizens of other countries. They hunt moose from a spotting aircraft; they shoot a unique old pheasant merely because its killing is a challenge; they can casually pile pieces of a human body "like cordwood". At worst they are trophy hunters — an Americanized African jazz-drummer seeking "a true African xylophone" ("Fulfilling our Foray"), or a "doctor of philosophy" who seeks one flying fish "to mount on my wall" ("Flying Fish"). At best they are greedy and self-indulgent — catching salmon, shooting moose, despoiling forests, not to meet need but merely to commit the frivolous acts of waste a disposable culture encourages.

The juxtapositional structure of Godfrey's fiction is one of the keys to his novel *The New Ancestors* (1970). The novel is composed of six sections told from the viewpoints of four characters. One of the characters (the British Council representative) is concerned exclusively with the present; a second (Michael Burdener) with the past; a third (Ama Burdener) with the future. An ambiguously narrated "Fifth City" section takes the viewpoint of visionary experience. Each section focusses on the same complex relationships, but from vastly differing personal perspectives. There are at least five 'central' characters. There is no 'orderly' development of plot. The book opens with a murder and a deportation, but their effects are noticeably unexplored. Instead, the various narrative sections report on the network of events and conflicts which have preceded the murder and deportation. Godfrey is interested not in the linear aspects of his tale, but rather in the textures of the individual lives which lie behind and contribute to political events. The ultimate reality of the novel's complex of political intrigues lies within the dreams, illusions, obsessions, and frustrations of its various participants; as the book's epigraph tells us, "We carry within us all the wonders we seek without us."

127

All of Godfrey's fiction resists easy interpretation. He aims to express subtle and elaborate perceptions and is willing to risk overworking and discouraging his readers in order to express these. Following the lead of post-Einsteinian physics, he sees truth not as absolute but as multifarious and variable; to Godfrey, phenomena viewed from differing systems of coordinates in motion relative to one another appear as different phenomena. The results of this theory so far have been brief and resonant short stories, and a diffuse and challenging novel, and for their writer a deserved reputation as a resourceful and uncompromising prose experimenter.

Godfrey, Dave.   *Death Goes Better with Coca-Cola.* Toronto: House of Anansi, 1967, reprinted Erin, Ont.: Press Porcépic, 1973.
       . *New Canadian Writing, 1968.* Stories by David Lewis Stein, Clark Blaise, and Dave Godfrey. Toronto: Clarke, Irwin, 1968.
       , ed. *Man Deserves Man: CUSO in Developing Countries* ed. Bill McWhinney and Dave Godfrey. Toronto: Ryerson Press, 1968.
       , ed. *Gordon to Watkins to You:* a Documentary of the battle for control of our economy, ed. Dave Godfrey and Mel Watkins. Toronto: New Press, 1970.
       . *The New Ancestors.* Toronto: New Press, 1970.
       . "Friday Afternoon at the Iowa City Airport," *Canadian Forum* 50 (January 1971), 340-342.
       , ed. *Read Canadian: a Book About Canadian Books,* ed. Robert Fulford, Dave Godfrey, and Abraham Rotstein. Toronto: James Lewis & Samuel, 1972.

Cameron, Donald.   "The Three People Inside Dave Godfrey," *Saturday Night* 86 (September 1971), 20-22.
       . "Myths and Gardens" (interview), *Conversations with Canadian Novelists* (Toronto: MacMillan of Canada, 1973), pp.34-47.
Coles, Don.   "Erotic? Forearms Never Had it so Good" (rev. of *Death Goes Better with Coca-Cola*), *The Globe and Mail Magazine,* Dec. 30, 1967, p.14.
Gibson, Graeme.   Interview with Dave Godfrey, in his *Eleven Canadian Novelists* (Toronto: House of Anansi, 1973), pp.155-179.
Grosskurth, Phyllis.   "Portrait of the Canadian Adam in a Buffalo Skin," *Canadian Forum* 51 (April-May 1971), 16-17.
Helwig, David.   "Stories Around Death," *Queen's Quarterly* 75 (Summer 1968), 347-350.
Laurence, Margaret.   "Caverns to the Mind's Dark Continent" (rev. of *The New Ancestors*), *The Globe and Mail Magazine,* Dec. 5, 1970, p.18.

Metcalf, John.   "Among the Best that Canada Has Produced," *Montreal Star,* February 27, 1971, "Entertainments", p.29.

New, William H.   "Equatorial Zones," in his *Articulating West* (Toronto: New Press, 1972), 216-233.

Sypnowich, Peter.   "Toronto Man Views His Writing as Weapon Against U.S. Empire," *The Toronto Star,* Jan. 9, 1971, p.49.

Thomas, Audrey.   "The Smell of Recognition," *Canadian Literature* 49 (Summer 1971), 78-80.

Woodcock, George.   "Borderland of Truth," *Canadian Literature* 38 (Autumn 1968), 92.

Gwethalyn Graham (1913-65)

Of Gwethalyn Graham's two novels, *Swiss Sonata* (1938) and *Earth and High Heaven* (1944), it is the latter which has proven to be of more enduring power. Highly publicized and praised at its initial publication, *Earth and High Heaven* has continued to be recognized as a profound and moving statement about the causes and implications of racial prejudice.

Graham was one of the earliest Canadian novelists to explore the issues of either anti-semitism or the alienation of ethnic minorities from Canada's two dominant cultures. Her novels stand at the beginning of a significant line of Canadian fiction which deals with alienation from the victim's point of view — Kreisel's *The Betrayal*, Marlyn's *Under the Ribs of Death*, Richler's *The Apprenticeship of Duddy Kravitz*, Wiseman's *The Sacrifice*. Her work, together with that of Klein and Layton, marks the beginning of our literature's concern with traditions other than the Anglo-Saxon one of Moodie, Connor, MacLennan, Pratt, Davies, and Atwood.

Graham's first novel, *Swiss Sonata*, is an awkward but passionate work involving the relationships between twenty students of various nationalities who attend a Swiss boarding school on the eve of World War II. The novel has a number of grave flaws: pages of unnecessary geography and floorplans; numerous unconvincingly staged conversations and confrontations; a diffuse plot which embraces twenty-seven allegedly "suffering" characters without managing to provide a single compelling centre; and a melodramatic ending of which the only credibility is derived from the incredibility of some of the events which have preceded.

Fundamental to the novel is the idea of international

129

cooperation. This idea is implicit in the Swiss setting, in references to the collapsing League of Nations, and in the headmistress's desire to have the school "inculcate the international idea in minds which are not yet too set, too limited by prejudice, too mired in conventional patriotism." The girls are intended to represent the world in microcosm: a Brazilian, a Canadian, a Québecois, a Norwegian, a Dane, an Italian, a Pole, a South African, two Armenians, a Jewish Saarlander, a Jewish American, several English, and several Jew-baiting Germans. Due to both world events and their own self-preoccupations, the girls live in considerable mistrust and tension until a fortuitous coincidence and one apparent "miracle" provides a partial solution.

In *Earth and High Heaven* Gwethalyn Graham adopts a much smaller and workable cast of characters and avoids most of the awkward effects of the earlier novel. Once again, however, the overall structure is one of increasing complication which is eventually resolved by a carefully prepared-for "miracle", and once again the conclusion contains more than a hint of melodrama. Despite this, *Earth and High Heaven* is an extremely intense, compelling, and satisfying novel. Its story is that of two upper-middle-class lovers, Marc Reiser and Erica Drake, who attempt to transcend the racial bigotry of Erica's family and WASP Montreal; it is told against the background of ongoing Nazi anti-semitism in World War II. The novel is particularly strong in making clear that the roots of racial prejudice lie in false generalizations and in irrational credence in totally impossible facts and stories.

The prejudice of Erica's father against Marc rests on preconceptions about "Jews" and on apocryphal stories and salacious jokes he has talked himself into accepting; the prejudice of ordinary Germans rests on similar lies and distortions taught them by their government. Basic to the prejudice of each is ignorance of individual Jewish people and of their particular circumstances. Graham cleverly exploits these aspects of prejudice in her narrative technique by letting the reader come to know Marc Reiser only through his words and actions, while having Erica's father continually both refuse to meet him and revile him on the basis of inaccurate generalizations and abstractions.

Regrettably, Graham has written no other novels, and the short stories that she contributed to *Macleans* and *Saturday Night* have been so far uncollected. A sequel to her novels and to her considerable interest in inter-cultural relations is provided by her exchange of letters with the French Canadian Solange Chaput-Rolland, published in 1963 under the title *Dear Enemies*.

Graham, Gwethalyn.   *Swiss Sonata*. New York: Scribner, 1938.
         . *Earth and High Heaven*. Philadelphia: Lippincott, 1944.
Reprinted Toronto: McClelland & Stewart, 1960 (New Canadian
Library no. 13)
         . *Dear Enemies: a Dialogue of French and English Canada*
by Gwethalyn Graham and Solange Chaput-Rolland. Toronto: Macmillan of Canada, 1964 (c. 1963).

Aitken, Margaret A.   "Gwethalyn Graham: a Canadian Author with a
Crusading Spirit," *Saturday Night* 60 (October 28, 1944), 36.
Anon.   Biography. In *Current Biography 1945* (New York: H.W.
Wilson, 1946), pp.246-247.
Anon.   Review of *Swiss Sonata, Times Literary Supplement,* February
19, 1938, p. 123.
Barry, Iris.   Review of *Earth and High Heaven, Weekly Book Review,*
October 8, 1944, p.3.
Benet, R.C.   Review of *Earth and High Heaven, Saturday Review of
Literature* 27 (October 7, 1944), 9.
Deacon, William Arthur.   "Bid on Books that will Last" (rev. of *Earth
and High Heaven*), *The Globe and Mail*, Dec. 3, 1960, "Review of
Books" p.16.
         . "Canadian Novel Challenges Montreal's Race Prejudice"
(rev. of *Earth and High Heaven*), *The Globe and Mail*, Oct. 7, 1944,
"Review of Books" p.10.
Gibson, Wilfrid.   Review of *Swiss Sonata, Manchester Guardian,*
February 11, 1938, p.7.
MacGillivray, J.R.   Review of *Earth and High Heaven, University of
Toronto Quarterly* 14 (April 1945), 267-269.
Mandel, Eli.   Introduction to *Earth and High Heaven* (Toronto:
McClelland & Stewart, 1960, New Canadian Library no. 13), pp.v-xi.
Rossbach, M.C.   Review of *Swiss Sonata, New York Times,* April 17,
1938, p.6.
Sloan, Thomas.   "Fluttering the Curtain of Prejudice" (rev. of *Dear
Enemies*), *The Globe and Mail Magazine*, Nov 23, 1963, p. 24.
Smith, A.D.H.   Review of *Earth and High Heaven, New York Times,*
October 15, 1944, p.6.
Stanley, Carleton.   "Voices in the Wilderness," *Dalhousie Review* 25
(July 1945), 173-181.

Ralph Gustafson (1909-   )

Nowhere better than in the poetry of Ralph Gustafson can the deleterious effect on Canadian poetry of the Eliot-Tate kind of modernism be seen. This movement's distaste for the physical universe and preference for a complex and intellectual poetic language had, by the forties, led to the dominant professional poetry being one of direct philosophical statement decrying human mortality in academic, tortured syntax and superbly recondite diction. In Britain, the U.S., and in Canada, numerous academically trained poets wrote, as Kenneth Rexroth has remarked, as if they were androids programmed in the Eliot tradition by Allen Tate and John Crowe Ransom.

Gustafson's first book of poetry, *The Golden Chalice* (1931) is a work of stereotyped Georgian romanticism. His next four — *Poems* (1940), *Epithalamium in Time of War* (1941), *Flight into Darkness* (1944) and *Rivers Among Rocks* (1960) — are modernist works, written in an overwrought, highly artificial 'poetic' language, cryptic, riddling syntax, and mechanical verse forms. With the exception of some poems in the last book, these are torturous poems that must be deciphered rather than read. They are nearly devoid of personal experience or evocative imagery, dwelling instead on the intricacies of philosophical and moral argument, occasionally half-heartedly documented by concrete reference.

The themes of the poems mostly concern the mutability of the physical world — its decay, rot, and death. Except for a few contrived flights of rhetorical passion in *Rivers Among Rocks*, however, Gustafson shows little personal anxiety or feeling for his subject. He takes the role of the uninspired but authoritative teacher, using

132

LYRICS
UNROMANTIC

BY RALPH GUSTAFSON

PRIVATELY PRINTED
NEW YORK CITY
1 9 4 2

Title page of *Lyrics Unromantic* by Ralph Gustafson.
Privately printed, 1942. One of 100 copies.

poetry as a platform for his own world view. Only in the last quarter of *Rivers Among Rocks* does he offer a few ballad stanzas in readable language and a few imagistic poems which confirm that he has the power of sight.

Certainly Gustafson is a dextrous, if uninspiring, verbal technician. The first substantial indication of this was his verse play *Alfred the Great* (1935). Its basic idiom is a somewhat accurate imitation of Elizabethan blank verse; it is ornamented with a number of authentically Anglo-Saxon alliterative verse passages. The imitations are not good enough, however, to give the play life. As in much of Gustafson's early poetry, the language fails to catch the tone of authentic human speech, appearing stilted and contrived.

In the sixties and seventies Gustafson has attempted a number of alterations in his style. *Rocky Mountain Poems* (1960) is written in short unmetered lines and an almost conversational idiom. There is an attempt here to deal with primary experience; unfortunately the descriptions of mountain landscapes are imprecise, and the thematic thrust of the poems is unclear. Most have the appearance of exercises on a topic rather than of high-energy writing. The syntax and diction of *Sift in an Hourglass* (1966) are also much less 'literary' than those of his early work; the metrical forms are more varied and include some free verse. For the first time a very few poems succeed in conveying Gustafson's feelings as well as his thoughts: "F.R. Scott","For Arthur Smith and Irving Layton, as if they All were Dead", "Dirge for a Penny Whistle", and "At Ned Pratt's Funeral". These poems, which are probably the best of his career, convey both his usual concern with mortality and an unusual joy in the juice and gusto of living. In *Ixion's Wheel* (1969) Gustafson continues his move toward a less formal vocabulary and syntax. This book, however, has none of the clear successes of *Sift in an Hourglass* . Most of the poems are travel poems which could have been written by an armchair tourist. Rather than being based, like the travel poems of Earle Birney, on keenly observed particulars, they are based mostly on secondary experience — on history, literature, art, and mythology. The tone is once again intellectual and moralizing.

His most recent publication, *Theme and Variations for Sounding Brass* (1972), consists of poems on the 1968 invasion of Czechoslovakia, the 1970 U.S. National Guard murder of four Kent State University students, the F.L.Q. terrorist bombings, abductions, and murders, and the Vietnamese war. This is the most colloquial verse of Gustafson's career, but one still unable to project an authentic personal voice. Much of the book has the ring of platitudinous journalism. Like most of Gustafson's poetry, they proceed from general to particular, here expressing 'correct' North American mid-

RALPH GUSTAFSON

RIVERS

AMONG

ROCKS

Rivers Among Rocks by Ralph Gustafson.
McClelland & Stewart, 1960.

dle-class liberal views on their chosen subjects. The poetry is unlikely to move those not already sharing its sentiments.

Gustafson's most important service to Canadian poetry has been as an international anthologist. He edited three anthologies of Canadian writing in the forties: *Anthology of Canadian Poetry* (Penguin, 1942), *A Little Anthology of Canadian Poets* (New Directions, 1943), and *Canadian Accent* (Penguin, 1944). These books served as the first notice to British and U.S. audiences that Canadian writing had moved past the Maple Leaf period and into the modernist one. In 1958 he edited *The Penguin Book of Canadian Verse.*

Gustafson, Ralph. *The Golden Chalice.* London: Nicholson & Watson, 1935.

. *Alfred the Great.* London: Joseph, 1937.

. *Epithalamium in Time of War.* New York: privately printed, 1941.

, ed. *Anthology of Canadian Poetry.* Harmondsworth: Penguin Books, 1942.

. *Lyrics Unromantic.* New York: privately printed, 1942.

, ed. *A Little Anthology of Canadian Poets.* Norfolk, Conn.: New Directions, 1943.

, ed. *Canadian Accent:* A Collection of Stories and Poems. Harmondsworth: Penguin Books, 1944.

. *Poetry and Canada:* A Guide to Reading. Ottawa: Canadian Legion Educational Services, 1945.

. *Flight Into Darkness.* New York: Pantheon, 1946.

, - ed. *The Penguin Book of Canadian Verse.* Harmondsworth: Penguin Books, 1958, rev. 1967.

. *Rivers Among Rocks.* Toronto: McClelland & Stewart, 1960.

. *Rocky Mountain Poems.* Vancouver: Klanak Press, 1960.

. *Sift in an Hourglass.* Toronto: McClelland & Stewart, 1966.

. *Ixion's Wheel.* Toronto: McClelland & Stewart, 1969.

. *Selected Poems.* Toronto: McClelland & Stewart, 1972.

. *Summer Storm.* Toronto: Roger Ascham Press, 1972.

. *Theme and Variations for Sounding Brass.* North Hatley, Que.: privately printed, 1972.

Coles, Don. "More Bunion than Heart" (rev. of *Selected Poems*), *The Globe and Mail*, Sep. 30, 1972, p.34.

Dudek, Louis. "Two Canadian Poets: Ralph Gustafson and Eli Mandel," *Culture* 22 (June 1961), 145-161.

Jones, D.G. "Voices in the Dark," *Canadian Literature* 45 (Summer

1970), 71-72.

Kirkconnell, Watson. "More Light, Please" (rev. of *Flight into Darkness*), *The Globe and Mail*, May 28, 1945, "Review of Books" p.19.

Lane, M. Travis. "The Fundamental Question About Poetry," *Fiddlehead* 96 (Winter 1973), 106-114.

MacCallum, Hugh. "Myth, Wit and Pop in Poems" (rev. of *Sift in an Hourglass*), *The Globe and Mail Magazine*, Jan. 7, 1967, p.13.

Mullins, S.G. "Ralph Gustafson's Poetry," *Culture* 22 (December 1961), 417-422.

Pacey, Desmond. Review of *Ixion's Wheel, Fiddlehead* 83 (January-February 1970), 80-81.

———. Review of *Sift in an Hourglass, Fiddlehead* 70 (Winter 1967), 62-65.

Skelton, Robin. "Possessed by Death," *Canadian Literature* 33 (Summer 1967), 85-86.

Hugh Hood

(1928-)

Hugh Hood was born in Toronto and lived there until completing his Ph.D. at the University of Toronto in 1955. He presently lives in Montreal where he teaches in the English Department of the University of Montreal. His parents were Roman Catholic — his father a Nova Scotian and his mother French-Canadian; most of his elementary and secondary education was acquired in Toronto's Catholic school system. Correspondingly, we find in his fiction little of the gloomy anxiety about protestant shibboleths — sin, conformity, and hard work — which characterizes the work of many of Hood's Toronto contemporaries, notably Margaret Atwood, Graeme Gibson, and Marian Engel. In contrast to the outlooks of these writers, Hood's vision of Canadian life is decidedly romantic.

In style, Hood is one of the most accomplished of his generation in the art of invisible craftsmanship. His work gives the illusion of being journalistic reportage — chatty, matter of fact, and unplanned; the casual voice of a somewhat unsophisticated but sensible narrator can be heard throughout. Nowhere in Hood does one find the verbal wit of an Atwood or the obvious straining for technical effect of a Graeme Gibson, Hood's casual style, however, cleverly creates a sense of credibility unavailable to the other two writers; the reader is led to trust every detail that Hood offers.

Part of this effect is achieved by Hood's abundant use of factual material. Many of Hood's stories are essentially autobiographical narrative essays — Hood as a schoolchild aspiring to musicianship, or Hood as a father taking his son to a summer resort. His novels and his less personal stories contain large amounts of factual or pseudo-factual material — sociological accounts of neighbourhoods, geographical descriptions of regions, quotations from newspapers, cameo appearances by famous personnages — so that there is always a pervasive and convincing tone of substantiality. In the novel *The Camera Always Lies* (1967), one character is even seen to be reading one of Hood's own books.

Hood's short stories have been gathered into three collections, *Flying a Red Kite* (1962), *Around the Mountain* (1967), and *The Fruit Man, the Meat Man, and the Manager* (1971). The characters of these stories are nearly all undistinguished 'ordinary' people — Hood's relatives, children, the caretaker of his apartment, a bank teller, an accountant, the fruit man, the meat man, and the manager. The challenges they face are the age-old everyday ones — sexuality, mutability, creativity, and death. Yet each of these characters is revealed to be in some sense extraordinary, suffering unique disillusionments or tragedies or making eccentric responses and adjustments. In many cases Hood seems to be asking us to see the character as a minor hero who milks small joys from a beautiful yet grudging world.

> That old woman on University had climbed and stood waiting for her green light; the tennis players chased their ball; and Monsieur Bourbonnais wanted it perfect. They were all within their rights. Human purpose is inscrutable, but undeniable.

In both the stories and the novels a strongly conservative sense of ethics pervades. The short stories celebrate the tenacious and the faithful — the married couple who defend their monogamous love, the young bank clerk who devotes himself to his career, the apartment caretaker who seeks perfection as both a worker and a father, the grocer who aims to offer "the best" goods and services possible. In two of Hood's four novels, *White Figure, White Ground* (1964) and *The Camera Always Lies*, the central figures struggle successfully to defend traditional romantic conceptions of marriage against the aggressive promiscuity which pervades the subcultures in which they work. Both figures are artists: Alex MacDonald of *White Figure, White Ground* is a painter, and Rose Leclair of *The Camera Always Lies* an actress. Both believe that sexual infidelity and promiscuity are bad for their art, that they encourage superficiality, cynicism, and economic pragmatism. In a third novel, *A Game of Touch* (1970), the sexually promiscuous characters, particularly Marie-Ange Robinson, the anglaise-canadienne who has fornicated her way to bilingualism and biculturalism, end up alone and rejected while the virginal Yvonne appears destined for a joyous, if conventional, marriage.

139

You Can't Get There from Here (1972), Hood's fourth novel, is a political fantasy set in the emerging African state of Leofrica. Despite the imaginary setting, the factual or pseudo-factual tone characteristic of Hood's writing continues. All of the elements of the story are parodies of people, places, institutions, and events common to world history in the 1970's. The title of the book is therefore ironic: you can get to Leofrica from "here", and Hood has. Leofrica's one large but divisive river echoes Canada's Ottawa-St. Lawrence; it's separation into two mistrustful ethnic areas echoes Canadian schizophrenia. Leofrica's total lack of competent native administrators with popular support parallels the initial dilemma of most recent independent African states — from Ghana to Uganda. The naiveté and misinformedness of the available cabinet ministers is unfortunately recognizable to misgoverned people the world over. To complete the familiar picture, American agents scheme for rights to rare minerals, Chinese-Albanian agents work to ignite a "people's" revolution. It is a humourous but bitter novel, rooted entirely in the global suspicion and hypocrisy peculiar to our times.

Of the better-known Canadian novelists, Hugh Hood most resembles Mordecai Richler. Both men have produced the satiric parable — *You Can't Get There from Here* and *Cocksure*. Both are conservative moralists, and both have tended to write fiction which vividly portrays contemporary society. Hood differs from Richler in not allowing his frequent passages of humour to damage his characterizations and in usually shunning the one-dimensional central character and bizarre secondary characters. Most of Hood's characters can be recognized from the reader's own experience. Many Canadian readers will find Hood the more interesting of the two because his portraits of Canadian life are more detailed and accurate than those of the long-term expatriate. I personally find Hugh Hood's total credibility, in characterization as well as setting, to be unexcelled in Canadian writing.

Hood, Hugh.   *Flying a Red Kite.* Toronto: Ryerson Press, 1962.
      . *White Figure, White Ground.* Toronto: Ryerson Press, 1964.
      . *Around the Mountain.* Toronto: Peter Martin Associates, 1967.
      . *The Camera Always Lies.* New York: Harcourt, Brace, and World, 1967.
      . *Predictions of Ice.* Agincourt: The Book Society of Canada, 1969.
      . *A Game of Touch.* Toronto: Longman Canada, 1970.
      . *Strength Down Center: the Jean Beliveau Story.*

Scarborough, Ont.: Prentice-Hall of Canada, 1970.

. *The Fruit Man, the Meat Man and the Manager.* Ottawa: Oberon Press, 1971.

. "Sober Coloring: the Ontology of Super Realism," *Canadian Literature* 49 (Summer 1971), 28-34.

. *You Can't Get There from Here.* Ottawa: Oberon Press, 1972.

. with Irving Layton, George Bowering, and Kerry Allard. "Conversation: Jewish Layton, Catholic Hood, Protestant Bowering," *Open Letter* (second series) 5, Summer 1973, pp.30-39.

. *The Governor's Bridge is Closed.* Ottawa: Oberon Press, 1973.

Cloutier, Pierre. "An Interview with Hugh Hood," *Journal of Canadian Fiction* II:1 (Winter, 1973), 49-52.

Dobbs, Kildare. "Memory Transfigured," *Canadian Literature* 16 (Spring 1963), 72-73.

Duffy, Dennis. "Grace: The Novels of Hugh Hood," *Canadian Literature* 47 (Winter 1971), 10-25.

. "A Quiet Rage" (rev. of *You Can't Get There From Here*), *The Globe and Mail,* Sept. 16, 1972, p.31.

Fulford, Robert. "Captain Canada," *Saturday Night* 85 (November, 1970), 47,49.

. "In Brightest Leofrica," *Montreal Star*, September 23, 1972, "Entertainments", p.4.

Godfrey, Dave. "Line and Form," *Tamarack Review* 35 (Spring 1965), 96-101.

. "Turning New Leaves (2)," *Canadian Forum* 42 (January 1968), 229-30.

Grosskurth, Phyllis. "There's No Doubt He Loves the Place," *Saturday Night* 86 (December 1971), 42-43.

Hale, Victoria G. "An Interview with Hugh Hood," *World Literature Written in English* XI:1, pp.35-41.

Kilgallin, Tony. "Hood's Montreal," *Canadian Literature* 36 (Spring 1968), 94-95.

Lane, Lauriat, Jr. "Fiction and Fact," *Queen's Quarterly* 70 (Autumn 1963), 451-452.

Mills, John. "On the Way Up," *Evidence 7 (1963), 107-110.*

Nowlan, Alden. Review of *The Camera Always Lies, Canadian Forum* 48 (May 1968), 46-47.

Rollins, Douglas. "The Montreal Storytellers," *Journal of Canadian Fiction* I:2 (1971), 5-6.

Simpson, Leo. "Masses of Fact Submit to Dazzling Prose" (rev. of *The Governor's Bridge is Closed*), *The Globe and Mail,* Oct. 13, 1973, p.35.

Stratford, Philip.   "The Artist's Life," *Saturday Night* 79 (October 1964), 30.
Warren, Michael.   "Artist's Passion," *Canadian Literature* 25 (Summer 1965), 76-77.
Weaver, Robert.   "Montreal Author Hugh Hood's Latest: A Convincing Reality Built on a Dream" (rev. of *You Can't Get There From Here*), *The Toronto Star*, Sept. 16, 1972, p.65.
       . Review of *White Figure, White Ground*, *The Toronto Star*, Aug. 8, 1964, p.28.

George Johnston

(1913 -   )

The poetry of George Johnston has had little in common with that of other Canadian writers of the sixties. Shunning both the cryptic formalism of a Finch or Gustafson and the adventurous experimentalism of a Bissett or Coleman, he has chosen his own deliberately limited poetic of deft quatrains and genial, conversational tones. His work has uniquely combined technical conservatism with a warmth and unpretentiousness of manner, and provided Canadian readers with some of the most purely delightful poems in all of their poetry.

The world of George Johnston's poetry is a small one, and as deliberately limited as his style. He writes primarily of domestic life — of his family and of a number of eccentric acquaintances ostensibly from within a narrow geographic area near Ottawa. To these latter he has given a variety of Dickensian names: Mrs. McGonigle, Mr. Murple, Farmer Elliott, Miss Belaney, Aunt Beleek, Mr. Goom. By means of gently satiric accounts of their lives and follies, and of their localized collisions with twentieth-century events, Johnston succeeds in giving a more convincingly representative picture of modern Canadian life than have most of Canada's poetic philosophers such as Dudek or Gustafson. He makes what he terms a comfortable "backwater" glow with both the eternal problems of humanity and the peculiar anguishes of the modern age.

In style and theme he has changed little throughout his three books: *The Cruising Auk* (1959), *Home Free* (1966) and *Happy Enough* (1972). His later works have been somewhat looser metrically than his earlier, and have contained several attempts at longer poems; however, his best work has remained the brief, conversational, and unobtrusively rhymed lyric. Johnston's feeling

George Johnston

that this planet and the life it allows its children are emphatically good — despite all human suffering, anxiety, duplicity, and death — has remained unchanged. As the title "Happy Enough" implies, he greets his unpredictable world with love and equanimity. He suggests through his tales of others' griefs and joys, that similar love and equanimity would bring relative pleasure and happiness to most of his fellow members of benighted humanity.

Vivid, humane, compassionate, and witty, Johnston's unambitious poetry has become one of the few indisputable successes of recent traditionalist writing in Canada.

Johnston, George.   *The Cruising Auk*. Toronto: Oxford University Press, 1959.

       . ed. *The Saga of Gisli the Outlaw*. Toronto: University of Toronto Press, 1963.

       . "Ned Pratt's Funeral," *Canadian Forum* 44 (June 1964), 53.

       . *Home Free*. Toronto: Oxford University Press, 1966.

       , ed. *The Church in the Modern World*, ed. George Johnston and Wolfgang Roth. Toronto: Ryerson Press, 1967.

       . *Happy Enough: Poems 1935-1972*. Toronto: Oxford University Press, 1972.

Dobbs, Kildare.   Review of *The Cruising Auk*, *Tamarack Review* 12 (Summer 1959), 99-101.

Jones, L.W.   "The Cruising Auk and the World Below," *Canadian Literature* 48 (Spring 1971), 28-36.

Livesay, Dorothy.   Review of *Home Free*, *Fiddlehead* 71 (Winter 1967), 65-69.

Nynych, Stephanie J.   "At Home with the World," *Books in Canada* I:12 (November-December 1972), 10-12.

Pacey, Desmond.   Review of *The Cruising Auk*, *Fiddlehead* 44 (Spring 1960), 45-46.

Robinson, Meredith.   "Deeper Water," *Alphabet* 3 (December 1961), 45-47.

Stevens, Peter.   "Achievement — this Light-Filled Equilibrium" (rev. of *Happy Enough*), *The Globe and Mail*, Jan. 27, 1973, p.29.

Whalley, George.   "George Johnson," *Canadian Literature* 35 (Winter 1968), 85-90.

D.G. Jones

(1929 -   )

The poetry of D.G. (Doug) Jones has occupied a middle ground between the formalistic poetry of Smith, Finch, and Gustafson and the 'natural voice' poetry of Layton, Atwood, and Bissett. Its subjects have been taken from both literature and experience. Its language has been direct and relatively informal, yet always subject to restraint which has prevented it from conveying intense feeling.

Jones's first book, *Frost on the Sun* (1957) is the most experimental and imagistic of his three collections, having much in common with the particularistic lyrics Louis Dudek and Raymond Souster had been writing in the early fifties. Most of the poems focus on a sharply described scene or object and succeed in giving this scene meaning without recourse to a general statement. In "A Problem of Space" Jones declares that he would "eliminate ... bombast, this / detail of type" and leave only "an image and a space". The poems celebrate the particulars their descriptions honour. To Jones, these particulars are the offspring of a vital, beautiful, and eternal cosmos which transcends individual mortality and gives meaning to all our petty destinies. In this cosmos "earth, air / water are one element, freedom / Engulfs the victim when he falls / disengaged / Among the rain of stars ...." Even so, a certain aloofness of tone is noticeable. Most of the poems involve impersonal landscapes and strangers observed at a distance; there are few glimpses of the poet's personal life, his family, or his friends. Almost all the poems have some faint formality in their opening which suggests that they are for the poet specifically 'literary' occasions — that they are separated from the larger day-to-day areas of the poet's life.

The Sun is Axeman (1961)   reprints nine of the most

145

successful imagistic poems of *Frost on the Sun*, but in its new poems moves in several different directions. Some, like "Disintegration in a Dream of Love" are abstract philosophical treatises; others like "Little Night Journey" take the imagistic lyric and extend it into diffuse and wordy multiple-section poems. Still others like "In the Present Mood" give a welcome taste of the poet's deeper feelings. As in the first book, the forms of the poems span both the traditional and the contemporary — quatrain, blank verse, and free verse. Underlying many of the poems is an insistent iambic rhythm which works against any sense of authentic, spontaneous emotion.

The theme of our cosmos being "a friendly nothingness" continues, as it does in his next volume *Phrases from Orpheus*. This collection moves entirely from traditional forms into organic ones, and is written in the most relaxed measures of Jones's career. The poems here are for the most part neither particularistic dramas nor philosophical declarations — instead they are personal meditations on people and events in his private life. Once again the shorter poems tend to be stronger in image and more intense in feeling than the longer ones. The long meditation requires that the poet establish a distinct and intriguing sense of his personal identity and worldview, which Jones fails to do. The lengthy central poem, "Phrases from Orpheus", suffers from a vague dramatic context and sketchy characterizations. The mythological elements in this poem appear arbitrary and imposed, since the reader is given no particular reality from which they could credibly have sprung forth. The strength of Jones's earlier work was the way in which he showed his few references to mythology to issue spontaneously from aspects of the environment.

Jones's most influential book has been his thematic study of Canadian literature, *Butterfly on Rock* (1970). Pursuing some of the implications of his own belief that man must, despite personal circumstances, view himself as a participant in a creative and benign cosmos, Jones examines here the attitudes toward nature betrayed by previous Canadian writers. He proposes that by and large these writers have viewed themselves as exiles, as in symbolic terms expellees from Eden, and have seen civilization's task as the setting up of enclaves against a hostile environment. A few writers, he suggests — notably Roberts, Lampman, and Sheila Watson — have moved beyond this in perceiving a paradoxical need to love that cosmos which ostensibly threatens one's own annihilation. *Butterfly on Rock* is a profound and potentially landmark work of creative criticism, one which not only informs much of subsequent Canadian criticism, such as Margaret Atwood's *Survival*, but which can also open new interpretive vistas to the non-professional reader.

146

Jones, D.G. *Frost on the Sun.* Toronto: Contact Press, 1957.

    . *The Sun is Axeman.* Toronto: University of Toronto Press, 1961.

    . "The Sleeping Giant," *Canadian Literature* 26 (Autumn 1965), 3-21.

    . *Phrases from Orpheus.* Toronto: Oxford University Press, 1967.

    . *Butterfly on Rock.* Toronto: University of Toronto Press, 1970.

    . "Between Mindscape and Landscape," *Canadian Literature* 53 (Summer 1972), 81-88.

    . "Myth, Frye and Canadian Writers," *Canadian Literature* 55 (Winter 1973), 7-22.

Barbour, Douglas. Review of *Phrases from Orpheus, Canadian Forum* 48 (August 1968), 119-120.

Buitenhuis, Peter. "Catching Deep-Fryed Butterflies" (rev. of *Butterfly on Rock*), *The Globe and Mail Magazine*, June 6, 1970, p.16.

Dudek, Louis. "The Misuses of Imagination", *Tamarack Review* 60 (1973), 51-67.

Livesay, Dorothy. Review of *Phrases from Orpheus, Quarry XVII:4 (Summer 1968), 41-42.*

New, W.H. "Quelques Arpents de Papillons," *Canadian Literature* 47 (Winter 1971), 94-97.

Pearson, Alan. "The Poetry of D.G. Jones," *Montreal Star*, April 27, 1968, "Entertainments", p.8.

Reaney, James. Review of *Frost on the Sun, Canadian Forum* 38 (July 1958), 95.

Spettigue, D.O. Review of *Butterfly on Rock, Queen's Quarterly* LXXVIII:1 (1971), 154-155.

Stevens, Peter. "The Poetic Vocation," *Canadian Literature* 39 (Winter 1969), 77-80.

Waddington, Miriam. "Five Without a Common Song" (rev. of *Phrases from Orpheus*), *The Globe and Mail Magazine*, Jan. 13, 1968, p.13.

Webb, Phyllis. Review of *The Sun is Axeman, Canadian Literature* 12 (Spring 1962), 58-59.

Woodcock, George. Review of *Butterfly on Rock, West Coast Review* V:3 (January 1971), 70-71.

Lionel Kearns

(1937-   )

Lionel Kearns began writing in the late fifties in Vancouver where he studied at the University of B.C. under the poet Earle Birney; in the early sixties he was loosely associated with the poetry newsletter *Tish*. In his early work, as represented in *Songs of Circumstance* (1963) and *Pointing* (1967), Kearns is a poet of the particular "circumstantial" scene. His poems present — in vivid concrete terms and exceptionally musical phrasing — concise personal testimony to the poet's interactions with his world. These poems are mostly brief, and often end ironically. Their emphasis on the poet's interaction with "circumstance" reflects the influence of the *Tish* group's interest in the "field theory" of the U.S. poet Charles Olson.

Also partially derived from Charles Olson and other writers studied by the *Tish* group was Kearns' interest in improving the printed notation of poetry. Having accepted the *Tish* premise that poetry was above all an oral art, Kearns went his own way in searching for a method of indicating accent and pitch on the printed page. The page, to Kearns, could be simply a score for the spoken poem, and contain something of the subtlety of the musical score. The one result of his investigations was the concept of the stress-axis, a vertical shaft across which the lines of a poem could be arranged so that the shaft, or axis, passed through the most heavily-stressed syllable of each line. Kearns used this system throughout *Songs of Circumstance,* but abandoned it when the poems of that limited-edition book were reprinted in *Pointing.*

Kearns's interest in poetic technique waned after most of the *Tish* editors moved from Vancouver in 1963. His next book, *Listen George* (1965), shows a continuing interest in testimonial poetry, but

Songs of Circumstance by Lionel Kearns.
Tishbooks, 1962. His first book.

little interest in the carefully articulated and notated poem. *Listen George* is a lengthy verse-letter to George Bowering, written in exceptionally long lines and affecting a spontaneity somewhat similar to that of Ginsberg's *Howl*. During the course of the poem Kearns reminisces about his youth in Nelson, B.C., and his brief career as a professional hockey player in Mexico City, outlines several film scripts, and writes a highly amusing continuation of Chaucer's *Cook's Tale*. The testimonial qualities of this book are very high, in the sense that it appears to give an accurate portrait of Kearns's state of mind at the time of writing. The book conveys extreme disillusionment with a system-valuing society and with order-oriented academics. Its loose form and seemingly impulsive structure provide a symbolic act of rebellion against the concepts of consciously crafted poetry which Kearns had partially acknowledged in his first two books.

By the time of the publication of his next book, *By the Light of the Silvery McLune* (1969), Kearns seems to have become even more disillusioned with purely literary values. Most of the work here is oversimplified parable in support of relaxed narcotics laws and left-wing politics. Only a few poems show the particularity of image and musicality of phrase characteristic of *Songs of Circumstance*. Instead of working, as art must, from the particular circumstance to the general observation, Kearns in the parables works from a general bias to stereotyped characterizations of narcotics detectives, marijuana smokers, Eskimos, etc. The result is for the most part superficial and unconvincing light verse.

The exception is "Transport", the story of one man's rise from amateur pimp to operator of a "come as you go" limousine/brothel service and finally to Minister of Transport, and a rollicking indictment of the cynical commercialism which so often elevates our governors to power. Kearns can write extraordinarily ironic and comic verse, as "Transport", his continuation of Chaucer's *Cook's Tale*, and many of the satiric poems of *Songs of Circumstance* attest. Among the varied kinds of work this impulsive and erratic writer has produced, these **are presently** his most important and interesting.

Kearns, Lionel. *Songs of Circumstance*. Vancouver: Tishbooks, 1963.
. "Stacked Verse — a Definition and Four Poems," *Evidence* 6 (*ca.* 1964), 96-104.
. *Listen George*. (*Imago* 3) Calgary, 1965.
. *Pointing*. Toronto: Ryerson Press, 1967.
. "If There's Anything I Hate it's Poetry," *Canadian Literature* 36 (Spring 1968), 67-70.

By the Light of the Silvery McLune: Media Parables, Poems, Signs, Gestures, and other Assaults on the Interface. Vancouver: Daylight Press and Talonbooks, 1969.

Bowering, George. "Unit Structure," *Canadian Literature* 37 (Summer 1968), 87-88.

Cogswell, Fred. "A World Set Forth," *Canadian Author and Bookman* 41 (Spring 1966), 11.

Coleman, Victor. "It's a Free Form Ain't It?" *Canadian Forum* 45 (October 1965), 164.

Davey, Frank. "The Limitations of Wit," *Canadian Literature* 44 (Spring 1970), 91-92.

Fetherling, Doug. "They Sing Singly and Apart but all Together" (rev. of *By the Light of the Silvery McClune*), *The Globe and Mail Magazine*, Aug. 1, 1970, p.16.

Fulford, Robert. "Parables and Fantasies," *Saturday Night* 85 (March 1970), 38, 40.

Waddington, Miriam. "Five Without a Common Song" (rev. of *Pointing*), *The Globe and Mail Magazine*, Jan. 13, 1968, p.13.

Henry Kreisel

(1922-   )

Henry Kreisel was born in Austria and lived there until Hitler's invasion in 1938. Both of Kreisel's novels concern the stories of Austrian Jews caught between 1933 and 1938 in Nazi Germany's fanatical assertions of Aryan superiority and *lebensraum*. Both view these stories from Canadian perspectives; in each some sense of unavoidable Canadian entanglement in the affairs of European man is implied. It should be noted, however, that Kreisel's 'Canada' is often culturally undistinguishable from the rest of North America.

In *The Rich Man* (1948) an aging and widowed Jewish Canadian, Jacob Grossman, who has spent 33 years working as a presser in a Toronto garment factory, travels back to Vienna to visit his mother and sisters. It is 1935. In Toronto Jacob's children — two married daughters and a son newly graduated as a medical doctor — are self-absorbed and marginally secure. In Vienna Jacob's sisters and their families live in fear of the first arrests and beatings of the impending holocaust. And while Jacob's children view him as a poor man squandering in travel the $700 savings which should be their inheritance, the Viennese relatives can see him only as a wealthy potential benefactor from the prosperous New World.

Jacob and Canada are continually linked by the imagery and dialectic of the novel. He participates in his country's general insularity and naiveté about European politics. Although a gentle and well-meaning man, he is disasterously prone to the North American penchant for appearing successful and prosperous — buying a white alpaca suit to wear on his journey, expensive gifts for his relatives, and on the voyage over being flattered to dine with ostensibly wealthy and cultured men. In Europe, his mother and sisters consistently associate him with the glamour of Chicago's gangsters, the Great Lakes, Niagara Falls, and the continent's breadth of four thousand miles. To them Canada is a rich country, and their Jacob therefore a "rich man" who could buy their way out of both financial and political disaster.

The tragic situation which ends the novel is a product of a variety of personal and cultural misunderstandings and illusions. Jacob goes to Vienna expecting the romantic city of North American cinema and finds instead unemployment, poverty, political repression, and religious persecution. He wishes to please his mother and sisters with the impression that he has done well in Canada, but succeeds only in giving them false hopes of his ability to help them. Conditioned by his years in Canada to have relatively optimistic expectations about life's comforts, he is utterly unprepared for the extent of suffering, brutality, and tragedy with which Vienna confronts him. At the core of the novel, then, is a contrast of cultures: naive and self-aggrandizing North America encounters a Europe pathetically and horrifyingly aware of human depravity. Kreisel's Canada is merely part of the standard American Dream; Jacob himself tends to refer to "America" rather than Canada as his adopted home.

This narrative pattern of developing seemingly innocent or harmless actions into humanly destructive and agonizing dilemmas is repeated in Kreisel's second novel, *The Betrayal* (1964). Its story is that of Theodore Stappler, who has pursued to Edmonton Joseph Held, the collaborator 'responsible' for Stappler's mother's arrest and death ten years before in Auschwitz. His quest for revenge or justice — he is not sure which — is complicated by his own partial guilt in the mother's arrest and by Held's partial lack of responsibility for his own actions. On Stappler's finding Held, it is further complicated by Held's pathetic "pot-bellied, middle-aged" appearance, and by Stappler's sudden falling in love with Held's daughter Katherine.

The Canadian perspective here is provided by the narrator, Mark Lerner, who is a Canadian-born professor of history at the University of Alberta. An arrogant and dispassionate man, Lerner finds himself asked to judge and advise the desperate Stappler. Like Jacob Grossman, Mark Lerner is a Canadian who takes for granted both his self-worth and the North American standard of living. He had served in World War II and had viewed his wounding in Italy as an adequate contribution to the cause of human liberty. While teaching history in classrooms far removed from the agony of world events in both place and time, he is in the habit of casually and pretentiously passing judgement on public figures. When the world of Nazi death-camps enters his life through the person of Theodore Stappler, it is the first time that human history has touched his life as an actual and personally-demanding phenomenon. Not surprisingly, he proves unequal to this challenge; his arrogance and superficiality are unchanged by both Stappler's story and its sordid aftermath. In fact, through a number of allusions to T.S. Eliot's poetry, Kreisel establishes the ineffectual Lerner as a Prufrock or "hollow man" figure.

Both novels are engrossing and convincing creations. If there is any flaw in *The Rich Man,* it is that the narrative becomes somewhat diffuse in the last third of the book when, as the omniscient narrator, Kreisel attempts to follow the actions and motivations of a number of characters. By giving the narration of *The Betrayal* to one of its characters, Mark Lerner, Kreisel achieves a much more concentrated narrative. This technique also allows him to develop Lerner into a major figure without involving him deeply in the the central action.

Henry Kreisel has also written a number of short stories, some of which have been anthologized in *The Klanak Islands* (1959) and *Stories from Western Canada* (1972).

Kreisel, Henry.   *The Rich Man.* Toronto: McClelland & Stewart, 1948, reprinted 1961 (New Canadian Library no. 24).

. "Joseph Conrad and the Dilemma of the Uprooted Man," *Tamarack Review* 7 (Spring 1958), 78-85.

. *Klanak Islands,* a collection of short stories by Henry Kreisel and others. Vancouver: Klanak Press, 1959.

. *The Betrayal.* Toronto: McClelland & Stewart, 1964, reprinted 1971 (New Canadian Library no. 77).

. "The Prairie: a state of Mind," *Royal Society of Canada Transactions,* Ser. 4, Vol. 6 (June 1968), 171-180, reprinted in Eli Mandel, ed., *Contexts of Canadian Criticism* (Chicago: University of Chicago Press, 1971), pp.254-266.

Carroll, John.   "Stirring Echoes of Conrad" (rev. of *The Betrayal*), *The Globe and Mail Magazine,* Nov. 7, 1967, p.13.

Child, Philip.   Review of *The Rich Man, Canadian Forum* 29 (February 1949), 263-264.

Macpherson, Hugo.   "Betrayal, Desertion, Atonement," *Tamarack Review* 34 (Winter 1965), 106-108.

Robertson, George.   "Guilt and Counter-Guilt," *Canadian Literature* 23 (Winter 1965), 72, 74.

Stedmond, John.   Introduction to *The Rich Man* (Toronto: McClelland & Stewart, 1961, New Canadian Library no. 24), pp.v-vii.

Stratford, Philip.   "The Colour of the Times," *Saturday Night* 79 (November 1964), 32-33.

Warhaft, S.   Introduction to *The Betrayal* (Toronto: McClelland &

Stewart, 1971, New Canadian Library no. 77), pp.v-x.

Robert
Kroetsch (1927-   )

The sense of a fragmentary, chaotic universe which has pervaded so much of Canadian writing since 1960 receives nowhere more powerful expression than in the novels of Robert Kroetsch. All aspects of these novels imply an immensely vital and unmappable world. Their narrative structures take unpredictable shifts and turns, and invariably terminate in ambiguity. Their language exuberantly interbreeds the bawdy, the literary, the poetic, and the colloquial. Their settings — northern Alberta and the Northwest Territories — appear as mythologic, Protean regions, regions where every journey a man takes is a voyage of discovery into both his unknown self and his unknowable environment. The leading characters are bewildered and impulsive giants; their doggedness and recklessness becomes absurdly delightful considering the instability and inconstancy that surround them.

All of Kroetsch's novels involve a male protagonist in a quest for his own identity and purpose. Peter Guy, the central character of the first novel, *But We Are Exiles* (1965), is a large man who has been "running and searching" all of his adult life. His inner chaos — especially a lack of both personal morality and personal goals — have caused him to acquiesce to his fiancée's defloration by a more violent man, Mike Hornyak, whom she eventually marries. His indecisiveness when he inadvertently stumbled into the girl's room during her first seduction, led him to retreat unnoticed. The next day he fled to the Mackenzie River waterway, both away from the complications of the immediate situation and toward some possible insight into his own behaviour.

Not until six years later, when Mike Hornyak is dead and Peter

155

Guy has pushed his corpse out of its "bed" on a drifting ice-coated barge on Great Slave Lake in order to get shelter for himself, does Guy begin to be free. The novel suggests that Guy's quest can end only when he has somehow re-enacted his moment of failure, challenged his usurper's right to occupy his bed, and successfully displaced him. It further suggests that his failure can be redeemed only by his lying in the bed of death, by his being willing to suffer a symbolic death in order to live again. At the book's end, his quest is completed but his actual life is in extreme jeopardy, and may well end within a few hours.

The Words of my Roaring (1966), the first novel of Kroetsch's 'Notikeewin' trilogy, also focuses on a large muscular man who can redeem the failures and mishaps of his life only via a route which passes through the beds of carnality and death. Johnny Backstrom is another man of inner chaos — a young, small-town undertaker who is prone to drunkenness and sexual adventure. His quest for enlightenment is totally accidental — the result of an impulsive decision to oppose the town doctor for election to the provincial legislature. What begins as a contest between death and life, between the undertaker who seduces the innocent and the doctor who has healed the sick and created a fertile private garden in the midst of parched farmland, is complicated when Backstrom inadvertently makes a promise of rain his major election plank, and totally confused at the novel's end when the doctor has failed to save a newborn infant and a freak rainstorm is about to give a repentant Backstrom the election. The novel implies that the undertaker's enormous vitality has propelled him not only to increased self-understanding but to relative invulnerability in an external chaos in which life and death are siblings rather than opposites. Far from being a source of death, Backstrom's wildly and promiscuously displayed creative energy may be a source of renewal for both a drought-stricken land and the 'parched', conventional lives of its people. But again the novel ends before the protagonist's fate is completely revealed — on the eve of election day.

The quest of Hazard Lepage in Kroetsch's third novel and the second of the trilogy, *The Studhorse Man* (1969), runs roughly parallel to that of Homer's *Odyssey*. After having served in the First World War, Lepage returns to Alberta to attempt to continue the Lepage line of blue roans. At the outbreak of World War II, the fate of this line rests on his being able to breed his virgin stallion Poseidon either with the virgin mares of his reluctant fiancée Martha Proudfoot or with other suitable mares. To find the latter, he leads Poseidon in an ironic journey across Alberta, encountering the Hades of a dark and moving boxcar, a Lestrygonian Edmonton, a Circaean nun who would seduce him with the security of a geriatric home, a Charybdis widow with whom he must serve his time in bed. In each episode, as in *The Words of My Roaring*, Kroetsch makes clear the contrast between convention and the power of impulsive and decisive sexuality. Poseidon's nickname of "Poesy", as W.H. New has observed, implies that in the Lepage semen rests the future of art and poetry.

Creativity and sexuality remain frustrated, however, until Lepage and Poseidon stumble back to their homes near his fiancée's farm. There Lepage is nearly burned to death in the house of a Mrs. Laporte (Nausicaa), is presumed dead, and is revived only when Martha visits his 'corpse' and notices and avails herself of its erect phallus. Like Peter Guy in *But We Are Exiles*, Lepage must undergo ritual death before his quest can be fulfilled. The coupling of Lepage and Martha presages that of Poseidon and Martha's mares, brought together by Martha's insane cousin Demeter, who narrates the novel. Although Hazard Lepage is accidentally kicked to death by passion-crazed Poseidon shortly after, and although Poseidon is subsequently shot by Demeter, the quest does terminate successfully. Both Martha and her mares carry within them the Lepage line.

The usual elements of a Kroetsch novel — a troubled and sexually anxious protagonist, a chaotic and dangerous landscape, an explicit link between art, creativity, and uncontrolled sexuality, and a quest for self-knowledge that can only be achieved by passing near death, if not symbolically through it — are present in his fourth novel, *Gone Indian* (1973). The protagonist is Jeremy Sadness, a young American graduate student equally obsessed with both life in the wilderness and his inability to have an erection while in a prone position. His inner chaos has expressed itself in a failing marriage, an inability after nine years research to write more than one sentence of his doctoral dissertation, and an infatuation with the writings of Grey Owl. The setting, to which Sadness is led after he has taken the wrong suitcase at the Edmonton airport, is a winter festival at Notikeewin, Alberta. The novel's reigning presence is the suggestively named festival king, Roger Dorck. It is Dorck whose luggage Sadness had taken in Edmonton, and it is Dorck's critical injury in a snowmobile mishap hours later which indirectly causes Sadness some unexpected complications. Art and convention are opposed throughout the novel in encounters between Sadness's 'Grey Owl' concept of the frontier and the real Indians, cowboys, and women of Alberta in the late 1960's. Sadness's quest for both increased sexual potency and his lost suitcase leads him late in the novel to sleep in a borrowed coffin and subsequently to play the role of a woman's long-dead lover. Through these events he literally does "rise again" —

becoming at long last able to make love while horizontal.

In addition, Kroetsch's theme from *But We Are Exiles* of the past having to be re-enacted and the dead displaced recurs. The teen-age husband of Bea Sunderman, the woman who restores Sadness's horizontal potency, had ostensibly plunged to his death twenty years before through the ice of Elkhart Pond. Jeremy Sadness not only reunites Mrs. Sunderman with this lover symbolically by making love to her, but literally by later causing a snowmobile accident in which both of them appear to plunge to their deaths through the ice of the river that drains into Elkhart Pond.

Gone Indian gains further complexity by being narrated by Sadness's pompous dissertation supervisor, Prof. R. Mark Madham of the State University of New York at Binghampton, in letters to Mrs. Sunderman's daughter, Jill, that contain long sections transcribed from tape-recorded reports that Sadness has sent to him. Thus eastern U.S. is juxtaposed to western Canada, Madham's cynical academicism to Sadness's vitality, Binghampton's sleepy sophistication with the bawdy and brutal energy of Roger Dorck's kingdom.

All four of Kroetsch's novels deliver partially crippled men from failure by means of cataclysmic immersion in natural process — particularly in carnality, passion, and death. Tragi-comic in tone, and comic in structure, they find in the 'green world' of the wild northern landscape and of unbridled human sexuality the healing forces which can counteract the paralytic effects of a pragmatic, mechanized culture and thus return meaning and joy to individual life. Even though three of the novels conclude with the actual, assumed, or probable deaths of the protagonists, these are optimistic works that run counter to traditional Canadian mistrust of the land. To Kroetsch mechanical centralizing technology is man's enemy and the land his friend; in *Gone Indian* a collision with a locomotive causes the apparent death of Jeremy and Bea; in *The Studhorse Man* it is the automobile and tractor that are closing the market for Hazard Lepage's services. Like most of Canada's innovative new writers since 1960, Kroetsch falls outside Margaret Atwood's *Survival* thesis. His novels show death to be a redeemer rather than a persecuter, and man to be victimized finally only by his own lack of will. Given this will, the Canadian landscape or passionate Canadian Venus-figures like Martha Proudfoot or Bea Sunderman can always find and unleash within the victim an indomitable and reckless creativity.

Kroetsch, Robert. *But We Are Exiles*. Toronto: Macmillan of Canada, 1965.

_____. *The Words of My Roaring*. Toronto: Macmillan of Canada, 1966.

. *Alberta*. Toronto: Macmillan of Canada, 1968.

. *The Studhorse Man*. Toronto: Macmillan of Canada, 1969.

. *Creation* by Robert Kroetsch, James Bacque, and Pierre Gravel. Toronto: New Press, 1970.

. "The Canadian Writer and the American Literary Tradition," *English Quarterly* IV:2 (1971), 45-49.

. *Gone Indian*. Toronto: New Press, 1973.

Brady, Elizabeth. "Novelist Completes Old West Series" (rev. of *Gone Indian*), *The Toronto Star*, Aug. 11, 1973, p.E7.

Brown, Russell M. "Odyssean Journey," *Canadian Literature* 45 (Summer 1970), 89-90.

Cameron, Donald. "The American Experience and the Canadian Voice" (interview), in his *Conversations with Canadian Novelists* (Toronto: Macmillan of Canada, 1973), 81-95.

Coles, Don. "Dreams of a Prairie Undertaker" (rev. of *The Words of My Roaring*), *The Globe and Mail Magazine*, Sept. 17, 1966, p.21.

. "A Rare Alberta Animal" (rev. of *The Studhorse Man*), *The Globe and Mail Magazine*, Jan. 31, 1970, p.15.

Dickson, Lovat. "Stinging and Gentle" (rev. of *Gone Indian*), *The Globe and Mail*, May 5, 1973, p.37.

Gelmon, Joseph N. "Cool and Simple Plot" (rev. of *But We Are Exiles*), *The Globe and Mail Magazine*, Dec. 18, 1965, p.19.

Gutteridge, Don. "No Reservations," *Books in Canada* II:2 (April, May, June, 1973), 55.

New, W.H. "Clichés and Roaring Words", *Canadian Literature* 31 (Winter 1967), 64, 66-67.

. "The Studhorse Quests," in his *Articulating West* (Toronto: New Press, 1972), pp.179-186.

Stratford, Phil. "A Fetus in Good Health" (rev. of *Creation*), *The Globe and Mail Magazine*, Mar. 27, 1971, p.37.

Irving Layton

(1912-   )

Irving Layton has had little direct influence on contemporary English-Canadian poetry. His idiosyncratic and rhetorical style and his persistent use of sexual imagery both have merely weakened the work of the few younger poets who have attempted imitation. Layton's indirect influence, however, has been large. Particularly effective have been his vigorous condemnations of academicism, gentility, and aestheticism in poetry. To Layton, the 'truth' of poetry is found not in the beautiful object but in the common, the vulgar, even the ugly. The rationalist or so-called 'Frygian' concept of the poet as a detached impersonal intellect creating linguistic structures of cold, static, and eternal beauty (as Smith, Gustafson, Finch, Macpherson) Layton has countered with passionate, personal lyrics whose form is determined by the rhetoric of his own emotion as the writing occurs. The fact that colloquial, open-form, and 'process' poetry has in the last decade come to dominate the older academic modes suggests that this poetry, plus Layton's various and well-publicized manifestos, have not been without effect.

Layton was born in Rumania, but came to Montreal with his parents (Lazarovitch) at the age of one. He attended Baron Byng High School and Macdonald College, where he earned a B.Sc. in agriculture. After serving briefly in the Canadian Army (1942-43) he did post-graduate work in economics and political science at McGill University. Although Layton had been writing poetry in Keatsian and Tennysonian styles while in college, his first knowledge of modern poetry came in 1942 when he met John Sutherland, who had just founded the magazine *First Statement,* and his sister Betty, whom he later married. He became an editor of *First Statement* in 1943, and remained with the magazine after it merged with *Preview* in 1945 to become *Northern Review.* He resigned in the 1950's when Sutherland became a Roman Catholic and adopted a conservative editorial direction. In 1952 he joined Louis Dudek and Raymond Souster in founding Contact Press. In 1955 he was invited by Charles Olson to teach at Black Mountain College in North Carolina and to become an editor of *Black Mountain Review,* but declined. He was, however, in close contact with several 'Black Mountain' writers — Robert Creeley, Cid Corman, and Jonathan Williams — throughout the 1950's, and in 1956 edited a Canadian issue of Corman's influential magazine, *Origin.* Despite these many connections with the little magazine and small press world, Layton rarely took interest in shaping long-term editorial policies. His dominating concerns were his own work and the creation, through enterprises like *Northern Review* and Contact Press, of a literary climate hospitable to this work.

Layton has built his poetry around a number of paradoxes. The most important is his belief in the interdependence of the Dionysian (raw energy) and the Apollonian (form and intelligence). In his view, these contraries are both incomplete in themselves; thus the intellectual must also be sensual, and the beautiful be grounded in passion and brutality. Lesser but related paradoxes concern good and evil, male and female. Again, in each pair the contraries are individually incomplete. All men contain within them the evil of Cain and Eichmann; the 'civilized' man who would deny his potential for irrationality and evil cuts himself off not only from humanity but from the very roots of human creativity. The male/female paradox has caused many readers to believe, quite rightly, that Layton has a sexist view of women. Briefly, Layton sees women as pragmatic, sensual, nature-loving, Dionysian beings most at home in the terrestrial world; he sees men as idealistic, intellectual, disdainful of matter — Apollonian spirits who yearn for the stars. Such a view is entirely consistent with his overall world view, and, as he remarks in "Teufelsdrokh Concerning Women",

> No male superiority is vaunted here;
> Both [conditions] are requisite poles
> In this enterprise humans are embarked on;
> . . . .
> If women were dreamers too, where would it end?
> It would simply end.

Men and women together constitute the human creative spirit and "the gorgeous flesh that holds it firm".

The one characteristic which distinguishes Layton's poetry

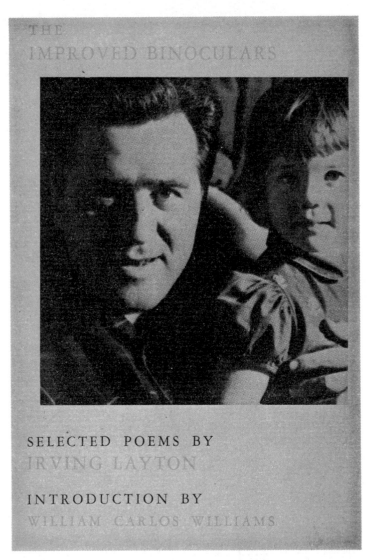

THE
IMPROVED BINOCULARS

SELECTED POEMS BY
IRVING LAYTON

INTRODUCTION BY
WILLIAM CARLOS WILLIAMS

The Improved Binoculars by Irving Layton.
Jonathan Williams, 1956.

(together with that of Souster, Purdy, Nowlan, Acorn) from equally colloquial and particularistic poetry in the next generation is the fact that Layton's poetry is essentially 'message' poetry — poetry meant to convey personal opinions, thoughts, feelings. That is, the explicit content of Layton's reflections is more important than their quality or tone, whereas in a Newlove, Bowering, or Atwood poem the tone of the reflections and the nature of the consciousness which they project is more important than their overt content. Layton has often identified himself with the prophetic poet — Isaiah, Blake, Coleridge, the Welsh bard — and I suspect from his work that he conceives of the prophet as a man who understands more than other men, and specifically understands his own prophecies. His poems are externally rather than internally focused, they speak in fluent and colloquial address rather than in the discontinuous language of thought process, they assume in the poet a perceptual and emotional superiority over other men, they appear designed to communicate their burden to the misinformed. In short, the concept of the prophet as knowing more than he understands — a concept essential to Bowering, Coleman, Gilbert, and Nichol — as speaking indirectly rather than directly, is probably foreign to Layton's aesthetic.

Layton, Irving. *Here and Now.* Montreal: First Statement Press, 1946.
. *Now is the Place.* Montreal: First Statement Press, 1948.
. *The Black Huntsman.* Privately printed, 1951.
. *Cerberus,* with Louis Dudek and Raymond Souster. Toronto: Contact Press, 1952.
. *Love the Conqueror Worm.* Toronto: Contact Press, 1953.
. *In the Midst of My Fever.* Mallorca: The Divers Press, 1954.
. *The Long Pea-Shooter.* Montreal: Lacoon Press, 1954.
. *The Blue Propeller.* Toronto: Contact Press, 1955.
. *The Cold Green Element.* Toronto: Contact Press, 1955.
. *Music on a Kazoo.* Toronto: Contact Press, 1956.
. *The Bull Calf and Other Poems.* Toronto: Contact Press, 1956.
. *The Improved Binoculars,* 1st ed. Highlands, N.C.: Jargon Press, 1956. Jargon 18.
. *A Laughter in the Mind.* Highlands, N.C.: Jargon Press, 1958. Jargon 28.
. *A Red Carpet for the Sun.* Highlands, N.C.: Jonathan Williams, and Toronto: McClelland & Stewart, 1959.
. *The Swinging Flesh.* Toronto: McClelland & Stewart, 1961.

. *Balls for a One-Armed Juggler.* Toronto: McClelland & Stewart, 1963.

. *The Laughing Rooster.* Toronto: McClelland & Stewart, 1964.

. *Collected Poems.* Toronto: McClelland & Stewart, 1965.

. *Periods of the Moon.* Toronto: McClelland & Stewart, 1967.

. *The Shattered Plinths.* Toronto: McClelland & Stewart, 1968.

. *Selected Poems,* ed. with a preface by Wynne Francis. Toronto: McClelland & Stewart, 1969.

. *The Whole Bloody Bird.* Toronto: McClelland & Stewart, 1969.

. *The Collected Poems.* Toronto: McClelland & Stewart, 1971.

. *Nail Polish.* Toronto: McClelland & Stewart, 1971.

. *Engagements* (essays). Toronto: McClelland & Stewart, 1972.

. *Lovers and Lesser Men.* Toronto: McClelland & Stewart, 1973.

Bowering, George. "Eli and Irving," *Canadian Literature* 39 (Winter 1969), 74-76.

Carruth, Haydn. "That Heaven-sent Lively Rope-Worker, Irving Layton," *Tamarack Review* 39 (Spring 1966), 68-73.

Davey, Frank. Review of *The Collected Poems, Open Letter,* (second series), no. 2, pp.50-52.

Dudek, Louis. "Layton, Now and Then," *Queen's Quarterly* 63 (Summer 1956), 291-293.

Francis, Wynne. Preface to *Selected Poems.*

Fulford, Robert. "Irving Layton as his Own Best Friend," *The Montreal Star,* Nov. 18, 1972, p.C3.

Hosein, Clyde. "Kicking Against the Pricks," *Books in Canada* II:1 (April, May, June, 1973), 4-5.

Mandel, Eli. *Irving Layton.* Toronto: Forum House, 1969.

, with Irving Layton. "Nietzche and Poetry: a Discussion," *The Malahat Review* 24 (October 1972), 23-29.

Reznitsky, Lawrence J. "Interview with Irving Layton," *Le Chien d'Or/The Golden Dog,* no. 1, n.p.

Skelton, Robin. "Personal Heresy," *Canadian Literature* 23 (Winter 1965), 63-65.

Smith, Patricia Keeney. "Irving Layton and the Theme of Death," *Canadian Literature* 48 (Spring 1971), 6-15.

Thomas, Clara. "A Conversation with Margaret Laurence and Irving

Layton", *Journal of Canadian Fiction* 1 (Winter 1972), 65-69.

Waterston, Elizabeth. "Apocalypse in Montreal," *Canadian Literature* 48 (Spring 1971), 16-24.

Williams, William Carlos. "A Note on Layton," in *The Improved Binoculars*. Reprinted in Dudek and Gnarowski, *The Making of Modern Poetry in Canada* (Toronto: Ryerson, 1967), 233-234.

Woodcock, George. "Grab at Proteus: Notes on Layton," *Canadian Literature* 28 (Spring 1966), 5-21. Reprinted in his *Odysseus Ever Returning* (Toronto: McClelland & Stewart, 1970), 75-91.

Dennis Lee (1939-   )

The unity of political and artistic action which has been believed in by most of Canada's avant-garde throughout the sixties and seventies finds exceedingly clear expression in the work of Toronto's nationalistic poet Dennis Lee. His commitment to this ideal has been manifested in his assisting to found Rochdale College (an ambitious but abortive attempt at a student-operated educational and residential cooperative), in his co-founding in 1966 of House of Anansi Press, and in his writing of the 'patriotic' poems *Civil Elegies* (1968). To Lee, all of these variously educational, commercial, and literary acts have been, before all else, political. Canadian nationalism, one of the strongest and most profound currents for Canadian writers of the sixties, informs them all.

Lee's first book, *Kingdom of Absence* (1967) established one of the dominant ideas of his work: that man lives on the edge of "vacancy", "absence", an "abyss", or "void" — a void which tends to make human effort seem futile and meaningless. This idea appears a borrowing from the post-war confrontations with 'nothingness' of the European existentialist philosophers; it is also not far removed from the obsession with mutability of older poets like Smith, Finch, and Gustafson, although it lacks their faith that beyond the decaying physical world lies Christian redemption. In style, *Kingdom of Absence* is awkwardly conservative. Lee seeks metrical, metaphorical, and allegorical equivalents for his ideas, writing poetry closer to the versified essay than to the transcription of powerful feelings. The book shows a marked preference for abstractions and generalizations over particular experiences, and for generalized emotion based on a vaguely delineated set of circumstances over those emotions that arise spontaneously from circumstantial fact. The reader never learns what basis there may be in actuality for the various states of alienation Lee continuously and extravagantly lays claim to. In the central "Kingdom of Absence" series Lee envisions himself allegorically stranded in the white void of Arctic icefields; however, what the actual circumstances are that this allegory is supposed to represent is not indicated. Further handicapping the ability of this book to communicate is Lee's awkwardness in using language with metrical form; unnatural inversions, archaisms, and vague rhetoric help shape too many of his lines.

In *Civil Elegies* Lee adopts a long flexible verse line in an attempt to deliver more authenticity to his feelings about the predicament of contemporary man. This work is one of the central documents of the new Canadian nationalism, although not one of its best achievements. Here Lee focuses on the Canadian portion of twentieth-century alienation, persuasively arguing Canada's consistent "emptiness" of purpose and moral commitment. He claims to be deeply troubled, even paralyzed, by his country's vacuity; unfortunately, the peaceful march of his long line tends to give the lie to these claims of anguish and despair.

Once again the basis of Lee's writing is generalized expression. Apart from three or four historic persons, the people seen in *Civil Elegies* are representative figures, faces in crowds. They are used to buttress abstract positions already taken by Lee, rather than allowed to shape the poem and the reader's response to it by their own particularity. The reasons for Lee's disaffection with Canada remain obscure; in twenty-two pages of poetry the only substantial issues he can cite are air pollution and Canadian support of the U.S. war effort in Vietnam. Furthermore, despite the relative freedom of the verse form, Lee still sprinkles his pages with empty and pretentious phrases: "psalm of being", "negative presence", "the texture of our being-here", "bitter droves".

Lee presents a revised version of the elegies in *Civil Elegies and Other Poems* (1972), but the revisions do not grapple with the graver weaknesses of the work. Historical inaccuracies are corrected, various awkwardnesses and pedantries in the language are removed, and additional generalized descriptions of landscapes and generic personnages are provided. The additional material brings two new sections into being and adds a third issue, the sellout of natural resources, to Lee's evidence for Canadian inadequacy. Only the nineteen pages of new lyrics suggest in this volume that Lee may be learning that the power of art is based on its particularity and vividness, and not on its grasp of abstract issues — however modish these may be. The lyrics reveal specific circumstances of Lee's interactions with himself, with women, and even with publishing ventures. They show his feelings of uncertainty and paralysis as having substance in the flesh of circumstance. Let us hope both as readers and as Canadians that he can eventually bring such specifity to his perceptions of Canadian malaise.

Lee, Dennis.　*Kingdom of Absence.* Toronto: House of Anansi, 1967.
　　　　. *Civil Elegies.* Toronto: House of Anansi, 1968.
　　　　, ed. *T.O. Now:* the Young Toronto Poets. Toronto: House of Anansi, 1968.
　　　　, ed. *The University Game,* ed. Dennis Lee and Howard Adelman. Toronto: House of Anansi, 1968.
　　　　. *Wiggle to the Laundromat.* Toronto: New Press.
　　　　. "Cadence, Country' Silence," *Liberté* XIV:6 (1972), 65-88.
　　　　. *Civil Elegies and Other Poems.* Toronto: House of Anansi, 1972.
　　　　. "Letter to David Helwig," *Quarry* XXI:3 (1972), 67-70.

Fulford, Robert.　"A Poet's View of Canada: a Nation of Losers and Quislings" (rev. of *Civil Elegies*), *The Toronto Star,* Apr. 15, 1972, p.77.
Helwig, David.　Review of *Civil Elegies and Other Poems, Quarry* XXI:3 (1972), 66-67.
Kearns, Lionel.　"If There's Anything I Hate It's Poetry," *Canadian Literature* 36 (Spring 1968), 68.
Newman, Christina.　"A Feeling for the Nation that Made Him," *MacLean's* 85 (June 1972), 88.
Schroeder, Andreas.　"Difficult Sanities," *Canadian Literature* 55(Winter 1973), 102-105.
Swan, Susan.　"From Minding to Feeling," *Books in Canada* I:10 (August 1972), 21-22.

Dorothy Livesay

(1909 -   )

The vividness, liveliness, and apparent spontaneity of Dorothy Livesay's verse placed it far from the mainstream of Canadian poetry from the beginning of her writing career in 1926 until the early 1960's. Unlike the academically fashionable poets of these years — Smith, Finch, Pratt, Gustafson, Jay Macpherson, P.K. Page — Livesay believed in the worth of the individual, the joy of sexuality, and the sufficiency of the physical universe. She wrote a poetry which passionately celebrated the common, everyday changing world — a poetry nearly the reverse of Smith's yearning for timeless pattern or Pratt's for the sub-divided and industrialized landscape.

In Livesay the open experimental verse forms and Heraclitean attitudes to nature characteristic of Canadian poetry in the sixties are foreshadowed as early as the late twenties. In *The Green Pitcher* (poems 1926-29, published in 1929) are poems in exquisitely phrased free verse and short-lined quatrains, completely free of both the decadent note of late Georgian poetry and the sterile aloofness of A. J.M. Smith modernism. In the best traditions of imagism, these poems skillfully avoid argument and philosophizing by making objects, events, and images become resonant with meaning. The craftmanship, as it is in most of Livesay's work, is deftly submerged; an illusion of spontaneous light-hearted speech is created out of an economical and precise choice of language. This latter characteristic alone distinguishes Livesay's work from the visibly crafted and erudite works of a Smith or Finch.

The themes of *The Green Pitcher* also prefigure dominant ones of recent times. Nature is seen as an intimate of the human world; "man has a kinship with each stone," one of Livesay's characters tells

168

us in the poem "Hermit". Much like Margaret Atwood forty years later, Livesay here implicitly condemns farmers who attack rocks and trees, who fear "wind and sun/rain, even, and snow". She denies both the traditional Canadian 'garrison mentality' ("this land grows like a garden in my heart") and the Finch-Gustafson fear of mortality ("There is no death: life is a constant sun.")

During the 1930's Livesay became increasingly indignant with the injustices and persecutions she saw heaped upon individual men and women whom she believed capable of the deepest feelings of beauty, joy, and love. The breadlines, riots, and police brutality of the depression in Canada, the rise of Hitler in Germany, the atrocities committed by the Fascists in the Spanish Civil War saw Livesay involved in left-wing political action. Her poems in this period serve the dual purpose of attacking cruelty and oppression and of exhorting the oppressed to continue to struggle for justice. Livesay here links her faith in a benificent cosmos with the social struggle. Those who fight the fascists in Spain fight not only for human freedom but for "leaf and light". Low-paid production-line tasks are an affront to the innate beauty of man and of the cosmos which spawned him ("Day and Night"). Livesay tells unemployed workers in "Depression Suite" that the natural beauty of the planet makes life worthwhile even in conditions which make that life barely sustainable. Most of these poems are energetic, vivid, and engrossing. However, because of conventionality in form and an occasional tendency to slip into the jargon and rhetoric of left-wing politics, they are somewhat less powerful than her early lyrics.

The wartime and postwar years saw Livesay write a variety of lyric, political, and dramatic poetry. These latter — "poems for voices" — are extremely weak, and suggest that Livesay is incapable of catching any voice except her own. Her own, however, she rendered with ever-increasing power; in recent years she has become almost exclusively a lyric poet of physical love, producing her two finest books, The Unquiet Bed (1967) and Plainsongs (1971).

Over the years Livesay's love poetry has centred on both the celebration of sexual fulfillment and the free woman's need to achieve this fulfillment without the sacrifice of her freedom and integrity. The man seeks to force his own concept of her upon her ("The Taming"); he prefers "an island" circumscribed, finite, and comprehensible ("Other"). The woman must keep both her spirit and her sexual delight concealed from her lover ("Blindness"). The lovers may merge physically but undergo separate and private spiritual alterations as a result of their mating ("The Touching"). Eventually the separate processes the individuals experience lead the lovers apart, and their loving becomes "a kind of disease" between them

NEW POEMS

Dorothy Livesay

New Poems by Dorothy Livesay. Emblem Books, 1955.

("The Operation"). Throughout, these poems possess a delicacy of image and a frankness and directness of language. Imagery from the cosmic world which Livesay cherishes is used to convincingly evoke the natural and proper beauty of surrender to sexuality. Dorothy Livesay is one of the most important Canadian poets of the last half-century. She successfully kept alive the direct and colloquial Heraclitean tradition in Canadian poetry throughout the thirties. Together with Layton, Souster, and Dudek, she provided the inspiration for the explosion of new natural voice poetry in the sixties. She is certainly the finest lyricist of her generation in Canada, eclipsing throughout her career the overtly fabricated creations of Pratt, Smith, Scott, Finch, Gustafson, and even early Birney. Among her works are the most sensitive and powerful poems of feminine sexuality in our literature.

Livesay, Dorothy. *Green Pitcher.* Toronto: Macmillan of Canada, 1928. . *Sign Post.* Toronto: Macmillan of Canada, 1932.
. *Day and Night.* Toronto: Ryerson Press, 1944.
. *Poems for People.* Toronto: Ryerson Press, 1947.
. *Call My People Home.* Toronto: Ryerson Press, 1950.
. *New Poems.* Toronto: Emblem Books, 1955.
. *Selected Poems.* Toronto: Ryerson Press, 1957.
. *The Colour of God's Face.* (Vancouver: privately printed, 1964?).
. "Livesayana," *Canadian Author and Bookman* 43 (Autumn 1967), 10-11.
. *The Unquiet Bed.* Toronto: Ryerson Press, 1967.
. *The Documentaries.* Toronto: Ryerson Press, 1968.
. *Plainsongs.* Fredericton: Fiddlehead Poetry Books, 1969.
. *Disasters of the Sun.* Burnaby, B.C.: Blackfish, 1971.
. "The Documentary Poem: a Canadian Genre," in Eli Mandel, ed., *Contexts of Canadian Criticism* (Chicago: University of Chicago Press, 1971), pp.267-281.
, ed. *Forty Women Poets of Canada.* Montreal: Ingluvin, 1971.
. *Plainsongs extended.* Fredericton: Fiddlehead Poetry Books, 1971.
. *Collected Poems: the Two Seasons.* Toronto: McGraw-Hill Ryerson, 1972.
. *Nine Poems of Farewell, 1972-73.* Windsor: Black Moss Press, 1973.
. *A Winnipeg Childhood* (stories). Winnipeg: Peguis Press, 1973.

Collin, W.E. "My New Found Land," in his *The White Savannahs* (Toronto: Macmillan of Canada, 1936), pp.147-173.

Crawley, Alan. "Dorothy Livesay," in W.P. Perceval, ed., *Leading Canadian Poets* (Toronto: Ryerson Press, 1948), pp.117-124.

Fetherling, Doug. "Canada, Country You Loved with Hate," *Saturday Night* 88 (March 1973), 36-37.

Francis, Wynne. "Poems of Wide Experience," *Montreal Star*, September 16, 1967, "Entertainments", p.6.

Geddes, Gary. "Livesay Towers over a Kitchen-Sink Pack" (rev. of *Collected Poems*), *The Globe and Mail*, Jan. 13, 1973, p.31.

Leland, D. "Dorothy Livesay: Poet of Nature," *Dalhousie Review* 51 (Autumn 1971), 404-412.

Pacey, Desmond. Introduction to *Selected Poems* (Toronto: Ryerson Press, 1957), pp.xi-xix.

———. Review of *The Unquiet Bed*, *Canadian Forum* 48 (April 1968), 21-22.

Pratt, E.J. "Dorothy Livesay," *Gants du Ciel* 11 (Printemps 1946), 61-65.

Rogers, Linda. "A Woman for All Seasons," *Books in Canada* II:1 (January-February 1973), 50.

Skelton, Robin. "Everything Lives," *Canadian Literature* 35 (Winter 1968), 91-92.

Steinberg, M.W. "Dorothy Livesay: Poet of Affirmation," *British Columbia Library Quarterly* 24 (October 1960), 9-13.

Stephan, Ruth. "A Canadian Poet," *Poetry* (Chicago) 65 (January 1945), 220-222.

Stevens, Peter. "Dorothy Livesay: the Love Poetry," *Canadian Literature* 47 (Winter 1971), 26-43.

———. "Ideas and Icons," *Canadian Literature* 40 (Spring 1969), 76-77.

———. "Out of the Silence and Across the Distance," *Queen's Quarterly* 78 (1971), 579-591.

Weaver, Robert. "The Poetry of Dorothy Livesay," *Contemporary Verse* 26 (Fall 1948), 18-22.

———. "Twenty Years of Irving Layton and 40 of Dorothy Livesay" (rev. of *The Documentaries*), *The Toronto Star*, Feb. 1, 1969, p.15.

Jack Ludwig
(1922-   )

Jack Ludwig's first two novels (*Confusions*, 1963, and *Above Ground*, 1968) appear to have been consciously written for a United States audience — so skilfully, in fact that there is little that is Canadian about them. In both cases the physical space of the settings and the psychological space of the characters are thoroughly American. Both narrators, even Joshua of *Above Ground* who is born in Canada, consider themselves representative of American experience.

Jack Ludwig was born in Winnipeg and educated at the University of Manitoba. At the end of the Second World War he moved to the United States to do graduate work at U.C.L.A. and did not return. He has, however, attempted to create the illusion of Canadian involvement by publishing articles and stories in such magazines as *Macleans, Canadian Literature,* and *The Tamarack Review,* by editing anthologies of Canadian Literature, and by writing *Hockey Night in Moscow* about the 1972 Canada-U.S.S.R. professional hockey series. Ludwig, like fellow-novelist Mordecai Richler, belongs to a generation of Canadians for whom New York and London set the only artistic fashions and standards worth observing. Unlike Richler, Ludwig spurned Canada not only as a place to live but, until his most recent novel, *A Woman of her Age* (1973), as a subject for literature.

Praised by its early reviewers for wit and humour, *Confusions* is a campus novel written in a pretentious first-person narrative style that aspires to those of Roth and Updike. Its narrator and central character, Joseph Golsky, is a Harvard Ph.D., Jewish and of New York City birth, who moves to a teaching post at a small California university. His "confusions", on which the novel centres, all concern cultural collisions peculiar to U.S. society: his old-world Jewish heritage meets Harvard's suave and genteel skepticism; his family's conservative sexual world meets America's sexual supermarket; later his Harvard blazer and flannels confront the Hawaian prints and Bermuda shorts of California's academic Disneylands. Consistently, the book insists on "America" as its topic and on the Americanness of the narrator: "I am no part-time member of contemporary American society," Golsky tells us. "I am in it and of it."

In *Above Ground,* Ludwig takes special care to suppress any Canadian elements which might alienate U.S. readers. The first third of the book, it can be determined with some detective work, is set in Winnipeg, and yet not one reference to the geography of this city or to the names of any Canadian city or landmark is given. In contrast, when the setting shifts to Los Angeles and New York, place references — Sunset Boulevard, Bel Aire, Bakersfield, Carson Sink, the Teton Mountains, Idlewild Airport, the East River, the Biltmore Hotel, the Empire State Building — occur on most pages. The narrator, whom Ludwig presents sympathetically throughout, has spent his first twenty-five years in Winnipeg, but thinks of himself as an American and views American history as his history. His psychological space contains no international boundary; even while he is in Winnipeg, its centre is in New York.

The theme of this book is again "confusion": the confusions suffered by a young man who abruptly moves from a childhood in hospital to a dying adult world of harassing sexuality. The images of this sexual world are American — jazz, the supermarket, the California freeway, the suntanned Malibu surfer-girl, the sullen rumble of the New York El. The narrator plunges into this noisy and frantic American world in a desperate and life-long attempt to forget his own mortality. His narrative style is as abrupt and rapid-fire as a street of flashing neon signs. Sudden transitions on almost every page parallel the mindless speed and variety that surrounds him in his American world.

A Woman of her Age is Ludwig's only novel with an overtly Canadian setting. It also differs from *Confusions* and *Above Ground* in lacking both a single narrative viewpoint and a prolonged linear plot-line; instead it takes place in one day and consists of juxtaposed stream-of-consciousness sections from the viewpoints of six characters - all members of Montreal's Jewish community. Ludwig's usual theme of individual confusion due to cultural differences and clashes is evident in the frantic yet unfulfilling lives most of the six characters lead. In the two central characters, eighty-five year old Doba Goffman and her widowed young daughter-in-law Shirley

Gordon, regret for having abandoned both working-class values and the spontaneity of working-class sexuality disrupts their enjoyment of wealth and status. Their ascent to wealth has brought the other four characters — Doba's suitor Barney, Doba's elder son Sidney, Shirley's ex-lover Maxie, and Shirley's second husband Neville — to sexual paralysis and frustration. It has also brought a seventh character, Jim Goffman, Doba's second son and Shirley's first husband, to a death symbolic of all their predicaments — crushed between two Bentley limousines in a Westmount fog.

A new theme of United States political and cultural domination of Canada — expressed intermittently by Franklin, a U.S. 'revolutionary' who has come to Montreal to aid the F.L.Q. — adds modish Canadian colour to this novel but has little relevance to the continuing crises of the six major characters. While it is true that all six are in some way victims of the capitalist economic system which Doba and Shirley have embraced in Westmount and which Franklin decries, it is fallacious to equate capitalism *per se* with the United States. Economic systems, although they can encourage various forms of cultural imperialism (mostly not evident in *A Woman of her Age*), are themselves meta-national phenomena.

With the exception of this poorly-integrated political element, *A Woman of her Age* is a mature and perceptive creation. The multiple viewpoints give rise to a variety and appropriateness of style and an equanimity of vision entirely absent in the acrobatic prose of Ludwig's earlier works. As for *Confusions* and *Above Ground,* the kind of 'hustling' after U.S. acceptance and excessive deference to American literary values that one sees in them are rare in serious Canadian fiction of the sixties, but certainly a common part of the overall Canadian experience. While these novels directly present little that is relevant to Canadian life, they do deserve to be read and discussed in Canada — if only as examples of Franklin's favourite target, cultural imperialism.

Ludwig, Jack. *Recent American Novelists.* Minneapolis: University of Minneapolis Press, 1962.

. *Confusions.* Toronto: McClelland & Stewart, 1963.

. "On Thermostats, Super-egos, Theatre Directors, and Cleaning Ladies," *Tamarack Review* 45 (Autumn 1967), 106-110, 112-113.

. *Requiem for Bibul.* Agincourt: the Book Society of Canada, 1967.

. *Above Ground.* Boston: Little, Brown, 1968.

, ed. *Soundings: New Canadian Poets,* ed. Jack Ludwig and Andy Wainwright. Toronto: House of Anansi, 1970.

    . *Hockey Night in Moscow*. Toronto: McClelland & Stewart, 1972.

    . *A Woman of her Age*. Toronto: McClelland & Stewart, 1973.

Buckle, Daphne.   "In American Confusion," *Evidence* 8 (1965), 133-134.

Buitenhuis, Peter.   "Conflicting Conclusions Reading Confusions" (rev. of *Confusions*), *The Globe and Mail Magazine*, Nov. 2, 1963, p.19.

Cameron, Donald.   Review of *Above Ground*, *Canadian Forum* 48 (January 1969), 231.

    . "Sleeping is a Criminal Activity" (interview), in his *Conversations with Canadian Novelists* (Toronto: Macmillan of Canada, 1973), pp.116-129.

Carroll, John.   "On Richler and Ludwig," *Tamarack Review* 29 (Autumn 1963), 98-102.

Fulford, Robert.   "On the Academic Jungle: Confusion, Identity, Smart Guys," *Maclean's* 76 (October 19, 1963), 81.

Gibson, Graeme.   Interview with Jack Ludwig, in his *Eleven Canadian Novelists* (Toronto: House of Anansi, 1973), pp.213-235.

Godfrey, Dave.   "Starved in the Hour of our Hoarding — the Conglomerate as Fiction," *Tamarack Review* 48 (1968), 73, 76-79.

James, Esther.   "Ludwig's 'Confusions'," *Canadian Literature* 40 (Spring 1969), 49-53.

New, W.H.   "Cock and Bull Stories," *Canadian Literature* 39 (Winter 1969), 83-84.

Pacey, Desmond.   "Light Weights," *Canadian Forum* 44 (April 1964), 22.

Stonehewer, Lila.   "The Anatomy of Confusion," *Canadian Literature* 29 (Summer 1966), 34-42.

Sutherland, Ronald.   "The Mainstream," *Canadian Literature* 53 (Summer 1972), 30-41.

Tallman, Warren.   "Performers and Entertainers," *Canadian Literature* 19 (Winter 1964), 49-50.

Waddington, Miriam.   "Avant-Garde Posture, But Academic in the Worst Way" (rev. of *Above Ground*), *The Globe and Mail Magazine*, June 1, 1968, p.19.

Gwendolyn MacEwen (1939 -)

One of the leaders in the movement of Canadian poetry in the sixties toward more indirect dramatic and concrete expression was Gwendolyn MacEwen. Like many earlier but less talented Canadian writers, MacEwen's perception of man and his cosmos has been coloured by the secrets of mythological lore, but, unlike her predecessors, she has continually sought the artistic means by which the mythological can be induced to appear within the phenomenal — by which the word can appear as flesh.

MacEwen's novels and short stories have all focused on characters who have attempted in some way to discover the divine by means of the actual. *Julian the Magician* (1963) tells of the life of a nineteenth-century European magician who comes to believe that his body is being taken over by Christ. Julian's early apprenticeship with the alchemist Kardin (during which he has learned of alchemy's goal of transmuting opposites into a supreme gold, the Christ/Mercurius, the god incarnate as man) plus his reading of such mystical texts as the Zohar, the Kabbalah, and the writings of Paracelsus, Albertus Magnus, and Jacob Boehme lead him to feel reluctantly obliged to welcome this divine entry into his own actuality. He consequently finds himself reliving the final years of Christ's life, and approaching the casual horror of its inevitable conclusion.

A more powerful novel is *King of Egypt, King of Dreams* (1971) which attempts to recreate the life of Egypt's 'monotheistic' pharoah, the fourteenth-century B.C. Akhenaton. This pharoah abandoned the traditional structures of Egyptian religion in order to discern and worship the purest essence of divinity, the sun-disc Aton. Unfortunately, Akhenaton's efforts lead him further and further from the actual world of his kingdom, its people, his wife, and his own flesh, and yet no nearer to outright perception of divinity and the description of its being. He has failed to realize the alchemist's truth that the divine can be apprehended only when fully integrated with terrestrial reality, and that it can be described only by means of earthly, concrete terms. Akhenaton dies literally and figuratively blind — having failed both to keep his kingdom in order and to articulate the essence of his ineffable deity. The artistic message of this book is clear: to fulfill Akhenaton's ambitions of speaking "the unspeakable" and explaining "the inexplicable", the artist must seek to find his truths fully-clothed in the flesh of the phenomenal world.

In her own work as an artist MacEwen has attempted much the same task as Akhenaton, but via the alchemist's way. Her novels and short stories reveal the sentences of divine law indirectly through the implications of the lives of such men as Julian, Akhenaton, or — in her short story collection *Noman* (1972) — through those of contemporary Toronto men and women. Her poems, particularly those of recent books, succeed in giving substance to myth by showing the poet living these myths in the mundane and domestic particulars of her life. Only the very early books of her poetry, *Selah* (1961), *The Drunken Clock* (1961), and *The Rising Fire* (1963), present myth in unconvincing, non-particular forms — as dogma, artifact or rhetorical statement of emotion. In *Breakfast for Barbarians* (1966) and *Armies of the Moon* (1972) mythology is kinetic, actively incarnate in realistic scenes, witty colloquial language, and explicit references to the personal life of the writer.

Throughout, the poetry assumes the binary structure of reality — at its highest level the celestial versus the terrestrial, at lower levels the sun versus the moon, light versus dark, man versus woman, sanity versus madness. The way to enlightenment can require the seeking of truth in its opposites: says MacEwen, "Only because my poems are lies do they earn the right to be truth." The greatest human attainments require the reconciliation of opposites — the divine with the profane, the beast with the lamb — until it becomes clear that "all worlds, all time, all loves are one." MacEwen's most frequent method of reconciliation is the paradox: "that wolf is stone, this/stone is wolf."

In the 1940's and 1950's the arbitrary, ornamental, and purely 'literary' use of myth in Canadian poetry had become so extensive that some poets, notably Louis Dudek, called on new writers to forsake mythology entirely. The work of MacEwen, more than that of any other writer, has restored the value of mythology to Canadian poetry. She has demonstrated that it need not be merely a system by

Gwendolyn MacEwen

which one escapes worldly events, but in fact can be found emanating from those events and providing understanding of our very real sensual and Heraclitean world. For Canadian writers, the most salutary union of opposites MacEwen has achieved is this one in which the mythological and the experiential become inseparable faces of one living reality.

MacEwen, Gwendolyn.   *The Drunken Clock*. Toronto: Aleph Press, 1961.
. "Genesis," *Teangadoir* II:1 (November 1961), 73-80.
. *Selah*. Toronto: Aleph Press, 1961.
. *Julian the Magician*. Toronto: Macmillan of Canada, 1963.
. *The Rising Fire*. Toronto: Contact Press, 1963.
. *A Breakfast for Barbarians*. Toronto: Ryerson Press, 1966.
. *The Shadow Maker*. Toronto: Macmillan of Canada, 1969.
. *King of Egypt, King of Dreams*. Toronto: Macmillan of Canada, 1971.
. *Armies of the Moon*. Toronto: Macmillan of Canada, 1972.
. *Noman*. Ottawa: Oberon Press, 1972.
. *Open Secret* (phonograph record), CBC Learning Systems, 1972.

Atwood, Margaret.   "MacEwen's Muse," *Canadian Literature* 45 (Summer 1970), 23-32.
Barrett, Elizabeth.   "A Tour de Force," *Evidence* 8 (1964), 140-143.
Bowering, George.   "The Canadian Poetry Underground," *Canadian Literature* 13 (Summer 1962), 66-67.
. "A Complex Music," *Canadian Literature* 21 (Summer 1964), 70-71.
Colombo, John Robert.   "Half Naive, Half Knowing" (rev. of *A Breakfast for Barbarians*), *The Globe and Mail Magazine*, Nov. 19, 1966, p.16.
Davey, Frank.   "Gwendolyn MacEwen: the Secret of Alchemy," *Open Letter* (second series) 4, Spring 1973, pp.5-23.
Dragland, Stan.   Review of *The Armies of the Moon*, *Quarry* XXI:4 (Autumn 1972), 57-62.
Fox, Gail.   Review of *The Shadow Maker*, *Quarry* XIX:2 (Winter 1970), 57-59.
Godfrey, Dave.   "Figments of a Northern Mind," *Tamarack Review* 31 (Spring 1964), 90-91.
Gose, E.B.   "They Shall Have Arcana," *Canadian Literature* 21 (Summer 1964), 36-45.
Grosskurth, Phyllis.   "Madness and Divinity in the Mundane World" (rev. of *King of Egypt, King of Dreams*), *The Globe and Mail*, Nov. 27,

1971, p.33.

Jones, D.G. "Language of our Time," *Canadian Literature* 29 (Summer 1966), 67-69.

Mandel, Eli. "The Real Reveals the Tiresome" (rev. of *The Shadow Maker*), *the Globe and Mail Magazine*, Sept. 27, 1969, p.18.

———. "Seedtime in a Dark May," *Alphabet* 4 (June 1962), 70.

Marshall, Tom. Review of *The Rising Fire*, *Quarry* 14 (1964-65), 54-55.

Mezei, Kathy. Review of *Noman*, *Quarry* XXII:2 (Spring 1973), 70-71.

Revell, Peter. "Images," *Alphabet* 13 (June 1967), 96-97.

Ringrose, Christopher. "Vision Enveloped in Night," *Canadian Literature* 53 (Summer 1972), 102-104.

Sowton, Ian. "To Improvise an Eden," *Edge* 2 (Spring 1964), 119-124.

Stevens, Peter. "In Word, in Act, and in Flux" (rev. of *The Armies of the Moon*), *The Globe and Mail*, Apr. 22, 1972, p.35.

Weaver, Robert. "Bold Language and Emotional Maturity" (rev. of *The Shadow Maker*), *The Toronto Star*, Aug. 2, 1969, p.27.

———. "Real Power Misused" (rev. of *Julian the Magician* and *The Rising Fire*), *The Toronto Star*, March 21, 1964, p.30.

David McFadden (1940 -   )

The poetry of David McFadden is rooted in the poet's family life in Hamilton, Ontario, but manages to contain most of the explosive themes of the later twentieth century: geological disaster, irremedial human brutality, human extinction. McFadden presents himself in his poetry as the common man of our time, paying his taxes, loving his children, renting summer cabins, driving his Volkswagen amid the tragi-comic ruins and creations of a Pepsi civilization. He deliberately avoids any associations with counter-culture values and 'avant-garde' writing by adopting the disarming, garrulous, and casual style of ordinary-joe speech and by openly acknowledging the lower-middle-class imagery of his day-to-day activities.

This ingenious and 'sloppily' colloquial style has led numerous reviewers to believe McFadden writes ingenuous and trivial poetry. They are wrong. McFadden's most original technique is to use his own professed ingenuousness — together with the ordinariness of his family's suburban life — as emblems of the little man's loves and dilemmas. McFadden's frequent jokes at his own expense, especially concerning the 'campy' activities which delight him, continually underline to the reader that the poet is not unaware of his own limitations, and that he is intentionally exploring these as means of illuminating the life of post-modern man.

Central to the poems of McFadden's three major collections, *Letters from the Earth to the Earth* (1968), *Poems Worth Knowing* (1971), and *Intense Pleasure* (1972) is his devotion to his wife Joan and his daughters Alison and Jennifer. In passages filled with the homey details of the changing of diapers, the repairing of toys, the cooking of meals, McFadden works to reinvest the alleged trivialities and banalities of all our lives with some unpretentious sense of ceremony and beauty. In other poems he brings to attention the fact that his family (and by implication our own families) live in a world in which Vietnamese children of equal charm are napalmed and bayonetted, in which Martin Luther King is shot through the neck, in which "Bruce Marsh" speaks on television for "Kraft Foods in Canada", or in which Hamiltonian "George Glidden, 26/married, father of three" drives at night into an unlighted stalled truck, dying instantly. In a world where sudden death stalks the saintly and the undistinguished alike, such small things of a man's life as listening to a child's song or watching a U.S. football game on television can give (as one McFadden title states) "intense pleasure".

McFadden's tendency toward good natured self-parody for his sentimental attitudes and his petit-bourgeois tastes, is amplified in his two part novel, *The Great Canadian Sonnet* (1970). Here he adopts a persona, Ricky Wayne, whose mind is even more than McFadden's innundated with the images of later twentieth-century pop and commercial culture. Wayne, who narrates the novel, is a

The Great Canadian Sonnet by David McFadden.
The Coach House Press, 1970.

media victim. Although he has ambitions to be a poet, and is undoubtedly a man of some perceptiveness and talent, every paragraph he writes is seduced from its real track by the predominantly American mythology of current international culture. All varieties of image assail him, from the intellectual fads of mysticism, orientalism, and Unidentified Flying Objects, to Mickey Mouse, baseball, Nazi insignia, dial-a-prayer, Billie Holiday and Coca-Cola. At the beginning of the novel, Wayne gives the reader a mileage chart of Hamilton's distance from thirty-two North American cities. As the novel unfolds, it becomes clear that these figures indicate invasion routes through which the various alien images are rushing to cripple Wayne and his "Great Canadian Sonnet". While the message of McFadden's poems is that individual man inevitably is forced to participate in both the *lumpen* culture and global political forces of his time, that of *The Great Canadian Sonnet* is that the larger forces can overwhelm the rootless individual. McFadden roots himself within the global sea of international image and events by means of the trivial particularities of his family, but Ricky Wayne has gone adrift and is wildly searching for stability and direction.

The Great Canadian Sonnet is an ingenious and emphatic statement of Canadian nationalism, in some ways more perceptive than the recent analyses of George Grant, Walter Gordon, or Margaret Atwood. The accompanying illustrations by Greg Curnoe repeatedly expand the implications of the writing. Less flamboyant, McFadden's poetry also makes a nationalistic statement in demonstrating one family's humourous and fumbling struggle for its own life within the media vortex. In all his work, McFadden shows himself to be a totally authentic and original voice of his time.

McFadden, David.   *The Poem Poem*. Kitchener, Ont.: Weed/Flower Press, 1967.
         . *The Saladmaker*. (*Imago* 9) Montreal, 1968.
         . *Letters from the Earth to the Earth*. Toronto: The Coach House Press, 1969.
         . "Drapes" (story), *Quarry* XIX:3 (Spring 1970), 22-28.
         . *The Great Canadian Sonnet*, Part I. Toronto: The Coach House Press, 1970.
         . "Here Are Some More Snaps" (story), *Fiddlehead* 87 (November-December 1970), 6-14.
         . *The Great Canadian Sonnet*, Part II. Toronto: The Coach House Press, 1971.
         . *Poems Worth Knowing*. Toronto: The Coach House Press, 1971.

    . *Intense Pleasure*. Toronto: McClelland & Stewart, 1972.
    . *The Ova Yogas*. Toronto: Weed/Flower Press and Ganglia Press, 1972.

Barbour, Douglas.   Review of *The Poem Poem*, *Canadian Forum* 48 (May 1968), 44-45.

Bowering, George.   "It's a Funny Thing: an Interview with David McFadden," *Copperfield* 3 (1971), 77-82.

Fisher, Carole.   "Suck Chomp Lick Yummy Slurp" (review of *Poems Worth Knowing*), *The B.C. Monthly* I:3 (December 1972), 90.

Gibbs, Robert.   Review of *The Saladmaker*, *Fiddlehead* 77 (Summer 1968), 97.

Helwig, David.   Review of *Letters from the Earth to the Earth*, *Quarry* XIX:2 (Winter 1970), 59-60.

Howell, Bill.   "That's My Boy!" *Books in Canada* I:10 (August 1972), 27-28.

Stevens, Peter.   "In Word, in Act, and in Flux" (rev. of *Intense Pleasure*), *The Globe and Mail,* Apr. 22, 1972, p.35.

Marshall McLuhan (1911 -   )

Through a series of aggressively messianic and typographically adventurous books on advertising, printing, language, and the electronic media, Herbert Marshall McLuhan became the internationally best-known Canadian writer of the sixties. His *Understanding Media* (1964), published in hardback, college paperback, and drugstore paperback editions, not only revolutionized the interpretation of television and other media but made McLuhan for several years a North American culture-hero — discussed in *Maclean's, Esquire,* and *Mademoiselle,* interviewed on national U.S. television, and caricatured in numerous cartoons.

McLuhan was born in Edmonton and spent most of his life there and in Winnipeg, where he received a B.A. from the University of Manitoba in 1933. He did graduate work at Cambridge University, obtaining an M.A. in 1940 and a PH.D. in 1942. During the thirties he also taught at the University of Wisconsin and St. Louis University; he joined Assumption University in Windsor, Ontario, in 1944, and St. Michael's College at the University of Toronto, where he presently teaches, in 1952. In 1953 he founded *Explorations*, an important magazine of culture and communications. In 1959-60 he served as director of a media project for the U.S. Office of Education and the National Association of Educational Broadcasters. He was appointed director of the University of Toronto's Centre for Culture and Technology in 1963, and to the Albert Schweitzer Chair in Humanities at Fordham University in 1966.

His central idea, expanded from Harold Adams Innis's perception of the central importance of communications in shaping the character of a culture, has been that the way in which information is communicated can be of greater significance than the content of the information. Changes in the dominant modes of communication, and of the human senses that these modes involve, can alter human consciousness and cause massive shifts in the course of history and culture. McLuhan identifies three major communication periods: the aural, from man's beginning to 1460; the Gutenberg, from 1460-1960; and the electric, from 1960-present. The aural period is one of multisensory communication and decentralized and communal living patterns. The Gutenberg is a print and eye-oriented time in which the logical, sequential, and single-track flow of the printed sentence becomes a model for mass production of uniform products, centralized organization, and compartmentalized intellectual disciplines. The electric sees the arrival of totally immersing multiphasic media — television, in particular — which once again demand multisensory response and encourage decentralized living patterns.

McLuhan's analyses of the ramifications of both the invention of movable type and the creation of the electronic media are always stimulating and usually convincing. McLuhan is at his best in bringing into perspective changes currently affecting his society — in discussing the effects of live television coverage on public response to the Vietnamese war, or the relationship between television and the changing intellectual perspectives of children. He is less successful in suggesting causal relationships between events; here he tends both to equate coincidence with cause and, in some cases, to distort historical facts. The credibility projected by his historical accounts is more often a product of this 'electric' style, his pseudo-scientific diction, his suggestive juxtapositions, and his invocation of famous names — Mallarmé, Proust, Eliot, Joyce, and Picasso — than of definitive documentation.

McLuhan has not been strong in predicting the future. He has on several occasions announced the obsolescence of the book. Meanwhile his own books have demonstrated numerous ways in which the power of the book's form can be expanded, and the new electronic technologies of teletype, photo-copying, xerography, and computer typesetting have tended to amplify the book's convenience and significance rather than diminish them. McLuhan has also clung to a perverse 'Gutenberg' conviction that the new media world requires human control. Rather than recognizing that the electronic technology increases the independence of the individual from centralized control, he has proposed that it offers a new "possibility of arranging the entire human environment." His vision of future society has been of a programmed mass, with "controls" extended "to all the sensory thresholds of our being".

Viewed from the seventies, McLuhan would seem to have been

more a symptom of his time than its master. He has had little influence on contemporary writing except in his role as an experimenter with print and the book form. He has had, however, a very important indirect influence on the acceptance of experimental and fragmented literary forms.

McLuhan, Marshall. *The Mechanical Bride: Folklore of Industrial Man.* New York: Vanguard, 1951.
. *Explorations in Communication*, with E.S. Carpenter. Boston: Beacon Press, 1960.
. *The Gutenberg Galaxy: The Making of Typographic Man.* Toronto: University of Toronto Press, 1962.
. *Understanding Media: The Extensions of Man.* New York: McGraw-Hill, 1964.
. *Voices of Literature*, ed. Marshall McLuhan and Richard J. Schoek. Two vols. New York: Holt, 1965, 1966.
. *The Medium is the Massage: an Inventory of Effects*, with Quentin Fiore. New York: Random House, 1967.
. *Through the Vanishing Point: Space in Poetry and Painting*, with Harley Parker. New York: Harper & Row, 1968.
. *War and Peace in the Global Village*, with Quentin Fiore. New York: McGraw-Hill, 1968.
. *Counterblast*, with Harley Parker. New York: Harcourt Brace, 1969.
. *Culture is Our Business.* New York: McGraw-Hill, 1970.
. *From Cliché to Archetype*, with Wilfred Watson. New York: Viking, 1970.
. *The Interior Landscape: the Literary Criticism of Marshall McLuhan*, selected, compiled, and edited by Eugene McNamara. New York: McGraw-Hill, 1970.
. *Take Today: the Executive as Dropout*, with Barrington Nevitt. New York: Harcourt Brace Jovanovitch, 1972.

Buitenhuis, Peter. "Marshall McLuhan: the Analogical Critic" (rev. of *The Interior Landscape*), *The Globe and Mail Magazine*, Feb. 14, 1970, p.15.
Crosby, Harry H., and George R. Bond, ed. *The McLuhan Explosion: a Casebook on Marshall McLuhan and Understanding Media.* New York: American Book Company, 1968.
Duffy, Dennis. *Marshall McLuhan.* Toronto: McClelland & Stewart, 1969. New Canadian Library, Canadian Writers no. 1.
Miller, Jonathan. *Marshall McLuhan.* New York: Viking, 1971.
Stearn, Gerald E., ed. *McLuhan Hot & Cool: a Critical Symposium with a Rebuttal by McLuhan.* New York: Dial Press, 1967.

Rosenthal, Raymond, ed.   *McLuhan Pro & Con*. New York: Funk & Wagnalls, 1968.

Theall, Donald F.   *The Medium is the Rear-View Mirror: Understanding McLuhan*. Montreal: McGill-Queen's University Press, 1971.

Eli Mandel

(1922 -   )

Since its first significant publication as one-third of the Contact Press anthology *Trio* (1954), the poetry of Eli Mandel has developed and expanded nearly as much as Canadian poetry itself. His first poetry was complex and erudite, its setting not in the actual world but one of literature and mythology, its voice that of a learned man discoursing cryptically to his peers. The first changes in this style became evident in *Black and Secret Man* (1964); here Mandel's syntax began to simplify and his attention move from the world of books to that of contemporary experience. A new and confident sense of his own individuality is projected; the poetry is consequently capable of eliciting emotional as well as intellectual response.

Mandel has remained a meditational poet throughout his subsequent books, *An Idiot Joy* (1966) and *Stony Plain* (1973), but one who can increasingly make his meditations carry rich emotional power. His new willingness to expose his self simply and directly in his poetry has led him to various adventures in the open, logically discontinuous forms of post-modern verse, including prose poems, found poems, and concrete poems. The academic sombreness of his first books has yielded totally to a new tone of terse, flexible commitment and ironic wit. The mythological references are no longer arbitrarily imposed on barely visible experience, but now are made to arise naturally from keenly perceived details of the phenomenal world.

Behind all of Mandel's poetry lurks an evil, devious, and vicious human community populated by suicides, murderers, torturers, and idiots. The poet/victim, variously incarnate as Houdini, Goya, Janis Joplin, Mandel himself, labours to absorb and transcend this community into some endurable artistic form. The gruesome atrocities which befell more than six million of Mandel's fellow Jews in World War II dominate his sense of man's reality; around these other

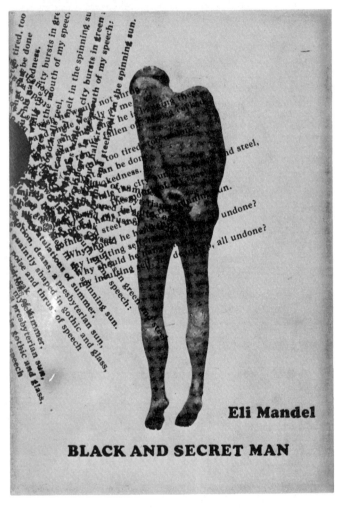

Black and Secret Man by Eli Mandel. Ryerson Press, 1964.

horrors orchestrate to form a ghastly and persuasive human music —
from Cain's murder of Abel to the tens of thousands of civilian deaths
by bombing, shelling and premeditated murder in Vietnam. To
Mandel even the Canadian landscape is a hostile presence filled with
"sharp rocks, screams, hawks, kites, and cranes"; the Saskatchewan
sun kills indiscriminately in its "poisoned slow air".

Mandel's can thus be loosely associated with the earlier pessimistic Canadian poetries of Finch and Gustafson; certainly his has
little in common with the affirmative poetry of Livesay, Souster,
MacEwen, Bowering, Coleman, or Bissett. However, his work is also
unrelieved by the hope for divine grace found in that of Finch and
Gustafson. Mandel's bleak worldview seems most firmly related to
European postwar literary and philosophical pessimism; its closest
analogues in Canadian poetry are the works of Michael Ondaatje,
John Newlove, and Phyllis Webb.

Since 1962, Mandel has been also one of the most important anthologists of poetry in Canada, instrumental in determining the
direction of Canadian poetry and the general reception of its poets.
His first anthology, *Poetry 62* (co-edited with Jean-Guy Pilon), introduced a number of the 1950's lesser known poets — Al Purdy,
Milton Acorn, D.G. Jones, Alden Nowlan, Leonard Cohen, and John
Robert Colombo. A recent anthology, *Poets of Contemporary
Canada* (1972), provided Joe Rosenblatt and Bill Bissett with their
first important college textbook appearance. Mandel's other an-
thologies are *Five Modern Canadian Poets* (1970), *Contexts of
Canadian Criticism* (1971), *English Poems of the Twentieth Century*
(1971), co-edited with D.E.S. Maxwell, and *Eight More Canadian
Poets* (1972).

Mandel's critical writings have included *Criticism: the Silent
Speaking Words* (1966), eight important essays that insist on an
emotional orientation and subjectivity in criticism, and a monograph
(1969) on his fellow poet Irving Layton. The latter makes a bold and
well-documented case for Layton being a poet of passionately held
"myth and idea"; it is without a doubt the most original study of
Layton to date.

Mandel, Eli.   *Trio*: First Poems by Gael Turnbull, Phyllis Webb, Eli
    Mandel. Toronto: Contact Press, 1954.
        . *Fuseli Poems*. Toronto: Contact Press, 1960.
        . "Giants, Beasts, and Men in Recent Canadian Poetry,"
    Queen's Quarterly 67 (Summer 1960), 285-293.
        , ed. *Poetry 62*, ed. Eli Mandel and Jean-Guy Pilon. Toron-
    to: Ryerson Press, 1961.

. "Lapwing You Are. Lapwing He — a Note on Icarus in Myth and Poetry," *Alphabet* 4 (June 1962), 59-62.
. *Black and Secret Man.* Toronto: Ryerson Press, 1964.
. "A Lack of Ghosts: Canadian Poets and Poetry," *Humanities Association Bulletin* 16 (Spring 1965), 59-67.
. *Criticism: the Silent-Speaking Words.* Toronto: CBC Publications, 1966.
. *An Idiot Joy.* Edmonton: M.G. Hurtig, 1967.
. *Irving Layton.* Toronto: Forum House, 1969.
, ed. *Five Modern Canadian Poets.* Toronto: Holt Rinehart and Winston, 1970.
, ed. *Contexts of Canadian Criticism.* Chicago: University of Chicago Press, 1971.
, ed. *English Poems of the Twentieth Century*, ed. Eli Mandel and Desmond Maxwell. Toronto: Macmillan of Canada, 1971.
, ed. *Eight More Canadian Poets.* Toronto: Holt Rinehart and Winston, 1972.
. "Nietzsche and Poetry: a Discussion" by Eli Mandel and Irving Layton, *The Malahat Review* 24 (October 1972), 23-29.
, ed. *Poets of Contemporary Canada 1960-1970.* Toronto: McClelland & Stewart, 1972.
. *Crusoe.* Toronto: House of Anansi, 1973.
. *Stony Plain.* Toronto: Press Porcépic, 1973.

Barbour, Douglas. Review of *Black and Secret Man, Quarry* XV:4 (August 1966), 46-47.
. Review of *An Idiot Joy, Canadian Forum* 48 (August 1968), 19.
Bowering, George. "Eli and Irving," *Canadian Literature* 39 (Winter 1969), 74-76.
Cook, Gregory M. Review of *An Idiot Joy, Dalhousie Review* 49 (Spring 1969), 147.
Dudek, Louis. "Two Canadian Poets: Ralph Gustafson and Eli Mandel," *Culture* 22 (June 1961), 145-151.
Geddes, Gary. "Lyrical Half-Mad Visions of a Bruised Eye" (rev. of *Stony Plain*), *The Globe and Mail*, May 5, 1973, p.37.
Gibson, Kenneth. Review of *An Idiot Joy, Quarry* XVIII:4 (Summer 1969), 54-56.
McMaster, R.D. "The Unexplained Interior: a Study of E.W. Mandel's *Fuseli Poems*," *Dalhousie Review* 40 (Fall 1960), 392-396.
Ower, John. "Black and Secret Poet, Notes on Eli Mandel," *Canadian Literature* 42 (Autumn 1969), 14-25.
Simms, Norman. Review of *An Idiot Joy, The Far Point* 2, pp.63-68.
Sonthoff, H.W. "Darkness and Experience," *Canadian Literature* 24

(Spring 1965), 66-68.
Waddington, Miriam.   "Five Without a Common Song," (rev. of *An Idiot Joy*), *The Globe and Mail Magazine*, Jan. 13, 1968, p.13.

Daphne Marlatt

Throughout the sixties and early seventies Vancouver has been the home of a large number of radically experimental writers — Daphne Marlatt, Judy Copithorne, Maxine Gadd, Gerry Gilbert, David W. Harris, and Bill Bissett; all except Bissett have found little Canadian readership east of the Rockies. Ontario readers especially, taught by Northrop Frye to read primarily for thematic content and attracted in recent years to the overt statements of literary nationalism, have showed little interest in the numerous expansions of technical resource achieved in Vancouver. As a result, the very precise, form-conscious poetry of Daphne Marlatt is better known to readers of little magazines in Vancouver and the U.S. than it is across most of Canada.

Daphne Marlatt first appeared to a national Canadian audience as the author of the very fine novella "Sea Haven" in Giose Rimanelli and Roberto Ruberto's anthology *Modern Canadian Stories* (1966). This was followed by four books of poetry: *Frames* (1968), *Leaf/leafs* (1969), *Rings* (1971), and *The Vancouver Poems* (1972). Marlatt's characteristic style involves a minute and painstaking examination of the processes of perception and of the moment-by-moment contents of consciousness. The narrative line of her work is entirely phenomenological: objects, words, images, sounds are recorded as they obtrude into consciousness. The author's reflections on these, which in a conventional writer's work would be primary, are recorded only as additional phenomena parallel, not superior, to the stimuli to which they respond.

Frames is a ritual poem in which the writer calls on Hans Christian Andersen's "The Snow Queen" to illuminate the solitary white room in which a personal crisis has trapped her. Each section of Andersen's tale not only leads her to re-live Gerda's literal dilemmas, choices, and hardships, but to re-examine and accept similar acts and events which are necessitated by her own loss. In no sense is Andersen's tale allowed to symbolize and distort her own experience. Rather it is used to initiate the poet into the realities of her own life: as she explains, "my thought was an acceptance of having to 'undergo' (be initiated in?) certain events so that the necessity lay in understanding why or what was going on."

The phenomenological method of *Frames* results in some extraordinarily elaborate and detailed evocations of consciousness, as the images of Andersen's tale and of Marlatt's past and present experiences weave and counterweave. Marlatt's next book, *Leaf/leafs*, similarly emphasizes the pre-reflective aspects of consciousness, but in much briefer and consequently less complex works. *Leaf/leafs* is a collection of sharply defined moments, each possessing the imagistic precision of a dark-veined leaf. Objects enter and leave these poems, as in the haiku, in simple, appositional syntax. In the absence of complex syntax, the sound and morphology of each assert themselves as unique and intrinsically important features; they create puns and surprise — rhymes that re-route both the poet's and reader's awareness. In this way, like the Andersen tale in *Frames*, they continually initiate the poet into meanings and perceptions of which she would have been otherwise ignorant.

The most powerful of Marlatt's books is the long prose-poem, *Rings*. This work is written from inside the eyes and mind of a woman whose marriage is becoming increasingly strained and untenable and whose first child is about to be born. The six sections of *Rings* present separate incidents that occur at intervals of a week or more. Each incident, including that of the birth, is recorded by the woman with total multi-sensory attention to every last available quality and nuance of the experience. The increasing arrogance and withdrawal from her of the husband is pushing the woman deeper into her own sensory world. Unattracted by the normal linear pull of another human's conversation, her mind has turned inward to dwell on every signal either her body or its immediate world emits. To evoke such a desultory but alert consciousness, the language of *Rings* becomes exceedingly rich in imagery and syntactic innovation. Marlatt's approach is again thoroughly phenomenological; every image and reflection of the woman's multiphasic consciousness is recorded — some by means of puns, metaphors, split words, parenthetical phrases. Fragmented syntactic structures free the reader to slow his pace and re-live the woman's experiences at the same rate that they have exploded upon her senses. The resultant linguistic structure is one of the most beautiful in our literature.

Vancouver Poems lacks the compelling dramatic context of *Rings*. The twenty-eight poems possess loose inter-relationships, the strongest one being that they are all set in Vancouver shortly after the author has returned there to live after several years absence. However, the depth of Marlatt's knowledge and feeling concerning Vancouver, combined with her linguistic talent for evoking the rhythms of ongoing awareness, create superb present-tense tapestries of the city's life. Its history, its climate, its geography, Marlatt's private recollections of love and pain, Indian mythology and the current phenomena greeting the poet's eyes all blend in the consciousness of each poem to form a profound, tangible, and living whole. Levels of myth, person, and history are revealed by Marlatt's relatively detailed and self-exposing technique to have a vital and continuing life concurrent with the mundane and often humiliating events of any late twentieth-century technological city.

In her most recent and unpublished work, *Steveston,* Marlatt returns to the extended prose-poem form she used so effectively in *Rings*. The book is a journal of her research into the history of Steveston, B.C., a fishing village in the mouth of the Fraser River which is presently the headquarters of B.C. Packers. The phenomenological method — by which the poems record the present-tense *process* of the poet's discovery of history — gives the book many foci: the exploitation of natural resource, the exploitation of early Japanese-Canadian fisherman who were eventually rescued from economic servitude to the fish packers by their internment at the start of World War II, the exploitation of all weaker groups (the Indian, the Chinese, the Nisei, the poor, the female) by wealthy and legally-sophisticated corporations, the heroic tenacity of the exploited in living their very real, sexual, and substantive lives in the mud and storm to which the abstract powers of corporate finance have confined them. History in these poems becomes both personal and contemporary; the 'political' implications of the facts Marlatt discovers reach into both her life and the reader's.

The most important ideas of Marlatt's poetry are implied by its form. Our world is a mélange of cues and signals, it tells us. They beat unmercifully upon our several senses, bearing messages not only of the physical world but of the personal, historical, mythological, psychological, and spiritual realms. The poetry asks the reader to abandon his logical, linear, and superficial attitudes toward experience and become open to the multiplicities of a Heraclitean, post-Einsteinian universe. Despite its lack of reference to most popular Canadian political issues, it is, much like the fiction of Dave

Daphne Marlatt

Godfrey and Matt Cohen, a truly relevant kind of writing that would initiate us into the intricacies and depths of the post-modern age.

Marlatt, Daphne.   *Frames*. Toronto: Ryerson Press, 1968.
                . *Leaf/leafs*. Los Angeles: Black Sparrow Press, 1969.
                . *Rings*. Vancouver: Vancouver Community Press, 1971.
                . *The Vancouver Poems*. Toronto: The Coach House Press, 1972.

Barbour, Douglas.   Review of *Frames, Dalhousie Review* 49 (Summer 1969), 289.
Coleman, Victor.   Review of *Rings, Open Letter* (second series), Winter 1971-72, pp.76-80.
Garnet, Eldon.   Review of *Rings, Saturday Night* 87 (June 1972), 38, 41-42.

John Marlyn

(1912 -   )

One of the three or four most powerful works dealing with the immigrant's experience in Canada is John Marlyn's novel, *Under the Ribs of Death* (1957). Set in Winnipeg in the first half of this century, *Under the Ribs of Death* tells the story of Sandor Hunyadi, as he grows from childhood to maturity in the north end slums of that city. The novel is straightforward and economical in narration, its dialogue is convincingly vital, and its depictions of slum life masterfully energetic and evocative.

The novel is constructed in two parts, the first showing us the twelve-year old Sandor in 1913-14, and the second Sandor as a young man during 1924-29. In the first, Sandor lives with his family in appalling poverty — a poverty compounded by his gentle father's incontinent generosity toward his fellow immigrants. While his father blames Canada's materialistic values for the immigrants' suffering and advocates a philosophy of "mutual aid", young Sandor comes to blame it on their foreign names, their poor command of English, and their unfashionable clothes. For his own family's misfortunes, he blames his father's generosity, his bookishness, his "failure" to callously seek wealth.

Sandor determines to rid himself of all traces of his Hungarian origin and his father's humanity and kindness. He aspires toward the cool, orderly, and gracious life he imagines is possessed by those of wealth and power. In Part II we see the result of this determination. Sandor is apprenticed to old Nagy, a notary and real estate broker who has become wealthy by exploiting the Hungarian community. Sandor is wearing fashionable clothes, and has changed his name to Alex Hunter. By various schemes and compromises he rises to

IMAGO
(sixteen)

featuring Daphne Marlatt

Imago, ed. George Bowering, 1964-1974.

manage Nagy's agency, but finds himself ruined, and his inspiring world of clean, graceful, and logical power unmasked to reveal its fundamental disorder and savagery when the 1929 stock market crash occurs.

Marlyn's novel is an implicit and convincing attack on the values of Canada's capitalist society. Those immigrants who live for money alone, like old Nagy or the widow Kleinholtz, become mean, wretched, and lonely in their old age. The calm and logical English-Canadian financiers are reduced to drunkenness, bigotry, and suicide when the plunging stock market takes their wealth from them. Materialistic values nearly turn Sandor Hunyadi into the cruel and withdrawn opposite of his cheerful and philosophical father. Yet through Sandor, Marlyn appears to offer some ambiguous hope. Sandor is not totally corruptible; even at the height of his financial successes he is unable to cheat an impoverished client of five dollars. He is instinctively attracted to and marries a girl who embodies all the values of his father. Only with the utmost self-discipline can Sandor keep himself dedicated to the money-lender's gods; ultimately, Marlyn hints, this discipline will fail, and perhaps the heartless commercial system itself will crumble.

Marlyn, John.   *Under the Ribs of Death*. Toronto: McClelland & Stewart, 1957, reprinted 1964 (New Canadian Library no. 41).

Foster, Ann.   "Winnipeg Hungarian Has Bitter Difficulties" (rev. of *Under the Ribs of Death*), *The Globe and Mail*, Nov. 23, 1957, "Review of Books" p.17.

Mandel, Eli.   Introduction to *Under the Ribs of Death* (Toronto: McClelland & Stewart, 1964, New Canadian Library 41), pp.7-14.

Owen, Patricia.   Review of *Under the Ribs of Death*. *Tamarack Review* 5 (Autumn 1957), 76-78.

Waddington, Miriam.   "Canadian Novelists," *Queen's Quarterly* 64 (Winter 1958), 627-628.

Alice Munro

(1931 -   )

Although Alice Munro has lived in Victoria B.C., for most of her writing career, the world of her fiction is her childhood home, Protestant rural Ontario. She chronicles that familiar Canadian conflict between the talented, sensitive adolescent and a rigid, self-limiting society. But unlike many other treatments of this conflict, Munro's displays no rage, hostility or even indignation toward the protestant ethic. Instead, her dominant attitudes are astonishment and compassion — astonishment at the lengths to which a small town goes to deny to its inhabitants joy and creativity, and compassion for those thus robbed and maimed.

Munro works best as a writer of short fiction. Of her two book-length works, one is a collection of short stories, *The Dance of the Happy Shades* (1968), and the other a 'novel', *Lives of Girls and Women* (1971) constructed of what are properly short stories that share a common setting and narrator. The latter work is a remarkable example of the kind of novel the short story writer can construct without having to work outside the strengths of her talent. The plot of each chapter is self-contained; no incident develops further in ensuing chapters. The book derives its unity from the unique perceptual qualities of its young narrator, Del Jordan, and from the chronological arrangement of its incidents. The result is an apprenticeship novel in which the apprentice is depicted as developing not in a continuous visible line, as does Richler's Duddy Kravitz, but in a series of intense but essentially distinct incidents.

Most of Munro's short stories are narrated by what appears to be the same young girl who narrates the novel. Her name is Helen rather than Del, her younger brother is called Laird rather than Owen. But her father in both books is a silver-fox farmer, Ben Jordan; her mother is an ambitious would-be-middle-class farm girl; her home town is Jubilee, Ontario; and the decade of most of her childhood and adolescence is the 1940's. Even more significant is the fact that the sensitivities and psychologies of Helen and Del are similar. Both are precociously perceptive, introspective girls, who are intensely analytical toward their experiences. They hunger for "particular facts and circumstances". Both feel strangely disconnected from both

Alice Munro

their families and their townfolk — as if these people were of some eccentric and alien race. They can stand back even from their own most intense feelings to make frank and dispassionate judgements.

The fact that these narrators view themselves as outsiders in a bizarre world contributes to the extreme richness of physical detail that is characteristic of Alice Munro's writing. Helen and Del report their experiences with the precision of explorers. They find the texture of curtains, the shape of an old woman's knuckles, the smell of an automobile fascinating and significant. To them the world defines itself in its shapes, colours, sounds, and odours; people define themselves by the peculiar objects they have collected and the gestures they perform. Even though this world is narrow, puritanical, bigotted, and mechanical, and therefore dangerous to the girls, its textures and motions make it appear beautiful to them in a way that few of their pragmatic friends and relatives can perceive. This sense of eccentric beauty dispassionately perceived, coupled with the 1940's setting, give both books a curious tone of alienation and nostalgia.

Munro, Alice. *Dance of the Happy Shades.* Toronto: Ryerson Press, 1968.

    . *Lives of Girls and Women.* Toronto: McGraw-Hill Ryerson, 1971.

    . *Something I've Been Meaning to Tell You*: Twelve Stories. Toronto: McGraw-Hill Ryerson, 1974.

Dahlie, Hallvard. "Unconsummated Relationships: Isolation and Rejection in Alice Munro's Stories," *World Literature Written in English* XI:1, pp.43-48.

Dobbs, Kildare. "This First Novel is Solid, Beautiful" (rev. of *Lives of Girls and Women*), *The Toronto Star*, Oct. 31, 1971.

Fischman, Shelia. "To Maturity Along a Rural Route" (rev. of *Dance of the Happy Shades*), *The Globe and Mail Magazine*, Oct. 19, 1968. p.24.

Gibson, Graeme. Interview with Alice Munro, in his *Eleven Canadian Novelists* (Toronto: House of Anansi, 1973), pp.241-264.

Grosskurth, Phyllis. "A Delight. Goodbye to Inhibitions" (rev. of *Lives of Girls and Women*), *The Globe and Mail Magazine*, Oct. 30, 1971, p.17.

    . "Our Short Stories Can Come Alive" (rev. of *Dance of the Happy Shades*), *The Toronto Star*, Nov. 2, 1968, p.27.

Helwig, David. Review of *Dance of the Happy Shades*, *Queen's Quarterly* 77 (Spring 1970), 127-128.

Kirkwood, Hilda. Review of *Dance of the Happy Shades*, *Canadian*

Forum 48 (February 1969), 260.

Metcalf, John. "Growing Up," *Montreal Star,* November 20, 1971, "Entertainments", p.6.

———. "A Conversation with Alice Munro," Journal of Canadian Fiction I:4 (1972), 54-62.

Rule, Jane. "The Credible Woman," *Books in Canada* I:4 (1971), 4-5.

Stainsby, Mari. "Alice Munro Talks with Mari Stainsby," *British Columbia Library Quarterly* 35 (July 1971), 27-31.

Thomas, Audrey. " 'She's Only a Girl,' He Said," *Canadian Literature* 39 (Winter 1969), 91-92.

Thomas, Clara. Review of *Lives of Girls and Women, Journal of Canadian Fiction,* 1:4 (1972), 95-96.

Thompson, Kent. Review of *Dance of the Happy Shades, Fiddlehead* 82 (November-December 1969), 71-72.

John Newlove

(1938 -   )

The most frequently offered concept of the poet in English-Canadian poetry since 1960 has been that of the self-deprecating, ironic near-failure who stands at or near the centre of all the economic, historical, and political debacles which twentieth-century humanity has created. Such an anti-heroic concept colours the work of poets such as Alden Nowlan, Michael Ondaatje, George Bowering, Al Purdy, Leonard Cohen, Margaret Atwood, Phyllis Webb, and Dennis Lee, and thoroughly dominates that of John Newlove.

By looking mercilessly within himself, Newlove has managed, through seven books of poetry, to discover most of the sicknesses and stupidities of his contemporary man. His work displays a self-loathing only slightly less strong than his loathing for the human race and its wretched and treacherous planet. Particularly does he detest the inability of man to recognize or admit the truth about himself and his world. Newlove's poetry has been a relentless quest for truth, attacking in poem after poem the deceits of our politicians, myth-makers, historians, and theologians. The title of his collection *Lies* (1972) insists that even his own searchings for truth become, because of man's innate incompetence, merely fumbling examples of the human capacity for self-deceit.

In his obsession with honesty, Newlove has developed one of the most direct and visually precise styles in twentieth-century poetry. He avoids metaphor, simile, overt symbolism, rhyme, and most of the other stock resources of poetry — presumably because of the potential for distortion such devices contain. He presents external event by means of an exact phenomenological vocabulary, and his reflections about such events by means of rigidly limited numbers of specific

205

abstractions. Both methods are evident in his longer meditational poems such as "The Pride". Taking the place of metaphor in Newlove's poetry is the dispassionately described drama of the poet's inner and outer lives. The bulk of his poems are autobiographical; in them we see Newlove bleeding, vomiting, lying, despairing, stumbling, fleeing, betraying, and being betrayed. His life becomes in these poems a metaphor for mankind's wretchedness; his thoughts and fears become those of everyman — were everyman to have the courage to confront them.

The poems appear structured by the perceptual processes on which they are based. In many poems the consciousness of the writing moves back and forth between the viewing of the event at hand and criticism of the poet's responses to the event. In these poems Newlove resembles the man of his poem "The Fat Man", whose insecurity and paranoia cause him to stand accusingly outside himself, stripping himself of all possible pretension. Newlove's line varies in length with the emotionality of the utterance. His most cautiously articulated poems have lines of from one to three words; his normal dispassionate poems have five to seven word lines; in poems of more intense feeling, especially contempt or anger, his line can grow almost without limit.

The titles of many of Newlove's collections — *Grave Sirs* (1962), *Moving in Alone* (1965), *Black Night Window* (1968), *The Cave* (1970), and *Lies* — indicate much of the 'blackness' of Newlove's vision. The terrain of most of his poems is hostile: rain-swept pavements crisscrossed by speeding cars, dark swamps concealing both dead and predatory beasts, fields of sharp stones, bedrooms of fleshy, smothering women. Newlove either moves through these scenes "alone", or is too paralyzed even to move. His fellow men are both weak and dangerous, having been deceived by the lies of history and mythology and having succumbed to the "joyless pleasures" of the conforming life. In most of the poems, Newlove wishes to flee both this "world of cigarette butts spinning about the sun to quickening gunfire" and his guilt at being unable to change and redeem the world.

Often Newlove appears to believe he is chronicling the decline and extinction of humanity. He describes Canadians as "ancestorless masses with ancestors / half a day old in the dirt", mankind as "rigorously dancing with fractured minds", himself as "unaware", "stupid", a bungler and a "liar", "the stupid one", "the one / who can not endure", history as "great heaps of captivating skulls". The few hopeful notes in his work occur in lyrics where some scrupulous care to details in his personal life has brought him momentary reward ("Warm Wind"), and in historical poems concerning men whose

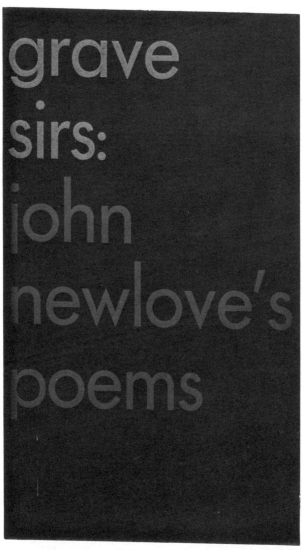

Grave Sirs by John Newlove. The private Press of
Robert Reid and Takao Tanabe, 1962. His first book.

surprising and often baffling grasp of events has brought about some of the few instances of nobility and achievement in man's history ("Crazy Riel", "Samuel Hearn in Winter Time", "The Pride").

Newlove, John.　*Grave Sirs*. Vancouver: Robert Reid and Takao Tanabe, 1962.
　　　.　*Elephants, Mothers and Others*. Vancouver: Periwinkle Press, 1963.
　　　.　*Moving in Alone*. Toronto: Contact Press, 1965.
　　　.　*What They Say*. Kitchener, Ont.: Weed/Flower Press, 1967.
　　　.　*Black Night Window*. Toronto: McClelland & Stewart.
　　　.　*The Cave*. Toronto: McClelland & Stewart, 1970.
　　　.　*Lies*. Toronto: McClelland & Stewart, 1972.

Atwood, Margaret.　"How Do I Get Out of Here: the Poetry of John Newlove," *Open Letter* (second series) 4, Spring 1973, pp.59-70.
Barbour, Douglas.　Review of *Black Night Window*, *Dalhousie Review* 49 (Summer 1969), 293, 295.
　　　.　"The Search for Roots: a Meditative Sermon of Sorts," *Literary Half-Yearly*, XIII:2, pp.1-14.
Bowering, George.　Review of *Black Night Window*, *Canadian Forum* 48 (November 1968), 187-188.
　　　.　"Where Does the Truth Lie," *Open Letter* (second series) 4, Spring 1973, pp.71-73.
Cook, Gregory M.　"The Subject of Poetry," *Canadian Literature* 39 (Winter 1969), 96-98.
Ferns, John.　"A Desolate Country," *The Far Point* 2, pp.68-75.
Jones, D.G.　"Moving in Alone: a Review Article," *Quarry* XV (1965-66), 12-15.
Kilgallin, Tony.　"Waiting for the End," *Canadian Literature* 37 (Summer 1968), 93-94.
Mandel, Eli.　"Mark More his Crushing Desire for Truth" (rev. of *Lies*), *The Globe and Mail*, Oct. 14, 1972, p.32.
　　　.　"The Poet as Animal — of Sorts" (rev. of *Black Night Window*), *The Globe and Mail Magazine*, Oct. 12, 1968, p.17.
Pacey, Desmond.　Review of *The Cave*, *Canadian Forum* 50 (November-December 1970), 309-310.
Purdy, A.W.　"Alienation and Aloneness," *Canadian Literature* 25 (Summer 1965), 70-71.
　　　.　"Calm Surfaces Destroyed," *Canadian Literature* 48 (Spring 1971), 91-92.
　　　.　Review of *Black Night Window*, *Quarry* XVIII:2 (Winter 1969), 43-45.

. "Who's Got the Emphasis?" *Canadian Forum* 44 (September 1964), 142-143.

Stevens, Peter. "Two Kinds of Honesty," *Canadian Forum* 45 (September 1965), 139.

Warkentin, Germaine. "Drifting to Oblivion," *Canadian Literature* 56 (Spring 1973), 121-122.

Weaver, Robert. "John Newlove Is Today's Poet" (rev. of *Black Night Window*), *The Toronto Star*, June 29, 1968, p.39

bp Nichol

(1944-   )

Of the many experimental poets of the last decade, only bpNichol has consciously adopted a symbolist and semioticist attitude to language and form. Nichol's work, however, is utterly unlike any Canadian symbolist writing of previous periods. It takes its inspiration not in the asceticism of William Morris or in the deliberately charged image structures of Baudelaire and Mallarmé, but in the linguistic experiments of Dada and Gertrude Stein and in the semiotic experiments of European and South American visual poetry.

In Nichol's view, the conventional usages of language by twentieth-century English-language poets have come to "a dead end". The realism of Williams, the clever symbol weaving of Eliot, the rhetoric of Dylan Thomas or Allen Ginsberg have all failed to provide a language for the increasingly disparate and fragmented human experiences of the sixties and seventies. Only an approach which abandons the conventional concept of language as a tool to convey meaning and regards it instead as itself intrinsically meaningful can begin to resolve the contemporary writer's problems.

Much of Nichol's poetry consists of experiment with the most basic signs of the language — the individual letters of the alphabet and the numerous morphemes which combine to make the English vocabulary. In these the attention of the reader is brought to the innate qualities of the letter or morpheme as *sign*. In *ABC, the Aleph Beth Book* (1970) Nichol redraws the alphabet so that from the unique properties of each letter a distinct "personality" is projected. In *Still Water* (1970) Nichol dismantles words to display within their morphological structure arcane signs closely related to the words' semantic significations; here too he uses words as objects within a visual field devoid of syntactic structure.

In other parts of his extraordinarily large and varied output since 1964, Nichol employs almost every conceivable part of language structure and book structure as signs and/or symbols. Broken syntax, wordiness, vagueness, blank pages, failed poems, all come to have significance based on their form quite apart from what is syntactically stated. Nichol regards every formal property of the book and the language as parts of a *machine* — parts which can be used either unobtrusively (as in conventional writing) or obtrusively so that they become not just means to an end but meaningful in themselves. In the conventional narrative, Nichol has observed, the pages are obstacles to the flow of the stories, obstacles which the writer conceals by distracting the reader through plot and image; in a Nichol novel the reader's turning of each page is potentially a significant event.

Nichol's fiction to date consists of two short novels, *Andy* and *For Jesus Lunatick,* published together in 1969. *Andy* is ostensibly an assemblage of found materials — letters from Nichol's friend Andy Phillips, and sections from a factually-narrated fantasy adventure story, a melodramatically-narrated pornographic detective novel, and a jargon-filled futuristic science-fiction novel. In about the middle of the novel the reader is offered respite from the variously colliding narratives in the form of four pages of cartoons, one of which comments, "Ultimately . . . one becomes totally frustrated with all this speaking." Toward the end only the Andy letters, written from Paris, maintain their integrity; the remaining narratives (one gathers that Nichol believes they indicate false realities) blur together into a single outrageous plot of soap-opera complexity. Hints contained in speeches by a character in the science-fiction plot (who proclaims a theory of mechanistic determinism) indicate that the contrast between the Andy letters and the blurred narratives is one between matter and "anti-matter", between true form and "pseudoform". In the juxtaposition of the words of real life and the literary words of bad art, the novel relates the "probable death of pseudoforms now revealed as constructs of anti-matter."

Andy implies a strong distrust of any fiction or poetry which assumes the one-dimensionality of plot and employs language as a totally manipulable tool to give this plot explicit narration. It suggests that melodrama, jargon, and superficial characterization are inevitable properties of such writing. In *For Jesus Lunatick* Nichol attempts an alternate way of fiction to those discredited in *Andy.* Here syntax and imagery are not used to convey semantic meaning, but instead to be in themselves extended symbols of the

210

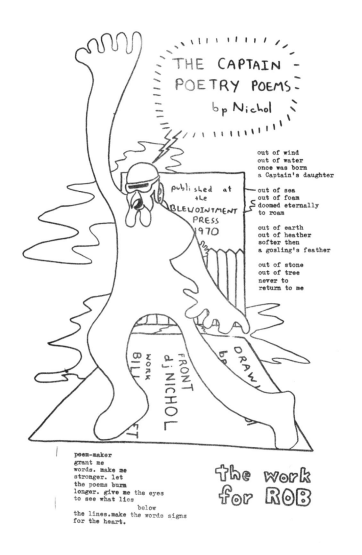

THE CAPTAIN -
POETRY POEMS -
bp Nichol

published at
the
BLEWOINTMENT
PRESS
1970

out of wind
out of water
once was born
a Captain's daughter

out of sea
out of foam
doomed eternally
to roam

out of earth
out of heather
softer then
a gosling's feather

out of stone
out of tree
never to
return to me

FRONT
WORK
BILL
dj NICHOL

DRAW
bp

poem-maker
grant me
words. make me
stronger. let
the poems burn
longer. give me the eyes
to see what lies
                below
the lines.make the words signs
for the heart.

the work
for ROB

The Captain Poetry Poems by bpNichol. Blewointmentpress, 1971.

psychological worlds of the characters. At the centre of *For Jesus Lunatick* is a young man, Phillip, who is obscurely involved with a totally reclusive youth Frank, and somewhat less obscurely engaged in a destructively neurotic affair with an unnamed girl. The plot is obscure because to Nichol it is not an important reality. (The various manuscript drafts of this novel show its plot deliberately being made more blurred and its characters less differentiated with each revision.) What is important is the texture of Phillip's fears — his anger toward the girl, his terror of being swallowed by her body, the paranoia felt by both him and Frank toward the "river" of dusty process that lurks outside each of their rooms to enclose them. The novel writhes with engulfing female imagery — the shadowy Victorian house in which Frank and Phillip have rooms, "the dark swollen waters murmuring voices of the river", the "blobby mass" of Phillip's girlfriend's breasts, the stabbed belly of a woman knifed and beaten by Frank's, or possibly Phillip's father. The latter scene devastatingly haunts Phillip and apparently has so crippled Frank that he will not even leave his room to attempt to fight clear of its memory.

bpNichol's central works of poetry are an interrelated series of reflective poems beginning with *Journeying and the Returns* (written 1963-66, published 1967), and continuing through *Monotones* (written 1967-70, published 1971), and *The Martyrology* (begun 1967 and still in process, Books I and II published 1972). *Journeying and the Returns* is the only one of these in which the physical world is substantially evoked — but only to demonstrate its uselessness to the spiritually lost man. The British Columbia rain and mountains, despite their beauty, cannot fill an internal silence. Man-made structures are alien, irrelevant. "This room will soon be empty/my having been here/made no difference." Only language speaks and endures: when a book is burned to start a beach fire "the black ash/print still visible" drifts out to sea.

In *Monotones* and *The Martyrology* there are no sharp imagistic pictures of the physical world. Language has become the only trustworthy reality in an otherwise instable "referenceless" world. Language no longer has any specific referentiality to the physical universe; it serves instead as the mystic instructor of the poet and as a field for symbolic display of the poet's anxieties, loves, and dilemmas. Numerous fragments and phrases indicate a profound suspicion of the earth's physical, Heraclitean, reality — "moment to moment the changes flow around me/it goes on too long"; "what'll we say ... after the fantasy that is north america crumbles". Man's supposed knowledge of this world is only deception: "of those things we understand this is the greatest mystery/knowledge deceives us/believing we move in our lostness purposefully". Men are "strangers on the earth" but not strangers in the realm of language:

always you are conscious the world is not encompassed only the
words you trust to take you there to what places you don't know.

Nichol's guides in *The Martyrology* are words which, in their
ability to symbolize for him the agonizing circumstances he shares
with the rest of humanity, have become the "saints" of his linguistic
cosmos. St. And represents the acausal disorders of three-dimen-
sional *non sequitur;* amid this confusing network of "and's" many
men merely "stand" in paralysis. St. Orm represents the vagaries of
elemental violence in which mortal man must live; St. Reat ("es-
treat"), the documentary records a man's past experiences become,
coughed up "in nightmares / screaming and babbling". Only St.
Rand offers any hope of unity and peace, and St. Rike any possibility
that man can "seize the moment" and live a significant present-tense
life free of the tortures of history, personal guilt, and instable
materiality.

The language of *The Martyrology* is not crafted into terse and
powerful poetic statements. In fact, what the language "says" in a
denotative sense is often irrelevant to the poem except as a symptom
of the writer's psychic condition. *The Martyrology,* particularly Book
I, is a sprawling, fragmented, disorderly, wordy, abstract, and private
work — openly testifying to vagueness, ignorance, indecisiveness,
alienation, and paralysis in its writer. Failed poems, pretentious passages of self-pity, obscure references to private people and events,
are all offered as evidence of the debilitating effects of the poet's
forced existence in a brutal, unpredictable, unloving world in which
"ignorance ... is a mercy god rewarded with heaven / hell a function of
wisdom / wisdom the quality of cursing." Nichol reaches for a further
level of symbolic meaning by claiming the universality of his
experience; his sense of despair and alienation are those of mankind:
"we are strangers on the earth / turn from each other in our silence /
hide behind our smiles our rage." The passage of his soul through
ineptitude and confusion in Books I and II of *The Martyrology*
becomes the necessary journey of the soul of post-modern man.

bpNichol's writing is the most courageous body of work in
Canadian literature today. It deserts the mainstream traditions of
twentieth-century writing, even the Williams-Olson tradition so important to Coleman, Bowering, Marlatt and the other members of the
Canadian avant-garde. It deliberately spurns the popular modes of
current Canadian poetry — the romantic realism of Purdy, Souster,
Layton, and Birney, the ironic pessimism of Ondaatje and Atwood,
and the vague romantic symbolism of Leonard Cohen. It risks, even

213

invites, condemnation by the conservative critic for triviality, banality, obscurity, wordiness, formlessness, privateness — all those 'vices' feared by the reasonable man because they so inform the human environment. To Nichol, however, these 'vices' are precisely what most need to be exorcised by their transformation into linguistic sign, so that the saints, rhymes, and secret rhymes of the language can move the poet to "greater vision", "other mysteries", and a reconciliation with Heraclitean process — a willingness to "allow what is to be".

The Four Horsemen
(bpNichol, Rafael Barreto-Rivera, Steve McCaffery, Paul Dutton),
a sound poetry collective, in concert at Erindale College, 1974.

Nichol, bp.   *Scrapture,* second sequence. Toronto: Ganglia Press, 1965.
          . *Calendar.* Woodchester, Eng.: Openings Press, 1966. Reprinted, London, Ont.: Rhinoceros Broadsheets, 1970.
          . *Scraptures, 3rd sequence.* Toronto: Ganglia Press, 1966.
          . *Scraptures, 4th sequence.* Niagara Falls, N.Y.: Press Today Niagara, 1966.
          . *Strange Grey Town,* by bpNichol and David Aylward. Toronto: Ganglia Press, 1966.
          . *Scraptures,* 11th sequence. Toronto: Fleye Press and Ganglia Press, 1967.
          . *Kon 66 & 67.* Toronto: Ganglia Press, 1967.

214

. *Konfessions of an Elizabethan Fan Dancer.* London: Writer's Forum Books, 1967. Revised edition, Toronto: Weed/Flower Press, 1973.

. *Journeying and the Returns.* Toronto: The Coach House Press, 1967.

. *Ruth.* Toronto: Fleye Press, 1967 (*Luv* 8).

. *The Year of the Frog.* Toronto: Ganglia Press, 1967.

. *Ballads of the Restless Are.* Sacramento: Runcible Spoon, 1968.

. *Dada Lama.* London: Tlaloc, 1968.

. *D.A. Dead.* Toronto: Ganglia Press, 1968.

. *Mother Love* (Phonograph record). Toronto: Allied Records, 1968.

. *Lament.* Toronto: Ganglia Press, 1969. Reprinted London: Writer's Forum Books, 1969.

. *Nights on Prose Mountain.* Toronto: Ganglia Press, 1969.

. *Two Novels: Andy and For Jesus Lunatick.* Toronto: The Coach House Press, 1969.

. *The Captain Poetry Poems.* Vancouver: Blewointment Press, 1970.

, ed. *The Cosmic Chef:* an Evening of Concrete. Ottawa: Oberon Press, 1970.

. *Still Water.* Vancouver: Talonbooks, 1970.

. *The True Eventual Story of Billy the Kid.* Toronto: Weed/Flower Press, 1970.

. *ABC: the Aleph Beth Book.* Ottawa: Oberon Press, 1971.

. *Beach Head.* Sacramento: Runcible Spoon, 1971.

. *Monotones.* Vancouver: Talonbooks, 1971.

. *The Other Side of the Room.* Toronto: Weed/Flower Press, 1971.

. *Adventures of Milt the Morph in Colour,* by bpNichol and Barbara Caruso. Toronto: Seripress, 1972.

. *Canadada* (phonograph record), as one of The Four Horsemen. Toronto: Griffin House, 1972.

. *Collbrations,* by bpNichol and Steve McCaffery. Toronto: Ganglia Press, 1972.

. *The Martyrology,* Books I & II. Toronto: The Coach House Press, 1972.

. *Aleph Unit.* Toronto: Seripress, 1973.

. *bpNichol* (tape recording). Toronto: High Barnett, 1973.

, ed. *The Pipe:* Recent Czech Concrete Poetry, ed. bpNichol and Jiri Valoch. Toronto: The Coach House Press, 1973.

. *Unit of Four.* Toronto: Seripress, 1973.

. *Love: A Book of Remembrances.* Vancouver: Talonbooks, 1974.

  . *Scraptures:* basic sequences. Toronto: Massasauga Editions, 1974.

  . *Zygal.* Toronto: The Coach House Press, 1974.

Barbour, Douglas. "Journey in a Mythic Landscape," *Canadian Literature* 56 (Spring 1973), 93-97.

  . Review of *Beach Head, Still Water,* and *The True Eventual Story of Billy the Kid, Quarry* XX:4 (Year End 1971), 61-63.

Bates, Pat Martin. "Two 'Lautegedichte' Singers," *Arts/Canada* 27 (April 1970), 64-65.

Bowering, George. "Cutting Them All Up: Interview with bpNichol," *Alphabet* 18-19 (1971), 18-21.

  . "A Lyrical Boom in Slim Volumes" (rev. of *Journeying and the Returns*), *The Globe and Mail Magazine,* Sep. 22, 1967, p.19.

  . Review of *Monotones, Open Letter* (second series) 2, Summer 1972, pp. 82-84.

Cohen, Matt. "Slicky Sensuous," *Saturday Night* 85 (June 1970), 35.

Colombo, John Robert. "New Wave Nichol," *Tamarack Review* 44 (Summer 1967), 100-104.

Davey, Frank. "At a Dead End," *Canadian Literature* 55 (Winter 1973), 118-119.

Garnet, Eldon. "Killing the Poem to Make it New," *Saturday Night* 88 (March 1973), 40.

Kearns, Lionel. "If There's Anything I Hate It's Poetry," *Canadian Literature* 36 (Spring 1968), 69-70.

Reaney, James. Review of *Journeying and the Returns, Quarry* 16 (Summer 1967), 46-47.

Scobie, Stephen. "A Dash for the Border," *Canadian Literature* 56 (Spring 1973), 89-92.

  . "Two Authors in Search of a Character," *Canadian Literature* 54 (Autumn 1972), 37-55.

Alden Nowlan

(1933-   )

The best-known writer from the Maritime provinces throughout the sixties and early seventies has been Alden Nowlan. Since 1958 he has published nine collections of poetry, a novel and a collection of short stories, and has been honoured with a Guggenheim Fellowship and a Governor-General's Award. Nowlan has not been an innovative or experimental writer; the power of most of his poetry and prose has depended on a careful and straightforward use of standard twentieth-century forms.

Throughout this century, Canada's Maritime provinces have been one of the country's most impoverished areas. Lacking in both heavy industry and good agricultural land, much of the Maritimes have been forced to subsist on the seasonal yields of fisheries and pulpwood forests and on the benificence of the federal government. Nowlan's childhood and adolescence was spent near Windsor, Nova Scotia, an area of subsistence farms and pulpwood forests characteristic of the worst of Maritime poverty. He left school at 15 to work in a lumber mill and at 18 left Nova Scotia for Hartland, New Brunswick, where he found work with the town's newspaper. In his writing since then he has made the people and the poverty of his home provinces his central concern.

The majority of Nowlan's poems are brief, conversationally related anecdotes about people and situations the poet has encountered in rural New Brunswick or Nova Scotia. The lives of these people have been constricted both by isolation from the thoroughfares of fashion and culture and by extreme poverty. Their reactions to their narrow circumstances have been eccentric and pathetic, but in Nowlan's eyes always thoroughly human. Nowlan's essentially sentimental attitude toward them is usually counterbalanced by brutally realistic accounts of their homes, customs, and deaths.

In his later poetry, particularly that of *The Mysterious Naked Man* (1969), *Playing the Jesus Game* (1970), and *Between Tears and Laughter* (1971), Nowlan often explores the complexities of the relationship between these benighted Maritimers and himself as the compassionate reporter of their lives. In "playing Jesus" to their Mary Magdalene, Nowlan must keep an honest perspective on his own limitations and failings. Although he is privileged to give words to their previously unarticulated joys and miseries, he is also one of their children, and potentially as treacherous, credulous and adulterous as they.

Nowlan's conviction that the wretchedness of his fellow Maritimers is not their own responsibility is made explicit in his two works of fiction, the short stories *Miracle at Indian River* (1968) and the novel *Various Persons named Kevin O'Brien* (1973). Their drunkenness, improvidence, and remarkable gullibility for evangelical Christianity are explainable, in Nowlan's view, almost entirely in terms of the infertility of their land and the brutality of the rural Maritime economy. Particularly fascinating to Nowlan is their propensity for escapism—to the joys of heaven via an hypnotic preacher, to those of Hollywood via cheap cosmetics and magazines, to those of the big city via *Reader's Digest* or a soldier's uniform.

Various Persons Named Kevin O'Brien explores, as do many of Nowlan's poems and stories, the writer's own life between 1933 and 1951 as a child of a penurious family in an isolated Nova Scotia village. The novel contains one of Nowlan's most adventurous workings with writing technique. Nowlan writes approximately one-third of the novel as a third-person perspective on his thirty year old persona Kevin O'Brien, who is revisiting his home sometime in the early 1960's; he gives the remainder as a series of first-person accounts that Kevin has been attempting to write in order to reconstruct various portions of his childhood. Thirty year old Kevin has a more sentimentalized view of the child Kevin than he has of himself; the external narrator sees at least two other versions of Kevin in his introductions to the young man's narratives. Unfortunately, the novel is too short to accommodate the number of shifts in point of view, and presents an unsatisfyingly incomplete account of Kevin both as a child and as a young man revisiting home.

The "various persons" or viewpoints, however, do represent a continuation of Nowlan's interest in the relationship between the writer and his subject. The young man not only writes about and distorts his past, but, in returning to its setting, must live with a number

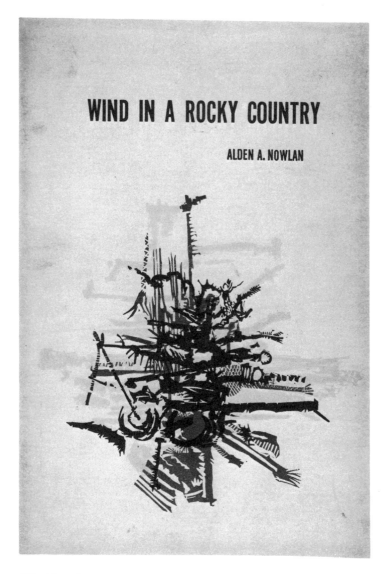

WIND IN A ROCKY COUNTRY

ALDEN A. NOWLAN

Wind in a Rocky Country by Alden Nowlan. Emblem Books, 1960.

of its personages and adjust to their customs. Nowlan the writer, who elsewhere shows himself forced, like Kevin, to accommodate the eccentricities of his fellow citizens and acknowledge their weaknesses within himself, undoubtedly distorts his portrait of the young man. In Nowlan's Maritimes, where illusion and escapist dreams are often the only tolerable aspect of a man's existence, no one can be sure of the authenticity of the reality he perceives. All life here becomes varieties of dream once the pain of the present has been evaded or left behind.

Nowlan, Alden.   *The Rose and the Puritan.* Fredericton: University of New Brunswick, 1958.
. *A Darkness in the Earth.* Eureka, Calif.: Hearse Press, 1959.
. "A Defence of Obscenity," *Delta* 9 (October-December 1959), 27-28.
. *Wind in a Rocky Country.* Toronto: Emblem Books, 1960.
. *Under the Ice.* Toronto: Ryerson Press, 1961.
, in *Five New Brunswick Poets.* Fredericton: The Fiddlehead, 1962.
. *The Things Which Are.* Toronto: Contact Press, 1962.
. *Bread Wine and Salt.* Toronto: Clarke Irwin, 1967. Paperback reprint, 1973.
. *Miracle at Indian River.* Toronto: Clarke Irwin, 1968.
. *The Mysterious Naked Man.* Toronto: Clarke Irwin, 1969. Paperback reprint, 1973.
. "Interview with Alden Nowlan," *Fiddlehead* 81 (August-September-October 1969), 5-13.
. *Playing the Jesus Game.* Trumansburg, N.Y.: New/Books, 1970.
. "Alden Nowlan's Canada," *Maclean's* 84 (June 1971), 16-17, 40.
. *Between Tears and Laughter.* Toronto: Clark Irwin, 1971. Paperback reprint, 1973.
. "My Advice to Fledgling Poets," *Atlantic Advocate* 61 (January 1971), 60-61.
. *Alden Nowlan's Maritimes* (phonograph record). CBC Learning Systems, 1972.
. *Various Persons Named Kevin O'Brien: a Fictional Memoir.* Toronto: Clarke Irwin, 1973.

Barbour Douglas.   Review of *Bread Wine and Salt. Quarry* XVIII:2 (Winter 1969) 45-46.
Barrett, Elizabeth.   "A Kind of Truth," *Evidence* 7 (1963), 105-107.

Bly, Robert. "For Alden Nowlan with Admiration," *Tamarack Review* 54 (1970), 32-38.

Buckler, Ernest. "Alden Nowlan: an Appreciation," *Fiddlehead* 81 (August-September-October 1969), 46-47.

Cameron, Donald. "Alden Nowlan, an 18th Century Tory in 20th Century Fredericton, is an Expatriate Who Never Left Home," *Saturday Night* 88 (May 1973), 29-32.

. Review of *Miracle at Indian River, Dalhousie Review* 48 (Winter 1968-69), 591-593.

Cockburn, Robert H. Review of *Bread Wine and Salt, Fiddlehead* 76 (Spring 1968), 74-76.

Coles, Don. "All is Not Apocalypse in a Big Portmanteau" (rev. of *Between Tears and Laughter*), *The Globe and Mail,* Jan. 8, 1972, p.29.

Cook, G.M. "New Wine, New Vessel, and New Bibber," *Fiddlehead* 81 (August-September-October 1969), 75-81.

Dudek, Louis. "Reading of Two Poems by Alden Nowlan," *Fiddlehead* 81 (August-September-October 1969), 51-59.

Fetherling, Douglas. "Sounding Time and Place," *Books in Canada* I:11 (October 1972), 33.

Fiamengo, Marya. "Puritans and Disbelievers," *Canadian Literature* 16 (Spring 1963), 76-78.

Ford, J.H. "Local Colour — the Myth and the Cult," *Fiddlehead* 81 (August-September-October 1969), 41-45.

Fraser, Keath. "Existence and Sonorous Art," *Canadian Literature* 45 (Summer 1970), 87-88.

. "Notes on Alden Nowlan," *Canadian Literature* 45 (Summer 1970), 41-51.

Fulford, Robert. "The Culture of Poverty," *Montreal Star,* June 2, 1973, C-3.

Greer, Ann. "Confessions of a Thesis Writer," *Fiddlehead* 81 (August-September-October 1969), 20-23.

. "Inside an Outsider," *Books in Canada* II:2 (April, May, June, 1973), 16-17.

Ives, E.S. "Alden Nowlan's Poetry: a Personal Chronicle," *Fiddlehead* 81 (August-September-October 1969), 61-66.

Livingstone, David. "In His Own Image," *The Far Point* 5, pp.67-69.

Lucas, Alex. Review of *Under the Ice, Fiddlehead* 51 (Winter 1962) 59-62.

Pacey, Desmond. Review of *Wind in A Rocky Country, Fiddlehead* 52 (Spring 1962), 61.

Pacey, Peter. Review of *Between Tears and Laughter, Fiddlehead* 93 (1972), 114-116.

Parr, D. Kermode. "The Interest of the Ugly," *Atlantic Advocate* 59 (September 1968), 71.

Reaney, James. "CPR (Canadian Poetry Railroad)," *Alphabet* 4 (June 1962), 72-73.
Rosengarten, Herbert. "Enjoyable Pessimism," *Canadian Literature* 40 (Spring 1969), 82-83.
Simpson, Leo. "The Magic's There — a Pity it's so Prim" (rev. of *Miracle at Indian River*), *The Globe and Mail Magazine*, Aug. 10, 1968, p.15.
Weaver, Robert. "Poetry: Nowlan's Bread, Wine, and Salt" (rev. of *Bread, Wine, and Salt*), *The Toronto Star,* March 23, 1968, p.37.
. "A Regional Poet Whose Place Is Poverty" (rev. of *The Mysterious Naked Man*), *The Toronto Star*, Jan. 31, 1970, p.43.

Michael Ondaatje

(1943 -   )

Among the various Canadian writers of the late sixties who have celebrated a dark, chaotic, but life-giving universe, the most direct and conventional in his techniques has been Ceylonese-born Michael Ondaatje. Unlike Victor Coleman, Gerry Gilbert, bpNichol, Daphne Marlatt, or even Gwendolyn MacEwen, Ondaatje has not believed that the form of his work must emulate the capriciousness or exuberance of the universe in which it is written. Man, in Ondaatje's poetry, exerts his own will — rationally or irrationally — amid the contradictory thrusts and pulls of his environment. Ondaatje is a deliberate craftsman, firmly controlling the pace of his lyric poems, and totally manipulating the structure and characterization of his longer narratives. His characters are artists who consciously modify their worlds: a Paris who sees himself "scar the city with his dreams", a Billy the Kid who reshapes his world with anger and bullets, spiders which "write their murderous art ... in the corners of rooms".

All of Ondaatje's poems reverberate with exotic violence. A camel can bite off a woman's breast; a bird collide with a ceiling fan during the night and splatter the sleeper with blood and feathers. Bizarre events lurk beyond everyday occasions: rats tear at a woman's umbrella on a London, Ontario, street; the exuberance of a friendly dog almost tears out the poet's "son's left eye". Even ordinary actions in his poems express themselves violently, as when Ondaatje's daughter "burns the lake / by reflecting her red shoes in it."

Ondaatje has a thoroughly disconcerting talent for presenting the ordinary in an extraordinary way. Most of his lyric poems (*The Dainty Monsters*, 1967, and *Rat Jelly*, 1973) focus on the domestic

Michael Ondaatje

223

lives of himself, his wife, their children and their pets. His matter-of-fact reportorial style gives little hint to the reader that a dragon is about to be entangled in the tennis net or a vulture to be shot down from the neighbourhood traffic light. In his vision the surreal becomes actual; the foetus "thrashes like a fish", a platoon of spiders carries his wife upward to their webs, a frantic moth trapped within his pyjamas frightens him from sleep — "my heart is breaking loose".

Throughout his work there is a strong photographic element. His lyrics are often well-composed photos in which small components suddenly change, and the "cell of civilized magic" breaks and horror enters. His longer poems are like skeletal movie scripts. In every poems something happens — a small boy steps on a live bird, a window "tries to split with cold" — which gives to the reader a world transformed, newly ominous with surprise and danger. The attempt to catch action in a cinematic manner is most obvious in Ondaatje's long narrative, *The Collected Works of Billy the Kid* (1970), which begins with a quotation from L.A. Hoffman, a western U.S. photographer contemporary to Billy the Kid, on the difficulty of obtaining a sharp image of a moving object.

Only in such long narrative poems does Ondaatje attempt any radical experiments in writing technique. *The Man with Seven Toes* (1969) is based on the story of a Mrs. Fraser who was shipwrecked among Australian aborigines and later led half-naked to civilization by an escaped convict. The narrative voice switches without overt signal from an omniscient narrator, to the convict, the woman, and back to the narrator. Each shift toward narration by the woman marks an intensification of the poem's drama. The setting of this poem is very much like the suburban Canadian world of Ondaatje's lyrics: corpses rot in the sun, birds' feathers are "caked with red vomit", leeches and worms can cover human skin.

Ondaatje's most celebrated work is *The Collected Works of Billy the Kid*. This book is a collage of altered and forged documents — diary entries, newspaper reports, interviews, reminiscences, even imaginary monolgues by Billy himself. As critic Stephen Scobie has revealed, *The Collected Works* is a highly conscious and researched achievement which makes use of a variety of older literary and cinematic treatments of the William Bonney legend. Ondaatje's purpose is not to illumine the historical gunman but rather to transform his story into a parable about the artist/outsider in North American society. His Billy is a careful, articulate, and extraordinarily perceptive hero — a man more eager for love and the pastoral dream of the Chisum ranch than for the bleeding, angry, and exploding forms that insist themselves upon him. He is brought into being by Ondaatje's deliberate alterations and additions to already suspect

Rat
Jelly

Michael Ondaatje

traditional material.

Ondaatje's openly subjective and symbolic treatment of history and document contrasts profoundly with other treatments of history in Canadian poetry. Both Pratt and Lampman distorted history in their narratives while insisting that they were being totally accurate. Among Ondaatje's contemporaries, George Bowering, Robert Hogg, Daphne Marlatt have often focused on the texture and limits of an individual's consciousness of the past and on the need to acknowledge distortion. Others like Victor Coleman, Gerry Gilbert, and bpNichol have preferred to write poems which are documents of their personal histories rather than of any delineated portion of 'history'; here the past has form only in its influence on the poet's life. John Robert Colombo in his historical poems has dealt with history by letting its unaltered documents speak for themselves.

In none of his work is Ondaatje a writer of personal consciousness or of submission to the found universe. Whether writing of his family or of legendary figures of past centuries, Ondaatje stands outside the experiences. In his sexual poems he becomes a voyeur to his own activity. In his love poems to his wife she remains a distinct and impersonally observed part of his landscape even "at half an inch". In a world as bloody and violent as Ondaatje perceives it, the poet can apparently never relax his self-control. In his own defence Ondaatje manipulates and watches, not only surviving, but creating a superbly tense, multicolour, explosive, macabre work as well — one entirely unique in our literature.

Ondaatje, Michael. *The Dainty Monsters.* Toronto: The Coach House Press, 1967.
          . *The Man with Seven Toes.* Toronto: The Coach House Press, 1969.
          . *The Collected Works of Billy the Kid.* Toronto: House of Anansi, 1970.
          . *Leonard Cohen.* Toronto: McClelland & Stewart, 1970. New Canadian Library: Canadian Writers no. 5.
          , ed. *The Broken Ark: a Book of Beasts.* Ottawa: Oberon Press, 1971.
          . *Rat Jelly.* Toronto: The Coach House Press, 1973.

Almon, Bert. "A Bitter Aspic," *Books in Canada* II:2 (April, May, June, 1973), 17.
Barbour, Douglas. "Controlling the Jungle," *Canadian Literature* 36 (Spring 1968), 86-88.
Davis, Marilyn. Review of *The Collected Works of Billy the Kid,* *Canadian Forum* 51 (July-August 1971), 34-35.

Fetherling, Doug. "A New Way To Do It," *Saturday Night* 86 (February 1971), 29-30.

——. "They Sing Singly and Apart, but All Together" (rev. of *The Man with Seven Toes*), *The Globe and Mail Magazine*, Aug. 1, 1970, p.16.

Geddes, Gary. "Astonishing: Blurred Visions Into His Fathomless Vault" (rev. of *Rat Jelly*), *The Globe and Mail*, April 21, 1973, p.23.

Hoar, Victor. "Outlawed in a Bestiary" (rev. of *The Collected Works of Billy the Kid*), *The Globe and Mail Magazine*, Feb. 12, 1971, p.16.

Lane, M. Travis. "Dream as History," *Fiddlehead* 86 (August-September-October, 1970), 158-162.

Pearson, Alan. "Ondaatje's Special Qualities," *Montreal Star*, September 21, 1968, "Entertainments", p.7.

Schroeder, Andreas. "The Poet as Gunman," *Canadian Literature* 51 (Winter 1972), 80-82.

Scobie, Stephen. "Two Authors in Search of a Character," *Canadian Literature* 54 (Autumn 1972), 37-55.

Skelton, Robin. Review of *The Collected Works of Billy the Kid*, *The Malahat Review* 18 (April 1971), 127.

Thompson, Kent. Review of *The Dainty Monsters*, *Fiddlehead* 76 (Spring 1968), 67-68.

Watson, Sheila. "Michael Ondaatje: The Mechanization of Death," *White Pelican* II:4 (1972), 56-64.

Weaver, Robert. Review of *The Dainty Monsters*, *The Toronto Star*, March 23, 1968, p.37.

Desmond Pacey

(1920-   )

A professional scholarship devoted to Canadian Literature has developed slowly. Only in the past decade has a literary history (Klinck *et al.*, *Literary History of Canada*, 1965) or an encyclopaedic reference guide (Norah Story, *The Oxford Companion to Canadian Literature and History*, 1966) been attempted. Still to be written are definitive studies of Canadian fiction, poetry, and short stories, as well as biographical studies of most of the major writers. Among the limited number of professional scholars of the literature, very few have had the knowledge or expertise to deal with contemporary writing. With mixed results, the appraisal of this work has fallen by default to Canadian poets. In consequence, Canada at the moment has a large number of poet/critics, with such distinguished writers as Eli Mandel, D.G. Jones, Margaret Atwood, George Bowering, James Reaney, Louis Dudek, and Dorothy Livesay among them.

Notable among the literary scholars who pioneered the study of Canadian writing has been Desmond Pacey. Since 1938 his numerous essays on Canadian writers and their public have argued, often prophetically, the significance of the literature as a subject of academic study. Much of Pacey's work has been, in his own words, "tentative and exploratory". In the absence of authoritative Canadian literary histories or of even preliminary critical appraisals of most Canadian writers, he has been obliged in much of his writing merely to establish the parameters of his subject.

Pacey became a scholar of Canadian literature in the early forties when a radio talk he had given on F.P. Grove grew into the monograph *Frederick Philip Grove* (1945). He followed this with the anthology *A Book of Canadian Stories* (1947) and with the important history of Canadian writing, *Creative Writing in Canada* (1952). The latter, revised in 1961, was the standard work of its kind until the publication of *Literary History of Canada* in 1965. In 1958 he published *Ten Canadian Poets,* biographical and critical essays on Sangster, Roberts, Carman, Lampman. D.C. Scott, E.J. Pratt, F.R. Scott, A.J.M. Smith, Earle Birney, and A.M. Klein. These are general and somewhat sociological essays, kept by their brevity from attempting extensive critical analyses; they were nevertheless the only widely available commentaries on most of the poets until the outburst of monograph publication at the end of the 1960's.

Pacey's recent publications include the anthology of criticism *Frederick Philip Grove* (1970), the monograph *Ethel Wilson* (1968), the posthumous edition of Grove's *Tales from the Margin* (1971), and *Essays in Canadian Criticism 1948-68* (1969). The latter provides a fascinating overview of the progress of our literature in the last forty years. Pacey's preferences throughout his career have been for a realistic, experiential writing, somewhat innovative in its styles and structures. Mildly nationalistic, he has demanded that the Canadian writer demonstrate his freedom from colonial mimicry by attending to Canadian experience and by modifying or replacing traditional forms. He has particularly admired the symbolic realism of Callaghan, the exuberant technical dexterity of Pratt, and the individualism of Livesay and Layton. He has defended regionalism in our writing as being the source of "the basic stuff of human nature" and of "the here and now" of our lives.

His leanings toward regionalism, realism, and particularism have made him one of the few academic critics to challenge the healthfulness of Northrop Frye's influence on Canadian poetry. He has accused the "clever, sophisticated, and brilliant as-all-get-out" work that Frye has encouraged of being "literature about literature rather than literature about life." He has suggested that the work of Jay Macpherson, Anne Wilkinson, Eli Mandel, James Reaney, Wilfred Watson, Daryl Hine, and Margaret Avison in the fifties was, under Frye's stewardship, "poetry ... led by criticism, rather than vice versa ... for the first time in English literary history and for that reason a rather dubious proceeding." The emergence of Canadian poetry in the sixties and seventies (including that of Avison, Reaney, Mandel, and Watson) out of Frye's confining shadow into an unprecedented variety of idiosyncratic forms may owe at least a small debt to Desmond Pacey.

Pacey, Desmond.   *Frederick Philip Grove.* Toronto: Ryerson Press, 1945.

, ed. *A Book of Canadian Stories.* Toronto: Ryerson Press, 1947, rev. 1950, 1962.

. *Creative Writing in Canada.* Toronto: Ryerson Press, 1952, rev. 1961.

. *The Picnic and Other Stories.* Toronto: Ryerson Press, 1958.

. *Ten Canadian Poets.* Toronto: Ryerson Press, 1958.

, ed. *Our Literary Heritage.* Toronto: Ryerson Press, 1966.

. *The Cat, the Crow, and the Kangaroo,* the collected children's verse of Desmond Pacey. Fredericton, N.B.: Brunswick Press, 1968.

. *Ethel Wilson.* New York: Twayne, 1968.

. *Essays in Canadian Criticism, 1938-1968.* Toronto: Ryerson Press, 1969.

. "Note on Major John Richardson," *Canadian Literature* 39 (Winter 1969), 103-104.

, ed. *Frederick Philip Grove.* Toronto: Ryerson Press, 1970.

. " 'Summer's Heat, and Winter's Frigid Gales ': the Effects of the Canadian Climate upon Canadian Literature," Royal Society of Canada, *Transactions,* fourth series, no. 8 (1970), 3-23.

. "In Search of Grove in Sweden: a Progress Report," *Journal of Canadian Fiction* I:1 (1971), 69-73.

, ed. *Tales from the Margin* by Frederick Philip Grove. Toronto: Ryerson Press, 1971.

. "The Mobility of English," *Canadian Literature* 53 (Summer 1972), 109-110.

. "The Study of Canadian Literature," *Journal of Canadian Fiction* II:2 (Spring 1973), 67-72.

Edwards, Mary Jane. "Bird's Eye View," *Canadian Literature* 45 (Summer 1970), 93-95.

Mandel, Eli. *"Creative Writing in Canada* Reviewed," *Fiddlehead* 53 (Summer 1962), 61, 63-64.

Richards, I.A. Review of *Creative Writing in Canada, University of Toronto Quarterly* 31 (July 1962), 479-480.

Sommerhalder, James. "Any Child," *Alphabet* 17 (December 1969), 71-72.

Sonthoff, H.W. "On Ethel Wilson," *Canadian Literature* 38 (Autumn 1968), 93-94.

P.K. Page

(1917-   )

Very similar to the work of A.J.M. Smith, Robert Finch, Ralph Gustafson, Leonard Cohen, and Phyllis Webb in its severe distrust of the physical universe is the poetry of Patricia Kathleen Page. Unlike Cohen and Webb, however, the rejection of the physical is not complete; for Page, this world can still be (as it can for Smith and Finch) a symbol of worlds less corrupt and inconstant than itself. Her poems search for visions of such symbolism within the tumult of day-to-day experience; her poetic techniques look to transform this tumult into the visually patterned stillness of art.

P.K. Page was born in England but spent her childhood and youth in Alberta; during the Second World War she was associated with *Preview* magazine, and later was a regional editor of *Northern Review*. She resigned from *Northern Review* in 1947 to protest John Sutherland's agressive review of Robert Finch's Governor-General's Award-winning collection *Poems*. She was most active as a poet during the forties and early fifties, publishing *As Ten as Twenty* (1946) and *The Metal and the Flower* (1954). In recent years she has devoted her time to a career as a graphic artist under her married name, P.K. Irwin. The retrospective selection of her poetry, *Cry Ararat!* (1967), contained seventeen new poems. A similar collection is *Poems Selected and New* (1974).

In Page's view, terrestrial life is an amalgam of deceit, pain, overpowering speed, and sin. Man is dragged into it like a fish into air "its mouth alive with metal". She finds its patterns disillusioning and temporary; the resplendent marching band "crumbles ... tired and grumbling / on the straggling grass." She sees its carnality and process as overwhelming and frightening in their randomness and power: a flight of "feathered and fiery" birds that go "pelting by".

Most of Miss Page's poems explore varieties of escape from op-pressive mortality. One escape is childhood innocence. For Miss Page, children live in "glass air" of illusory immortality; they are "white with running and innocence", on their wishes "innocence / has acted as a filter". Unfortunately, the children grow into a world of actuality and sin, into the "unfamiliar blood". The adult, however, can seek to recapture childhood's simplicity through his imagination. In "Cook's Mountains" a voice merely has to pronounce "Those are the Glass Mountains up ahead" and "sudden surrealist" shapes take on the geometric familiarity of "mirror", "mica", and "diamond". In "Only Child" a mother's voice works to turn living birds into "statues", "brittle as little sticks". In "Photos of a Salt Mine" the adult can transform the workman's terrible labour into "a child's / dream of caves and water", to "Aladdin's cave".

Obviously, such illusion can prove grossly deceptive. Many of Miss Page's poems demonstrate the sinister dangers lurking within this quest for innocence. The false pictures of the salt mine, she tells us, are inspired by "not innocence but guilt". The cold, snow-white, unchallenging geometric landscape of childhood is for the adult "a landscape without love" ("The Snowman"), a "way to death" ("Stories of Snow").

Nevertheless, the reduction of experience into simple, artistic pattern remains one of Miss Page's most frequent themes and her dominant technique. In "After Rain" she exults to see that snails have turned cabbage leaves to "green lace" and that the rain has made the entire garden appear a "garden abstracted, geometry awash — an unknown theorem argued in green ink". In "Brazilian Fazenda" the vitality of Brazilian life sees her cry out "Oh let me come back on a day / when nothing extraordinary happens / so I can stare / at the sugar white pillars / and black lace grills / of this pink house." Pure geometry, colour, and pattern are apparently preferable to the rough passions of actuality. Many of her poems actively transform a living scene to the lifeless permanence of glass, ice, snow, lace, metal, or pattern. "Bark Drawing" reduces Australia to a landscape of "cross hatch and serif"; "Blowing" reduces a windy Australian hillside to "light". In "No Flowers" the sea becomes "angular shapes across your eyes"; in "The Permanent Tourists" humans become through Miss Page's eyes "sculptured immemorial stone" and "placid glass".

Two other modes of escape from life suggested by Page are retreat into subconscious reverie and flight into a realm of divine, pre-lapsarian innocence. The former is expressed in numerous sea poems ("Boy with a Sea Dream", "Element", "Portrait of Marina", "The Stenographers", and "In a Ship Recently Raised from the Sea").

P.K. Page

233

In these the sea represents the green innocence of the Jungian unconscious, where one is "freed and whole again" among "finely fretted archipelagoes" and "the deep clear bottle green" of "ocean thought". The heavenly realm is less approachable for Page, and yet is glimpsed in a number of poems in images of "white and gold", "tall suns and sunflowers". The title poem of *Cry Ararat!* expresses yearning for that lost morning of our world's redemption into innocence when the dove led Noah onward to Ararat.

P.K. Page is unmistakenly one of the most readable of the various 'anti-life' poets of twentieth-century Canadian poetry. Her vision of a corrupt world is based on fairly detailed and realistic portraits. Her images are precisely and economically presented; her syntax, while not colloquial, is free of rhetoric and pretentious complication. Her symbolic patterns are straightforward almost to the point of being formulaic; white, snow, glass, and ice for childhood; foliage, fire, and birds for the physical and sensual; the sea for the subconscious; metal, gems, lace, geometry and pattern for the welcome permanence and simplicity of art; sunlight and gold for that celestial world "more real than flowers".

Page, P.K. *The Sun and the Moon* (novel) by Judith Cape [pseud.]. Toronto: Macmillan of Canada, 1944. Reprinted with eight short stories in *The Sun and the Moon and Other Fictions,* Toronto: House of Anansi, 1973.
    . *Unit of Five.* Poems by Louis Dudek, Ronald Hambleton, P.K. Page, Raymond Souster, James Wreford, ed. Ronald Hambleton. (Toronto: Ryerson Press, 1944), pp.39-52.
    . *As Ten As Twenty.* Toronto: Ryerson Press, 1946.
    . *The Metal and the Flower.* Toronto: McClelland & Stewart, 1954.
    . *Cry Ararat!* Poems New and Selected. Toronto: McClelland & Stewart, 1967.
    . "Questions and Images," *Canadian Literature* 41 (Summer 1969), 17-22.
    . "Traveller, Conjuror, Journeyman," *Canadian Literature* 46 (Autumn 1970), 35-42.
    . "Darkinbad the Brightdayler: Transmutation Symbolism in the Work of Pat Martin Bates," *Arts/Canada* 28 (April-May 1971), 35-40.
    . *Poems Selected and New.* Toronto: House of Anansi, 1974.
    . *Leviathan in a Pool.* Vancouver: Blackfish Press, 1974.

Bruce, Charles. "The Poetry of P.K. Page" (rev. of *As Ten, As Twen-*

ty), *The Globe and Mail,* Dec. 7, 1946, "Review of Books" p.10.

Cook, Gregory M. Review of *Cry Ararat!, Dalhousie Review* 48 (Spring 1968), 151, 153.

Francis, A. "P.K.," *Canadian Art* 20 (January-February 1963), 42-45.

Meredith, W. "A Good Modern Poet and a Modern Tradition," *Poetry* (Chicago) 70 (July 1947), 208-211.

Shaw, Neufville. "The Poetry of P.K. Page," *Educational Record* 64 (July-September 1948) 152-156.

Smith, A.J.M. "New Canadian Poetry," *Canadian Forum* 26 (February 1947), 252.

————. "The Poetry of P.K. Page," *Canadian Literature* 50 (Autumn 1971), 17-27.

Sutherland, John. "The Poetry of P.K. Page," *Northern Review* 1 (December-January 1946-47), 13-23. Reprinted in his *Essays, Controversies and Poems,* ed. Miriam Waddington (Toronto: McClelland & Stewart, 1972, New Canadian Library no. 81), pp.101-112.

Waddington, Miriam. "Five Without a Common Song" (rev. of *Cry Ararat!*), *The Globe and Mail Magazine,* Jan. 13, 1968, p.13.

Weaver, Robert. Review of *Cry Ararat!, The Toronto Star,* March 23, 1968, p.37.

Al Purdy

(1918 -   )

Al Purdy's colloquial and self-deprecating poetry has been one of the most popular of the past fifteen years. Like that of Layton, it has been indirectly rather than directly influential on the work of other writers. The uniquely homespun wit of Purdy has been uncapturable by imitators, although his dominant subject matter — the everyday experiences of an ordinary man wandering through the small towns, farms, and tourist stops of the nation — has reappeared in the work of numerous younger writers, among them Pat Lane, Sid Marty, Tom Wayman, and Ken Belford.

Purdy was born in Wooler, Ontario, not many miles from Ameliasburgh where he now lives. He attended school in Trenton and Belleville, Ontario, but was never able to attend university. In the late thirties he rode a freight train to Vancouver, and in the Second World War served in the Air Force. Between the war and the early 1960's he held a variety of casual jobs; since then he has been able to earn a marginal living from his writing, editing, and poetry readings.

In Purdy's work, as in Layton's, the personality of the writer is prominently displayed — through the diction, the rhythms, and the openly subjective point of view. Poems which appear to present the Canadian landscape in fact present Purdy's reactions to the landscape; poems which begin as static descriptions end up as documents of Purdy's self-questioning consciousness ("Trees at the Arctic Circle"). Purdy's tendency to self-deprecation is an essential and attractive part of his general self-absorption. He presents himself in comical, semi-humiliating situations — attacked with a butcher knife by his wife, caught by Eskimo dogs with his pants down, ridiculed in the Quinte Hotel tavern for expecting a poem to be worth

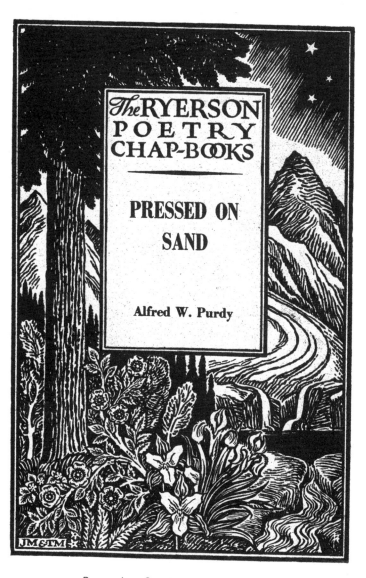

The RYERSON
POETRY
CHAP-BOOKS

PRESSED ON
SAND

Alfred W. Purdy

Pressed on Sand by Al Purdy. Ryerson Press, 1955.

a beer. In Purdy we are made to see the fate of the romantic in our materialistic society, and allowed to laugh at the humilations anyone who values beauty, love, and heroism is made to face in an insistently mundane world.

Purdy is frequently struck by the ways in which nature utterly dwarfs mankind. The mice walk unconcernedly across the floor of his Roblin Lake home. An arctic tree displays superhuman persistence in its century-long battle with permafrost. A dinosaur skeleton testifies to the puniness of the human body, the brevity of human history, the immensity of geologic time. Man, in Purdy's poems, is a visitor, an interloper. His creations, as in "My '48 Pontiac", look forward "at death" or backwards into the completed events of life. Yet there is no despair in Purdy's poems, and certainly no retreat into gnosticism or aestheticism. There is only joy in the continuing struggle to survive and understand.

As in "My '48 Pontiac", Purdy comes to the end of most of his poems "puzzled by things". He offers few conclusions about life, and his poetry — as in "Lament for Robert Kennedy" — tends to falter when he attempts to do so. Purdy's talent is not the prophetic one of Layton or the polemic one of Acorn. He is at his best exposing the complexities of situations and the unanswerableness, the futility, of our questions about them. Even the relationships between American, Canadian, and Eskimo culture "resists" him and leaves him "feeling stupid / rejecting the obvious" ("At the Movies").

Lately Purdy's nationalist sentiments and subject matter have made him one of the most attractive of contemporary writers to nationalist literary critics. This has made him the object of much reductive and unconsciously colonial criticism in which Roblin Lake becomes Walden Pond and Purdy himself the Canadian Whitman. In addition, as Leslie Mundwiler points out, this critical view works to transform Purdy's dynamic, random, and questioning writings into a static caricature of some national Canadian archetype. Purdy does not deserve this, for his sense of history, especially geologic history, and of the impenetrability of cultural and inter-cultural realities, is much more sophisticated than that of most of the nationalist analysts.

Purdy, Al.   *The Enchanted Echo.* Vancouver: Clarke and Stuart, 1944.
             . *Pressed on Sand.* Toronto: Ryerson Press, 1955.
             . *Emu, Remember!* Fredericton, N.B.: Fiddlehead Books,
      1957.
             . *The Crafte So Long to Lerne.* Toronto: Ryerson Press,
      1959.
             . *The Blur in Between.* Toronto: Emblem Books, 1962.

. *Poems for All the Annettes.* Toronto: Contact Press, 1956; second edition enlarged and revised, Toronto: Anansi, 1968; third edition enlarged and revised, Toronto: Anansi, 1973.

. *The Cariboo Horses.* Toronto: McClelland & Stewart, 1965.

. *North of Summer.* Toronto: McClelland & Stewart, 1967.

. *Wild Grape Wine.* Toronto: McClelland & Stewart, 1968.

, ed. *The New Romans.* Edmonton: Hurtig, 1968.

, ed. *Fifteen Winds.* Toronto: Ryerson Press, 1969.

. *Love in a Burning Building.* Toronto: McClelland & Stewart, 1970.

, ed. *Storm Warning.* Toronto: McClelland & Stewart, 1971.

. *Hiroshima Poems.* Trumansburg, N.Y.: The Crossing Press, 1972.

. *Selected Poems.* Toronto: McClelland & Stewart, 1972.

. *Sex and Death.* Toronto: McClelland & Stewart, 1973.

Atwood, Margaret. "Love is Ambiguous...Sex is a Bully," *Canadian Literature* 49 (Summer 1971), 71-75.

Bowering, George. *Al Purdy.* Toronto: Copp Clark, 1970. Studies in Canadian Literature 6.

Bromige, David. "Craftsmen and Others," *Canadian Literature* 4 (Spring 1960), 85-86.

Geddes, Gary. "A.W. Purdy — Interview," *Canadian Literature* 41 (Summer 1969), 66-72.

. "No Brew Like Home-Brew," *Canadian Literature* 40 (Spring 1969), 87-89.

. "A Victim in Darker Reality," *The Globe and Mail,* Oct. 20, 1973, p.34.

Lee, Dennis. "Running and Dwelling: Homage to Al Purdy," *Saturday Night* 87 (July 1972), 14-16.

MacCallum, Hugh. "Letters in Canada: 1965," *University of Toronto Quarterly,* XXXV:4 (1965-1966), 358-362.

Mundwiler, Leslie. Review of *Selected Poems, Open Letter,* second series, no. 3, pp.75-78.

Stevens, Peter. "In the Raw: the Poetry of A.W. Purdy," *Canadian Literature* 28 (Spring 1966), 22-30.

Webb, Phyllis. "Magnetic Field," *Canadian Literature* 15 (Winter 1963), 80-81.

Joe Rosenblatt (1933-   )

Joe Rosenblatt is a poet of wit and contrivance — along with John Robert Colombo one of the few to emerge among Canadian experimental poets of the past fifteen years. He delights in outrageous effects — in the juxtaposition of the sublime and the frivolous, the sacred and the obscene, sophisticated surrealism and the blatancies of pure sound.

Since his second book, *The LSD Leacock* (1966), his predominant theme has been the essential unity of cosmic life. To Rosenblatt, the human, animal, vegetable, and mineral realms share and interchange even their individual atoms of being. As the title of *The LSD Leacock* implies, he casts himself as a visionary who sees beyond the false and orgulous barriers man has placed between himself and the rest of creation. Like Leacock, he makes cynical note of human hypocrisy, but adds to this an absurd and horrific view of the insect and animal kingdoms as humanity unmasked — humanity stripped of its pretensions to decorum, tradition, etiquette, decency, chivalry, cleanliness, etc. He shows us our fragility in the smear of an egg yolk, our gluttony in the spider's feast.

The direct and exuberant lines of much of *The LSD Leacock* give place to more delicate and often less powerful writing in *The Winter of the Lunar Moth* (1968). The strongest poems comprise an opening section on the humanity of fish (and, correspondingly, the piscine nature of man); with a few outstanding exceptions, the book's other poems on bats, insects, and mirrors are uninspiringly formulaic. In this book Rosenblatt often dwells on man's murderous repudiation of his kinship with other sentient beings. One poem depicts two semi-deranged soldiers slaughtering fox bats from a helicopter with the aid of radar and napalm. Another portrays the remorse of a deceased fishmonger uncle when he finds himself "reincarnate in a minnow's whisper".

Bumblebee Dithyramb (1972) collects most of the poems of the previous volume and adds almost fifty-three pages of new work. The latter mark a return to the spontaniety of *The LSD Leacock*. Most of them celebrate the sharing by man and the rest of nature of a single soul of surpassing fertility and creativity. Many are chant poems in praise of the bumblebee ("the bee is breathing in th' womb / the bee is breathing in th' womb / the bee is breathing in th' womb / ...") which, together with the flower, comes to symbolize for Rosenblatt the eager submission to sexuality characteristic of non-human life. The poems of *Blind Photographer* (1973), however, have little of this energy and flamboyance. They are controlled, tightly written pieces that present the same worldview but in ironic and dispassionate terms. Most seem like minor variations on earlier and stronger work.

Rosenblatt's claim to originality is the rich view of the living cosmos his bestiary of bats, spiders, moths, men, fish, and penguins provides. Unfortunately, since *Winter of the Lunar Moth* he has had much difficulty in extending this view without appearing to repeat himself. He has displayed no firm sense of his own style, even in his early work. His recent books show him to be groping for technical solutions to the personal limits he has encountered. The chants of *Bumblebee Dithyramb* are transparently modelled on the sound poetry of Bill Bissett; the spare, ironic verse of *Blind Photographer* on the poetry of Margaret Atwood — to whom it is dedicated. Nevertheless, even the narrow range of Rosenblatt's present accomplishment adds 'a profound and arresting voice to Canadian poetry.

Rosenblatt, Joe.   *The Voyage of the Mood.* Toronto: Heinrich Heine Press, 1963.
          . *The LSD Leacock.* Toronto: The Coach House Press, 1966.
          . *The Winter of the Lunar Moth.* Toronto: House of Anansi, 1968.
          . *Greenbaum* (drawings). Toronto: The Coach House Press, 1970.
          . *Bumblebee Dithyramb.* Erin, Ont.: Press Porcépic, 1972.
          . *Blind Photographer.* Erin, Ont.: Press Porcépic, 1973.

Barbour, Douglas.   "Petit Four," *Books in Canada* I:11 (September-October 1972), 19.
          . Review of *Winter of the Lunar Moth, Dalhousie Review* 49

(Summer 1969), 289, 291.

Cameron, Allen Barry.　Review of *Winter of the Lunar Moth, Canadian Forum* 48 (March 1969), 286.

Cogswell, Fred.　"One Touch of Nature," *Canadian Literature* 40 (Spring 1969), 71-72.

Coleman, Victor.　"The Orangutan Inside Joe," *Canadian Forum* 44 (April 1964), 22-23.

Garnet, Eldon.　Review of *Bumblebee Dithyramb, Open Letter* (second series) 3, Fall 1972, pp.87-88.

Harrison, Keith.　"Poetry Chronicle," *Tamarack Review* 42 (Winter 1967), 72.

Mandel, Eli.　"The Poet as Animal — of Sorts" (rev. of *Winter of the Lunar Moth*), *The Globe and Mail Magazine*, Oct. 12, 1968, p.17.

Rhind, P.E.　Review of *Bumblebee Dithyramb, Quill and Quire* XXXVIII:11.

Snider, Norman.　"A Delight for Bibliophiles" (rev. of *Blind Photographer*), *The Globe and Mail*, May 12, 1973, p.35.

Stevens, Peter.　"Facts, To Be Dealt With," *Canadian Forum* 47 (September 1967), 139-140.

⸻ . "Undulating on a New Press" (rev. of *Bumblebee Dithyramb*), *The Globe and Mail*, Nov. 25, 1972, p.31.

Raymond Souster

Raymond Souster was born in Toronto, served in World War II — in his retrospective view a commercial struggle between industrial powers — and has lived in Toronto since. His poetry has concerned itself entirely with urban, industrial man — with the dehumanization this man suffers as a result of burgeoning technological and institutional structure. He has made his own quiet middle-class life — a job in a bank, a love of baseball, a home in the suburbs — into a parable for the 'little man's' life in the middle part of the the twentieth century.

All aspects of his writing have emphasized the unpretentiousness and ordinariness of his life — his prosody, his imagery, his language, his subjects, his themes. His poems have the external innocence of not being poems at all but recorded moments of casual speech. His diction is that of a literate working-man, his syntax direct, homey, and colloquial. He avoids the genteel forms of poetic tradition, preferring a breath-punctuated free verse modelled on the writings of another humanitarian poet, William Carlos Williams. His imagery is drawn not from literature, mythology, or science but from the common objects of the downtown street or suburban home — the house-cat, the market basket, the "egg hopping on a griddle". Souster's most frequent image for himself is the groundhog or other burrowing animal barred from shelter, awaiting a trap's spring, or already dead by gunshot.

Souster expresses extreme dissatisfaction with twentieth-century life, but unlike his contempories Gustafson, Newlove, and Webb, he makes no blanket condemnations. The wilderness and the countryside are innocent; only the city and the industrial and financial institutions that built it are to Souster irredeemably brutal. Individual men have a capacity for compassion and love, but must struggle against the "tomb" that is the city in order to give these expression. Most of the figures of Souster's landscapes have been defeated by the city — waitresses, cripples, soldiers, prostitutes, beggars, strippers, alcoholics.

The forces which vulgarize humanity also, in Souster's eyes, despoil the natural world. Within Souster's "cold hateful city" a symbolic battle is waged between the industrial grime and pigeons, ducks, trees, and a few hardy flowers. Animal imagery links man's victimization with that of the animal world; in the groundhog shot by technology's rifle or the bears imprisoned by Toronto's Riverdale Zoo, Souster invariably sees himself ("wonder what fate you have in store for me") and by extension his fellow man.

A further enemy of man in Souster's poetry is time. The city's power lies in the present and the future; that of nature and man in a nostalgic past of childhood excursions to the Toronto Islands or of innocent games of baseball in now-demolished stadia. Nevertheless, Souster sees a variety of alternatives to the city's spiritless machines. Sometimes Souster finds joy in escape to the country or even in close attention to the trees and birds of a residential street. Other times he delights in the pleasure of a good marriage, or of jazz music, or of nostalgic memories of youth. Perhaps the most attractive moments of his world for Souster are those in which some spark of compassion or love passes between his benighted fellow citizens. However, more of his poems deplore the failures of men, particularly himself, to achieve such moments than celebrate their occurrence.

Souster demands of that we sing "when there's really no reason why". He asks that we face the impermanent and tawdry modern world, if not hopefully, at least (like the last patch of April snow) "dirty-white / but defiant". In a world where large beauties have long ago succumbed to the towering forms of modern architecture, he celebrates the small beauties that remain. In numerous imagistic poems he draws attention to the sound of acorns falling, "small birds' gossip", bathwater glistening on a woman's "slight buttocks". He sings of the minimal, the familiar, the easily overlooked, reminding us that despite the vainglorious size and power of institutional oppression, the human and the natural survive in unspectacular ways.

Souster's editorial contributions to Canadian literature have been among the most influential of the century. His distaste for commercialism, established traditions, and institutions — academic or otherwise — led him to be a strong advocate of little magazines

WHEN WE ARE YOUNG

RAYMOND SOUSTER

NEW WRITERS SERIES NO.4 FIRST STATEMENT MONTREAL

When We Are Young by Raymond Souster.
First Statement Press, 1946. His first book.

and small presses. He has given much time and money to assisting young writers to come into print without having to submit to the tyrannies of financial pragmatism and academic conservatism. He helped found the little magazine *Direction* in 1943; he founded and edited *Contact* (1952-54) and *Combustion* (1957-60). He co-founded Contact Press with Louis Dudek and Irving Layton — a press which almost single-handedly kept a tradition of experimental poetry alive in the late 1950's. In 1965 he edited a courageous anthology of young writers, *New Wave Canada: the New Explosion in Canadian Poetry*. Recently he has edited *Generation Now* (1970), an anthology of poetry for schools, and co-edited with Douglas Lochhead *Made in Canada: New Poems of the Seventies* (1971).

Souster, Raymond. *Unit of Five*. Poems by Louis Dudek, Ronald Hambleton, P.K. Page, Raymond Souster, James Wreford, ed. Ronald Hambleton (Toronto: Ryerson Press, 1944), pp.55-67.

. *When We Are Young*. Montreal: First Statement Press, 1946.

. *Go to Sleep World*. Toronto: Ryerson Press, 1947.

. *The Winter of Time* (novel) by Raymond Holmes [pseud.]. New Toronto: Export Publishing Enterprises, 1949.

. *City Hall Street*. Toronto: Ryerson Press, 1951.

. *Cerberus*. Poems by Louis Dudek, Irving Layton, Raymond Souster. Toronto: Contact Press, 1952.

. *Shake Hands with the Hangman*. Toronto: Contact Press, 1953.

. *A Dream that is Is Dying*. Toronto: Contact Press, 1954.

. *For What Time Slays*. Toronto: Contact Press, 1955.

. *Walking Death*. Toronto: Contact Press, 1955.

. *The Selected Poems*, chosen by Louis Dudek. Toronto: Contact Press, 1956.

. *Crêpe-Hanger's Carnival*. Toronto: Contact Press, 1958.

. *A Local Pride*. Toronto: Contact Press, 1962.

. *Place of Meeting: Poems 1958-60*. Toronto: Gallery Editions, 1962.

. *At Split Rock Falls*. Vermont: American Letters Press, 1963.

. *The Colour of the Times:* Collected Poems. Toronto: Ryerson Press, 1964.

. *12 New Poems*. Lanham, Md.: Goosetree Press, 1964.

. *Ten Elephants on Yonge Street*. Toronto: Ryerson Press, 1965.

, ed. *New Wave Canada*. Toronto: Contact Press, 1966.

. *As Is*. Toronto: Oxford University Press, 1967.

The Winter of Time by Raymond Souster.
Export Publishing Enterprises Ltd., 1949.

. *Lost and Found:* Uncollected Poems 1945-65. Toronto: Clarke Irwin, 1968.

. *So Far, So Good:* Poems 1938/1968. Ottawa: Oberon Press, 1969.

, ed. *Generation Now,* ed. Raymond Souster and Richard Wollatt. Don Mills, Ont.: Longman Canada, 1970.

, ed. *Made in Canada,* ed. Raymond Souster and Douglas Lochhead. Ottawa: Oberon Press, 1970.

. *The Years.* Ottawa: Oberon Press, 1971.

. *Selected Poems.* Ottawa: Oberon Press, 1972.

. *On Target* (novel) by John Holmes [pseud.]. Toronto: Village Book Store Press, 1973 (c. 1972).

, ed. *100 Poems of Nineteenth-Century Canada,* ed. Douglas Lochhead and Raymond Souster. Toronto: Macmillan, 1974.

ANON. "The Private World of Raymond Souster," *Time* (Canada Edition) June 12, 1964, reprinted in Louis Dudek and Michael Gnarowski, ed., *The Making of Modern Poetry in Canada* (Toronto: Ryerson Press, 1967), pp.241-242.

Barbour, Douglas. Review of *Lost and Found, Canadian Forum* 48 (February 1969), 260-261.

Bell, Don. "Canada's Poet in a Cage," *Weekend Magazine,* April 15, 1972, p.24.

Bevan, Alan. "Whither Now?" *Evidence* 6 (1963), 113-115.

Bowering, George. Review of *Place of Meeting, Canadian Forum* 42 (May 1962), 44.

. "Sun, Seasons, City," *Canadian Literature* 28 (Spring 1966), 79-80.

Carruth, Hayden. "To Souster from Vermont," *Tamarack Review* 34 (Winter 1965), 81-95.

Cogswell, Fred. "Poet Alive," *Canadian Literature* 13 (Summer 1962), 70-71.

. Review of *Lost and Found. Fiddlehead* 79 (March-April 1969), 110-111.

Colombo, John Robert. "Attempting to Remake Civilization" (rev. of *New Wave Canada*), *The Globe and Mail Magazine,* Sept. 10, 1966, p.19.

. "A Poet for the Forlorn" (rev. of *Ten Elephants on Yonge Street*), *The Globe and Mail Magazine,* Nov. 27, 1965, p.24.

Cook, Hugh. Review of *As Is, West Coast Review* III:3 (Winter 1969), 72.

Curnoe, Greg. "Down 401," *Alphabet* 9 (November 1964), 80.

Dudek, Louis. "Groundhog Among the Stars: The Poetry of Raymond Souster," *Canadian Literature* 22 (Autumn 1964), 34-49.

. Review of *A Local Pride* and *A Place of Meeting, Delta* 20 (February 1963), 30-31.

Fetherling, Doug. "The Cities Within," *Saturday Night* 88 (January 1973), 36-38.

Finnigan, Joan. "Flowers Gathered and Given," *Canadian Author and Bookman* 41 (Spring 1966), 9.

Fulford, Robert. "On Raymond Souster: A Good Toronto Poet Toronto Never Discovered," *Maclean's* 77 (April 18, 1964), 59, reprinted in Louis Dudek and Michael Gnarowski, ed., *The Making of Modern Poetry in Canada* (Toronto: Ryerson Press, 1967), pp.245-246.

. "The Poet Laureate of the Toronto Streets Looks Sadly Backward" (rev. of *Selected Poems*), *The Toronto Star*, Oct. 7, 1972, p.65.

. "War-novel Recalls Flak-filled Skies Over Ruhr Valley" (rev. of *On Target*), *The Toronto Star*, July 7, 1973, p.67.

G., M.R. Review of *Go to Sleep, World, Canadian Forum* 27 (August 1947), 119-120.

Geddes, Gary. "A Cursed and Singular Blessing," *Canadian Literature* 54 (Autumn 1972), 27-36.

Gibbs, Robert. Review of *The Years, Fiddlehead* 94 (1972), 129-135.

Gibson, Kenneth. "The Curate's Egg," *Alphabet* 17 (December 1969) 67.

Jonas, George. "It is Hard Not to be Affected by his Spell," *Saturday Night* 86 (December 1971), 35-36.

Jones, B.W. Review of *A Local Pride, Queen's Quarterly* 69 (Winter 1963), 646-647.

Lane, Lauriat, Jr. "Raymond Souster's Poetry," *Fiddlehead* 54 (Fall 1962), 62-64.

Livesay, Dorothy. "Odd Poet Out," *Canadian Literature* 36 (Spring 1968), 81-82.

. Review of *When We Are Young, Canadian Forum* 26 (September 1946), 142.

McNamara, Eugene. Review of *The Years, Quarry* XXI:2 (Spring 1972), 61-63.

Mandel, Eli. "Internal Resonances," *Canadian Literature* 17 (Summer 1963), 62-65.

Marshall, Tom. Review of *Ten Elephants on Yonge Street, Quarry* XV:2 (November 1965), 44.

Mullins, S.G. Review of *A Local Pride, Culture* 23 (December 1962), 428-429.

Purdy, Alfred. "Some of the Colours are Fast," *Canadian Author and Bookman* 39 (Summer 1964), 15-16.

Solecki, Z.S. Review of *The Years, Queen's Quarterly* 79 (1972), 274-

275.

Stratford, Philip.   "A Song for Souster," *Saturday Night* 79 (November 1964), 32.

Taylor, Michael.   Review of *The Colour of the Times, Edge* 3 (Autumn 1964), 108-111.

Waddington, Miriam.   "Five Without a Common Song" (rev. of *As Is*), *The Globe and Mail Magazine,* Jan 13, 1968, p.13.

Watt, F.W.   "Toronto's Poet Laureate" (rev. of *The Colour of the Times*), *The Globe and Mail Magazine,* May 23, 1964, p.14.

Weaver, Robert.   "A Generous Writer" (rev. of *The Colour of the Times*), *The Toronto Star,* Apr. 4, 1964, p.29.

. "A Poet Speaks for the Lonely" (rev. of *Ten Elephants on Yonge Street*), *The Toronto Star,* Oct. 30, 1965, p.17.

Weeks, Robert Lewis.   "Picked Clean and Unpurple," *The Far Point* 1, pp.76-79.

Wilson, Milton.   Review of *Selected Poems, Canadian Forum* 36 (October 1956), 164-165.

Ronald Sutherland (1933-   )

The most significant and portentuos insight achieved by Canadian criticism in the last decade has been that English-Canadian and French-Canadian literatures have, despite their mutual isolation, developed in parallel, and often congruent, manners. This insight is implicit in the introduction of D.G. Jones's overview of Canadian Literature, *Butterfly on Rock* (1970). It is implicit also both in the concept of the scholarly periodicals *Ellipse* (founded by Jones in 1969 to introduce through criticism and translation English-Canadian writers to Quebec and French-Canadian writers to English-Canada) and in the symbolism of its title: the bilaterally symmetrical shape of an ellipse is determined by two fixed points within it. The insight has generated in the high schools and colleges of English Canada increased interest in Quebec Literature, for it implies that English-Canadians can perhaps study their own identity in the works of their *autre culture*.

The theory that the writing of the two Canadas form roughly duplicate images of each other was researched during the sixties by Ronald Sutherland while directing a new programme in comparative Canadian literature at the University of Sherbrooke. He proposed it in a number of articles published between 1967 and 1970 and collected in his extremely important book-length study *Second Image* (1971). The fundamental part of Sutherland's thesis, documented by reference to large numbers of English-Canadian and Quebec works, is that the two peoples have settled in equivalent physical environments, have reacted to this environment with similar "garrison" responses, have had similar colonial histories, and have had parallel histories of puritan belief. He suggests that in the novel

251

both literatures have evolved through the same three major themes in the last forty years: The Land and Divine Order (Louis Hemon, Ralph Connor), The Breaking of the Old Order (Gabrielle Roy, John Marlyn), and The Search for Vital Truth (Hubert Aquin, Leonard Cohen).

Despite a dubious claim that only English-Canadian writing which, like that of Hugh MacLennan, shows an awareness of French Canada and contains specifically French-Canadian references and characters can be considered "mainstream" Canadian literature, Sutherland builds a strong case for the thesis that serious Canadian writing of all regions and cultures grapples with themes and ideas central to both founding cultures. He exploits this case to make a persuasive appeal for greater respect and communication between the two cultures — specifically for recognition that only the creation of a unilingual Quebec within confederation can save a rich, bipolar, and unexpectedly symmetrical heritage for future Canadians.

Sutherland, Ronald.   *Frederick Philip Grove*. Toronto: McClelland & Stewart, 1969.

. *Lark des Neiges* (novel). Toronto: New Press, 1971.

. *Second Image:* Comparative Studies in Quebec/ Canadian Literature. Toronto: New Press, 1971.

. "Catching Up: Notes on Some Recent Cataclysms," *Saturday Night* 87 (August 1972), 12-14.

. "Cultural Identity and the Literature of French Canada," *Literary Half-Yearly* XIII:2 (1972), 193-209.

. "Tabernacles à Douze Etages: The New Multi-Cultural Nationalism in Canada," *Journal of Canadian Fiction,"* II:2 (Spring 1973), 72-77.

. "White Christmas in Montreal" (story), *Journal of Canadian Fiction* II:1 (Winter 1973), 16-18.

Cameron, Donald.   "Second Image: First Try," *Canadian Literature* 53 (Summer 1972), 94-97.

Conron, Brandon.   Review of *Second Image, Literary Half-Yearly* XIII:2, pp.44-45.

Downes, G.V.   Review of *Second Image, The Malahat Review* 22 (1972), 123-125.

French, William.   "Discovering Things We Have in Common" (rev. of *Second Image*), *The Globe and Mail Magazine,* July 26, 1971, p.15.

Giguere, Richard.   Review of *Second Image, University of Toronto Quarterly* 41 (1972), 406-409.

Lennox, John Watt.   Review of *Second Image, Open Letter* (second series) 2, Spring 1972, pp.73-76.

Livingstone, Donald.   Review of *Second Image, Antigonish Review* 9 (1972), 112-113.

Nesbitt, Bruce.   Review of *Frederick Philip Grove, West Coast Review* V:2 (October 1970), 72.

Phelps, Arthur L.   "Appraising a Passionate Enigma" (rev. of *Frederick Philip Grove*), *The Globe and Mail Magazine*, Nov. 29, 1969, p.15.

Remple, Jean.   "Trying to Prove a Myth," *Montreal Star,* July 17, 1971, "Entertainments", p.12.

Roiter, Howard.   "Bi-Lingua Franca," *Books in Canada* I:3 (1971), 7-8.

————. Review of *Larks des Neiges, Journal of Canadian Fiction* I:2 (1972), 91-92.

Spettigue, D.O.   Review of *Frederick Philip Grove, Quarry* XIX:3 (Spring 1970), 56-57.

Audrey Thomas

(1935-   )

Most of Audrey Thomas's life has been spent in the U.S., England, and Ghana; much of her fiction reflects this fact. Very little of her first two books, *Ten Green Bottles* (1967) and *Mrs. Blood* (1969), is specifically 'Canadian'. The characters are all American, African, or English; the narrator's point of view is usually that of a young woman of distinctly 'American' preconceptions, education, and family background. Her first work to deal with Canadian experience is *Munchmeyer and Prospero on the Island* (1971).

As a narrative stylist, Audrey Thomas is a technical adventuress. Syntax, paragraph structure, and narrative structure all must work in a Thomas creation toward an extreme kind of psychological realism. From a reader's point of view, the stories and novels can seem bafflingly idiosyncratic in idiom and fragmentary in detail, for she does not aim to recount 'complete' stories in rational and confident prose. Her narrators are confused, misinformed, and frequently tortured individuals. They know at best only a fragment of the story which they are living; their speech can be garbled by their confusion and pain. It is not their lives that Audrey Thomas presents, but the condition of living such lives, and she does this vividly.

Ten Green Bottles is a collection of ten short stories, most from the point of view of women or young girls, probably the same person. This girl or woman suffers in nearly all her experiences — being bullied as a child by elders, working as a nurse's aid in a mental hospital, living alone as a student in Scotland, losing a child by miscarriage in Africa. The stories centre on her bewilderment, suspicion, pain, and terror.

Most of these experiences are brought together and re-explored in Thomas's first novel, *Mrs. Blood*. A woman (apparently the same one as in the stories) lies for several weeks bleeding in bed to await an inevitable miscarriage. Her agonized and wandering thoughts reveal two views of her self; one as the nervous incompetent, inconsequential housewife and mother, "Mrs. Thing", who cannot even carry her fourth child to full term, and the other the passionately careless "Mrs. Blood", whose generosity toward life has often earned her embarrassment and disaster. On almost every page, as bold-letter titles indicate, the woman reverts from one self-image to the other.

Audrey Thomas continues her examination of the feminine experience and expands her range of narrative experiment in *Munchmeyer and Prospero on the Island*. This is an exceedingly complex work, which, on first examination, appears to be two novellas, "Munchmeyer" and "Prospero on the Island". The first is the story of a British-born graduate student in English literature who lives in Vancouver and abandons his wife Martha and their three children to attempt a career as a novelist. He rents a suite from Maria and Tom Lodestone, a painter and sculptor, and takes a materialistic middle-class girl named Mavis as his mistress. Munchmeyer's fiction is appallingly romantic, and reflects the same lack of perceptiveness evident in his choice of a wife and a mistress and in his reflections about Tom and Maria.

"Prospero on the Island" appears at first to be a separate work — the diary of a young woman (Miranda Archer) temporarily separated from her painter/sculptor husband (Fred Archer) in order to live on the B.C. Gulf Islands and write a novel. A number of casual remarks, however, reveal that she is engaged in writing the novella "Munchmeyer". Again, as in all of Audrey Thomas's fiction, the full 'story' does not emerge. We are given images and rhymes. Martha, Maria, Mavis, Miranda, are all various consorts of artist or would-be artist, and possess varying degrees of understanding and selfishness. The three married couples, Munchmeyer and Martha, Tom and Maria, Fred and Miranda, face similar difficulties, and resolve these by living partially or completely apart. The novella Miranda writes reveals the people she fears becoming — Martha, Mavis, Munchmeyer — and the marriage she suspects she is living, that of Tom and Maria. Meanwhile, her diary entries show that her island experiences are helping her to lose her previous insecurity and self-consciousness (her "Mrs. Thing" image) and to be gaining an equanimity toward life that the self-loving and self-deceiving Munchmeyer could not find.

The novel *Songs My Mother Taught Me* (1973) is the most straightforward of Audrey Thomas's fiction despite its somewhat non-linear narrative structure in which children's jokes, snippets of conversation, and well-plotted chapters are bluntly juxtaposed in an apparent attempt to evoke the atemporal flavour of childhood as well as relate its stories and progressions. The chapters are arranged chronologically, and the entire book is given a firm overstructure by being divided into two sections entitled "Songs of Innocence" and "Songs of Experience". The story is narrated by a girl named Isobel Cleary and follows her from early childhood to her initiation into womanhood. This girl provides another face of both Mrs. Blood and the young woman of *Ten Green Bottles;* she has the same upstate New York background, the same pretentious and spendthrift mother, the same weak father, the same cataclysmic entry into adult life through a job as a nurse's aid in a mental hospital.

Audrey Thomas

The Blakean subtitles, however, place the focus of *Songs My Mother Taught Me* on the pastoral idyll around which the "innocence" of Isobel's childhood centres. Every summer until she is seventeen she escapes with her family from the poverty and social ostracization of her normal life to her grandfather's summer cottage, "Journey's End". These summers allow her to remain "innocent", unaware, of the true failure of her parents' marriage and of the desperate confusion within her own self. Until the grandfather unexpectedly sells it, the cottage both allows the family to evade facing itself and prevents Isobel from reaching "experience" and adulthood. Thomas's metaphor here for adult responsibility is openly sexual; to approach maturity Isobel must abandon the false and escapist joys of innocence by experiencing sexual intercourse joyfully, impetuously, and with full risk of pregnancy. While the innocent and stagnant "Journey's End" had frustrated her growing subconscious eagerness to surpass her virginity, the real and vulgar world of the mental hospital can not only initiate her into dealing with pain, suffering, irrationality, and personal injury but release her into the experience of her own body. Once again Audrey Thomas's subject is womanhood and the precarious balance of joy and pain necessary for a woman to experience feelings of self-worth and affirmation.

Thomas, Audrey.   *Ten Green Bottles.* Indianopolis: Bobbs-Merrill, 1967.
        . *Mrs. Blood.* Indianapolis: Bobbs-Merrill, 1969.
        . *Munchmeyer and Prospero on the Island.* Indianapolis: Bobbs-Merrill, 1971.
        . *Songs My Mother Taught Me.* Vancouver: Talonbooks, 1973; Indianapolis: Bobbs-Merrill, 1973.

Boxill, Anthony.   Review of *Mrs. Blood* and *Munchmeyer and Prospero on the Island, Fiddlehead* 95 (Fall 1972), 113-117.
Coldwell, J.   "From the Inside," *Canadian Literature* 50 (Autumn 1971), 98-99.
Dobbs, Kildare.   "A Novelist Explores the Circles of Hell" (rev. of *Munchmeyer and Prospero on the Island*), *The Toronto Star,* Apr. 1, 1972, p.59.
Stephens, Donald.   "Mini-Novel Excellence," *Canadian Literature* 38 (Autumn 1968), 94-96.
Rosegarten, Herbert.   "Writer and Subject," *Canadian Literature* 55 (Winter 1973), 112-113.

Fred Wah

(1939 -   )

At first it seems difficult to rationalize the inclusion of Fred Wah in this critical survey. His work has not been included in educational anthologies; his five books have been neither widely reviewed nor distributed. Even among his fellow Canadian poets he is almost totally unknown outside British Columbia.

Wah's obscurity, however, is almost a necessary extension of his poetic — a poetic which constitutes one of the most extreme forms which the recent movement in Canadian poetry toward decentralization has taken. The concept which dominates Wah's writing is that the geographic and human particulars which immediately surround a man not only contain all place and all history but together form a place that is for that man the true centre of the cosmos. Wherever a man stands is the essential earth, the essential cosmos, and can yield to him the Pleistocene, medieval Europe, Franklin's Arctic, Attic Greece, or whatever. All of Wah's writing has been dedicated to the evoking of the 'sublime' which he believes resident in the most narrowly local and ordinary of phenomena, to making his voice contain man's cosmic condition by staying within a day's walk of its home.

> ... so I told myself I would go out wandering not over the world but in the world until I found instant upon instant of that minute contact with a piece of it, say a twig, or a woman but with no other intention than an afternoon walk or a job might be in getting some work done and that at any place along the way I could dwell there forever in a state of property....

The closest analogue to Wah's writing in contemporary Canadian literature is the work of David McFadden. Both build their poetries around the commonplace in their immediate environment: McFadden around middle-class Hamilton, Wah around a few miles of hills, trees, and water-courses that extend from his farmhouse on the banks of the Kootenay River. Both see in the banalities of family life and in the lives of their children elements (as distinct from symbols) of man's eternal condition. Both have chosen to spend their adult lives within the general geographic boundaries of their childhood and youth. Wah came to the Kootenay region of British Columbia when he was four years old, left to do undergraduate work at the University of B.C. and graduate work at Albuquerque and Buffalo, then (forsaking the excitement of the latter city's post-Black-Mountain writing scene) returned to teach at Selkirk College in Castlegar, B.C. Like McFadden, Wah uses the unadorned particulars of a landscape in which his roots go back to childhood not as metaphors for man's life, as is the practice of more traditional writers, but *as* human life. The particulars 'stand for' nothing but *are* man "himself, the mountains, creeks / & many other creatures / anywhere."

At the heart of Wah's work is the concept of "home". One guesses that one of the reasons he could return from Buffalo to the relative isolation of the Kootenay Valley is that to him there can be no exile; every place in the universe is potentially central, potentially where mind and place "meet to provide name and home". Wah tells us,

> Memory of having been anywhere on earth embellishes the particulars of those instants of specific step or touch and forms a living picture with all the referents of home, roots, heart, core.

There is a kinship between man and the "nutrient rock", the "creek song", "the skins of the Mountain's earth", the "trees (that) hum and whistle".

Wah's five books, *Lardeau* (1965), *Mountain* (1967), *Among* (1972), *Tree* (1972), and *Earth* (1974) are all set "among" the multiple phenomena that move from Wah's Kootenays outward in space to the stars and in time to the planet's geologic history. All of these books attempt to render the 'song' of a man amid his circumstances. The style of the earlier books, particularly *Mountain,* tends to be overly descriptive and artificially dramatic. *Tree* and *Among* occasionally are marred by distinct borrowings from the vocabulary and syntax of one of Wah's most powerful teachers, Charles Olson. Yet throughout Wah moves toward the relaxed voice of one "at home", not needing to rhapsodize or describe but merely to speak from out of his own ongoing activity. It is this style that he achieves in *Earth*, a book which could be used as a writing manual for direct and accurate expression.

For one so little known, Wah's editorial activities in little magazines have been extensive and at times decisive. He has edited *Sum* (1964-65) and *Scree* (1970-   ) and served on the editorial boards

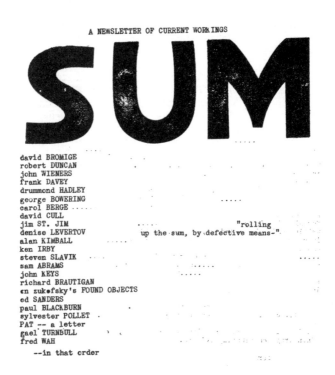

of *Tish* (1961-63), *Niagara Frontier Review* (1965-66). *The Magazine of Further Studies* (1966-67), and *Open Letter* (1965-   ).

Wah, Fred.   *Lardeau.* Toronto: Island Press, 1965.
        . *Mountain.* Buffalo: Audit East/West, 1967.
        . *Among.* Toronto: The Coach House Press, 1972.
        . *Tree.* Vancouver: New Star Books, 1972.
        . *Earth.* Canton, N.Y.: The Institute of Further Studies,
1974. Curriculum of the Soul no. 6.

Phyllis Webb

(1927-   )

In the poetry of Phyllis Webb, Canadian literature reaches its greatest depths of both worldly and metaphysical desolation. For her, the humanist dreams of Erasmus and Marx have crumbled, Christian hope is only a junkyard of reusable metaphor, and cosmic hope an impossible offspring of lifeless atoms.

Her early work, anthologized in *Trio* (1954) and collected in *Even Your Right Eye* (1956), takes a wide view of the pain and absurdity of man's physical existence. The mentors of this poetry are men in whom the anguish of mortality found its keenest expression: Aeschylus, Lear, Van Gogh, Edgar Christian, Gide. Its poet lives in a "tree of hell", and finds in poetry "the poet's curse". In these poems Webb sees the phenomenal world as a place of casual but relentless torture. It were best escaped all together: "to hell with that eternal circulation / of night, day, life, death, and love all over." Human love, she suggests, will bring tomorrow only "a slow terrible movement of scars".

Throughout these early poems there is a restraint of image and a directness and economy of language that is remarkably consistent with a philosophy that disdains worldly artifice and pomp. They contain no ornamental use of metaphor or mythological reference. There are no attempts at evocative description or at flights of rhetoric; all of the resources of the writing are given to unostentatious testimony of despair.

The Sea is Also a Garden (1962) marks a further retreat by Phyllis Webb from the world of matter, morality, and process. "What are we whole or beautiful or good for," she asks, "but to be absolutely broken." In such circumstances only extreme withdrawal — "sitting perfectly / still / and only / remotely human" — can appear a logical action. She would now surrender everything external to her skin. "Nakedness" ("nakedness is our only shelter") becomes a dominant theme, a nakedness both of the spirit amid the world of flesh and of the individual in a world that has capitulated to ostentatious acquisition.

The culmination of her work has been the brief, understated and ironic Naked Poems (1965) and the seven years of silence that have followed. Her distrust of materiality had always included a distrust of the efficacy of language; in Naked Poems this distrust brings about a language so private, cryptic, fragmentary, and "naked" that it almost abandons communication. The context of these poems — a room, a lover, the poet's white skin, moonlight, "waves of Event" — is left undefined. Only the emotions of futility, despondency, and occasional small pleasure are strongly evoked. The penultimate section is entitled "Suite of Lies", further emphasizing the fact that the crippling insufficiencies of the terrestrial penetrate even within the poet and her language. The cynicism displayed toward the self and its writing exceeds that of John Newlove. Newlove writes in a bitterly achieved sense of equanimity, resigned to extreme limitations in his world, his self, and his art, yet able to produce painful but significant work within these limitations. Phyllis Webb in Naked Poems collapses into a series of gnomic questions and answers in which, as respondent to some misunderstanding interlocutor, she successfully evades response. "Why are you standing there staring?" this figure asks her. "I am watching a shadow / shadowing a shadow," she replies. The last word and poem of the book is the questioner's puzzled "Oh."

As John Mays has argued, Phyllis Webb's work is vain, private, and inconclusive. It aspires not to greatness but to the simple recording of its own small melodramas and failures. It rejects certainty and "longs to slam the door on matter" — to free its self of historicity, morality, law, and words themselves. Its voice seeks to become amoral and amaterial, to transcend all extra-subjective considerations. This position, as Mays contends, is Gnostic in its seeking both transcendence without elevation to a celestial kingdom and purification of the soul by the abasement of the body.

Webb's severe pessimism and distrust of materiality is distinct from the earlier pessimism of Smith, Finch, and Gustafson in a number of ways. Most important, she scrupulously avoids the contradiction of fashioning poems of elaborate technical artifice while claiming to believe in the vanity of such worldly creations. Almost as important, she finds no solace in the Christian alternative to the terrestrial realm; the myth of heaven is as meaningless to her as a row of housewives "standing ... in queues for meat". Moreover, unlike her predecessors she does not attempt to intellectualize and order her despair. Not believing in the competence of the human intellect, and disillusioned by the examples of 'order' which the everyday world provides, she trusts only the naked fragments of experience — and

Phyllis Webb

trusts even these not enough to forge from them an extensive speech.

Phyllis Webb's poetry stands at the juncture between the modernist and post-modernist sensibilities. In it the modernist's rejection of the secular and material and his campaign to purify the language have reached their ultimate end. Beyond lie only suicide and silence. From the fragments and silences of this end, however, the post-modern recognition of a vast, disjointed, but sufficient cosmos can begin. In Canadian poetry, Webb's desperation clears the way for the creative junk-gatherers — bp Nichol, Gerry Gilbert, Victor Coleman — who will ask much less of the world than she, but find much more.

Webb, Phyllis.   *Trio: First Poems by Gael Turnbull, Phyllis Webb, Eli Mandel.* Toronto: Contact Press, 1954.
.   *Even Your Right Eye.* Toronto: McClelland & Stewart, 1956.
.   *The Sea Is Also a Garden.* Toronto: Ryerson Press, 1962.
.   *Naked Poems.* Vancouver: Periwinkle Press, 1965.
.   *Selected Poems 1954-1965.* Vancouver: Talonbooks, 1971.
.   "Phyllis Webb's Canada," *Maclean's* 84 (October 1971), 8-9, 47, 49.
.   "Letters to Margaret Atwood," *Open Letter* (second series) 5, Summer 1973, pp.71-73.

Barbour, Douglas.   Review of *Selected Poems, Quarry* XXI:1 (Winter 1972), 61-63.
Cogswell, Fred.   "Good But Not Great," *Fiddlehead* 55 (Winter 1963), 68.
Hulcoop, John.   Introduction to *Selected Poems* (Vancouver: Talonbooks, 1971).
.   "Phyllis Webb and the Priestess of Motion," *Canadian Literature* 32 (Spring 1967), 29-39.
Lane, M. Travis.   "Rare Mountain Air," *Fiddlehead* 92 (Winter 1971), 110-114.
Mays, John Bentley.   "Phyllis Webb," *Open Letter* (second series) 6, Fall 1973, pp.8-33.
Ronan, Tom.   Review of *Selected Poems, Tuatara* 8/9, pp.107-108.
Seaman, Roger.   Review of *Naked Poems, Quarry* XVI:4 (Summer 1967), 40-42.
Sontoff, H.W.   "Music Was Made, Arises Now," *Canadian Literature* 15 (Winter 1963), 81-82.
.   "Structure of Loss: The Poetry of Phyllis Webb,"

Canadian Literature 9 (Summer 1961), 15-22.

Stainsby, Mari. "An Interview with Phyllis Webb," *British Columbia Library Quarterly* XXXVI:2&3 (October 1972 and January 1973), 5-8.

Stevens, Peter. "Creative Bonds in the Limbo of Narcissism" (rev. of *Selected Poems*), *The Globe and Mail,* Dec. 4, 1971, p.33.

. "Shaking the Alphabet," *Canadian Literature* 52 (Spring 1972), 82-84.

Weaver, Robert. "A Puritan Dudek, An Efficient Webb," *Saturday Night* 86 (November 1971), 50, 52.

Zitner, S.P. "Peeling Off," *Books in Canada* I:4 (November 1971), 21.

Rudy Wiebe (1934 -)

Among recent serious Canadian writers, Rudy Wiebe is the only overtly Christian advocate. This advocacy has given to his novels a considerable tension between the didactic messages which they attempt to argue and the implications of their action and characterization. The extent to which Wiebe has increasingly reduced this tension in his third and fourth novels is one measure of his development as a novelist.

Wiebe belongs to the Mennonite branch of the Anabaptist faith; his family fled to Canada from the Soviet Union in 1930 in order to escape the religious persecution that had followed the Russian revolution. Much of Wiebe's writing has been concerned with one of the fundamental tenets of the Mennonites: that a Christian should attempt to live entirely in the spirit of Christ's teaching and example. Wiebe is particularly aware that institutional Christianity, even that of the Mennonites, can smother Christ's spirit beneath no-longer-relevant traditions and doctrines. To him, the spirit of Christianity must always take precedence over its forms.

In his first two novels, *Peace Shall Destroy Many* (1962) and *First and Vital Candle* (1966), Wiebe seemed as much concerned with religious teaching as with the craft of writing. In *Peace Shall Destroy Many* the characterizations are colourless and shallow and the dialogue contrived and literary. The novel's point of view wanders from character to character at the convenience of Wiebe's magisterial aims. The action leaps forward a month or more at a time, each leap mechanically bridged by one or more flashbacks. Yet *Peace Shall Destroy Many* is a fascinating novel despite its awkwardness. The fascination comes both from its plot, which is compelling, and from the intricacies of the religious issues which the novel embraces without totally resolving, as well as from its vivid portrayal of life in a part of Canada's Mennonite community. *First and Vital Candle* is also a compelling novel of plot and action. It again suffers from numerous technical problems. While its central character, the failed Presbyterian Abe Ross, is a deep though conventional portrayal, the supporting characters are puppets for particular points of view. The dialogue is often more suitable for religious tracts than for the mouths of spontaneously acting human beings. *First and Vital Candle* picks up the theme of the earlier novel: how should a Christian act toward his fellow man in the contemporary world? How can he resist war, lechery, avarice, exploitation, without acting contrary to Christ's pacifistic teachings? To Wiebe, faith and love are the only Christian means; not violence, cunning, economic pressure, or even withdrawal and retreat. Unfortunately, faith and love triumph in the novel only at the cost of a number of peculiar and most unlikely scenes.

Wiebe's third novel, *The Blue Mountains of China* (1970), comes very close to solving the artistic problems which his need to be both teacher and writer poses. Here Wiebe abandons the conventional narrative structures he used in the earlier novels, and with them the unconvincing imposition of religious theses on marginally appropriate events and characters. *The Blue Mountains of China* looks superficially like a collection of short stories. Each 'story' recounts an episode in the struggle of a number of Mennonite families, between 1870 and 1967, to flee religious oppression in Europe and to establish a new life, according to their faith, in Canada or South America. These are told from the points of view of nine characters, and are arranged in a loosely chronological order. As the book unfolds, it gradually becomes apparent that the stories collectively centre on one man, Jakob Friesen, and on one cluster of incidents in Russia in the autumn of 1929. Unlike in the other novels, no one character possesses Wiebe's evangelical message. Instead, the characters and stories together illustrate vividly the extreme difficulties the practicing Christian faces when living in seductively materialistic societies.

In a fourth novel, *The Temptations of Big Bear* (1973), Wiebe experiments again with a decentralized narrative structure. All of the characters of this novel are historical; the events are those preceding and immediately following the Northwest Rebellion of 1885. Wiebe attempts literally to recreate the worldviews of his central character, the Plains Cree chieftain Big Bear, and numerous lesser characters — Big Bear's sons Kingbird, Lone Man, and Little Bad Man, his warriors Wandering Spirit and Miserable Man, the factor's daughter

266

Kitty Maclean, and various federal government and Hudson's Bay Company representatives. Most of these characters contribute to Wiebe's narrative — through found documents such as letters and courtroom testimony or through Wiebe's attempts to envision their consciousness of particular events. In an interview by Donald Cameron, Wiebe claims there is "no narrator" in the novel; however, many passages, particularly toward the end of the book, are much too broad in scope for any single character and clearly imply the presence of an omniscient narrator.

The passages narrated from Big Bear's point of view dominate the book and are its strongest component. They persuasively present a portrait of a man who loves life, mankind, and the natural world with generosity and understanding. Though the poetry of these passages risks both cliché and grandiloquence, its effect is to imbue the un-cultivated western landscape and the Cree way of life with a stunning beauty. In the latter half of the book where Big Bear's lyrical vision is presented only occasionally, the writing is — with the exception of Kitty Maclean's narrative and several found documents — flat and mechanical.

The tone of *The Temptations of Big Bear* is elegiac and es-chatological: its time is that of the end of most things for the Indian people — the end of their culture, their rituals, their sacred places, their open grasslands, and the end of the buffalo and of the Cree's buffalo-centred economy. In these cataclysmic circumstances Big Bear emerges as another of Wiebe's conscience-ridden heroes, only too painfully aware of the responsibiltiies the death-throes of his world have placed upon him. Two principal temptations work to draw him away from his quasi-Christian faith in the brotherhood of man and the possibility of some equitable communal sharing of the western prairie by Indian and white man. One is the white man's treaty with its promise of reserved land, police protection, blankets, farm implements, food, and assistance in adapting to an agrarian way of life. The other is the way of violent resistance already followed with partial success by the Sioux under Sitting Bull. Big Bear (and the reader) come to see that both these temptations can offer nothing but ignoble sorts of death to the Cree culture.

In Wiebe's view, there is no escape for the Crees from the vise-grip of circumstance; only Big Bear's continuing refusal to follow the tempting ways of total surrender or total resistance can temper the inevitable Indian collapse with dignity and nobility. In this refusal to accept the conventional human responses to persecution, Big Bear takes on the role of the Christian martyr; like Christ himself he stub-bornly clings to a non-violent but fixed moral stance that with equanimity accepts the risk of death. Thus the least Christian of

Wiebe's novels in its overt content is the most powerful in its Christian implications. Through Big Bear's story Wiebe resolves the tension between didactic purpose and literary credibility more successfully than at any other time in his career. Given the subtlety and grace of this novel by comparison to the awkwardness of *Peace Shall Destroy Many*, plus the overall diversity of Wiebe's technical approaches to writing, Wiebe has to be considered among today's Canadian writers to be one of the most versatile, resourceful, and promising of further development.

Rudy Wiebe has also been active as a writer and editor of short stories. He is editor of *The Story Maker* (1970) and *Stories from Western Canada* (1972). His own stories are anthologized here and in *Fourteen Stories High* (1971) and *The Narrative Voice* (1972).

Wiebe, Rudy.   *Peace Shall Destroy Many*. Toronto: McClelland & Stewart, 1962, reprinted 1972 (New Canadian Library no. 82).
.... *First and Vital Candle*. Toronto: McClelland & Stewart, 1966.
.... *The Blue Mountains of China*. Toronto: McClelland & Stewart, 1970.
.... , ed. *The Story-Makers*. Toronto: Macmillan of Canada, 1970.
.... "Songs of the Canadian Eskimo," *Canadian Literature* 52 (Spring 1972), 57-69.
.... , ed. *Stories from Western Canada*. Toronto: Macmillan of Canada, 1972.
.... *The Temptations of Big Bear*. Toronto: McClelland & Stewart, 1973.

Cameron, Donald.   "The Moving Stream is Perfectly at Rest" (interview), in his *Conversations with Canadian Novelists* (Toronto: Macmillan of Canada, 1973), 146-160.
Christy, Jim.   "A Personal Christianity," *Saturday Night* 86 (April 1971), 26, 28.
Doerksen, Daniel W.   Review of *The Blue Mountains of China*, *Fiddlehead* 88 (Winter 1971), 98-102.
Jackson, Marni.   "Mennonites on the Move" (rev. of *The Blue Mountains of China*), *The Toronto Star*, Jan. 2, 1971, p.47.
Kostash, Myrna.   "A White Man's View of Big Bear," *Saturday Night* 89 (February 1974), 32-33.
Muggeridge, John.   "The Last of the New Mohicans is a Radical in Buckskin" (rev. of *The Temptations of Big Bear*), *The Toronto Star*, Nov. 17, 1973, p.F7.
Pomer, B.   Review of *First and Vital Candle*, *Canadian Forum* 47

(January 1968), 235-236.

Read, S.E. "Maverick Novelist," *Canadian Literature* 31 (Winter 1967), 76-77.

———. "The Storms of Change," *Canadian Literature* 16 (Spring 1963), 73-76.

Robinson, J.M. Introduction to *Peace Shall Destroy Many* (Toronto: McClelland & Stewart, 1972, New Canadian Library no. 82), pp.1-6.

Adele Wiseman

(1928-   )

Adele Wiseman's *The Sacrifice* (1956) is one of the finest novels written by a Canadian — profound in its characterizations, disturbingly realistic in its action, austere and evocative in its prose. Although the novel encompasses three generations of a Jewish immigrant family, it is essentially the story of Abraham, the family's would-be patriarch. Having been forced by the early death of his father to give up dreams of a rabbinical education and take up the trade of butcher, Abraham has become accustomed to think of himself as a man of unfulfilled, unrecognized greatness. His name and his marriage to a woman named Sarah lead him further to see himself in terms of the Biblical Abraham — an outcast who became the father of Jewry. Like his Biblical namesake, Abraham's personal lack of recognition, he believes, is to be made up many times over by the greatness of his descendants.

The structure of the novel places most weight on approximately twenty years of Abraham's life as an immigrant in Winnipeg between the two world wars. When the book opens, his two oldest sons are already dead (victims of a pogrom in Abraham's native Ukraine), his youngest son Isaac is weakened by typhoid, and his wife is broken by grief. We learn of the preceding years in Europe only through Abraham's reminiscences and reveries; we learn of the development of the third generation, Isaac's son Moishe, only in the final chapter which leaps forward ten years to provide a brief 'coda' to the central action.

Although Abraham is obsessively troubled by the fate of his oldest boys, what is most striking about him is his faith that, like the earlier Abraham, he is still special in the eyes of God, and that a

269

miracle or miracles are certain to befall him. He tends to see portents, blessings, and even miracles where there are none. His enthusiasms slowly kill his remaining son who must overwork to live up to his father's inflated image of his genius and destiny.

The Biblical legend of Abraham and Isaac is used by Wiseman throughout the novel to confirm the dimensions of Abraham's *hubris* and of the terrors it brings to his children. Abraham believed that his first sons were a promise made "in another place, another lifetime." He imagined their abilities to be almost super-natural; appropriately they died at a height above the sons of other men — hanged from long poles when their enslavement to their father's happiness caused them to risk death in a pogrom in order to be with their parents at Passover.

Imagery of climbing accompanies Abraham and his third son to other heights of sacrifice. From his arrival in Winnipeg, Isaac fears the "Mad Mountain" that looms over the city, and sees in it all his vague fears of the future. When their synagogue catches fire, Isaac, in a spontaneous attempt to be his father's "Miracle" child, rescues the Torah and emerges in flames "like a revelation bursting from the flaming heavens". After Isaac's death, a distraught, childless Abraham climbs the stairs of a prostitute's apartment to another mountain-top encounter with destiny: here he impulsively and ritualistically murders the woman in an insane attempt to expiate his growing feelings of self-revulsion. Found incompetent to stand trial, he is committed to a psychiatric hospital located on the "Mad Mountain" which Isaac had feared. It is here, in the last chapter, that the only hopeful mountain-top father and child encounter occurs, when the grandson, Moishe, visits him. Although Abraham still appears in love with miracles and believes his grandson's appearance after ten years to be one, the child, for the first time in the novel, descends the mountain not only unharmed but suddenly matured — "a different person from the boy who had gone up the hill."

Enriching the book are numerous ironies. Abraham, who continually suspects his son Isaac of atheism, ultimately commits the pagan act of human sacrifice that the Biblical Abraham had condemned and halted. One who has prided himself on being an unrecognized holy man, who is only by accident a butcher, performs the most appalling act of butchery. A man who has loved God for his mercy — particularly as expressed in the Abraham and Isaac legend — proves most unmerciful toward his sons and his fellow man. In addition, Canada, a "promised" and promising land in terms of the novel's imagery, rewards a father's *hubris* with death in the same way as did the Ukraine from which he had fled.

An indication of the richness of this fine novel is its openness to

270

auxiliary interpretations. Abraham's obsession with divine recognition and religious orthodoxy can be read — as Margaret Atwood reads it — as an immigrant's rejection of the Canadian reality. He neglects to learn English; he rejects the immigrant world of bootleggers, vulgar small-businessmen, and garrulous women as tawdry and degrading. Isaac's death can be read as the victimization of a son by a father — although such a reading deprives the relationship of most of its complexity and horror. Moishe's visit to "Mad Mountain" can be seen as implying the third generation's adjustment of the new world to old values. Such readings are valid, but they say very little about the central depths of Wiseman's novel.

Wiseman, Adele. *The Sacrifice.* New York: Viking Press, 1956. Reprinted Toronto: Macmillan of Canada, 1968 (Laurentian Library no. 8).
————. "Duel in the Kitchen" (story), *Maclean's* 74 (January 7, 1961), 22-23, 74.
————. *Old Markets, New World.* Drawn by Joe Rosenblatt, described by Adele Wiseman. Toronto: Macmillan of Canada, 1964.
————. "Montreal and French-Canadian Culture: What They Mean to English-Canadian Novelists," *Tamarack Review* 40 (Summer 1966), 49-50.
————. "English Writing in Canada: the Future," Royal Society of Canada, *Proceedings* 4th series, vol. 5 (June 1967), 45-51.
————. "A Brief Anatomy of an Honest Attempt at a Pithy Statement about the Impact of Manitoba Environment on My Development as an artist," *Mosaic* 3 (Spring 1970), 98-106.

ANON. Review of *The Sacrifice, Times Literary Supplement,* November 9, 1956, p.661.
Johnson, Vernon. Review of *The Sacrifice, Manchester Guardian,* November 20, 1956, p.4.
Keate, Stuart. Review of *The Sacrifice, New York Times,* September 16, 1956, p.4.
Mallory, Robert. Review of *The Sacrifice, Chicago Sunday Tribune,* September 16, 1956, p.3.
Maloff, Saul. Review of *The Sacrifice, New Republican* 135 (November 12, 1956), 20.
Mullins, Stanley E. "Traditional Symbolism in Adele Wiseman's *The Sacrifice,*" *Culture* 19 (September 1958), 287-297.
Weaver, Robert. "A Canadian 'First'," *Queen's Quarterly* 63 (Winter 1959), 632.

George Woodcock

(1912-   )

One extremely important event which furthered the variety and assurance of Canadian writing in the sixties and seventies was the founding in 1959 by George Woodcock, in cooperation with the University of British Columbia, of the scholarly magazine *Canadian Literature*. Competent literary criticism is essential for the maturity of any modern literature. Its summaries, explanations, and evaluations not only open the literature to wider general readership but bring its shape into focus for the teachers of literature in high schools and universities. In addition, the writer can receive intelligent readings of his own works and some sense of the range of accomplishment of his contemporaries.

George Woodcock has been the appropriate editor to preside over Canadian criticism during the recent diverse and fertile years. A rationalist who believes in the creative and moral potential of undirected individuals, he has made *Canadian Literature* into a truly national magazine free of authoritarian direction and open to divergent opinions and regional eccentricity. His background in the lively English literary world of the thirties has enabled him to regard with tolerant equanimity the angers and enthusiasms of Canadian writers. His confidence that the well-argued and documented thesis will dominate its inferiors has allowed him to keep the magazine open to critics and writers of all ages and persuasions. His contributors have included historians, poets, professional academicians, novelists, editors, and representatives of radio, television and theatre. *Canadian Literature* has consequently become a fascinating record of the cross-currents, conflicts, controversies, and new arrivals of its time.

Woodcock was born in Winnipeg to British immigrants who returned to England while he was still a child. During the thirties and forties he was active in the London literary scene and acquainted with many of its leading figures — Forster, Eliot, Thomas, and Orwell. His publications in this period reflect his interwoven interests in both literature and society, a book on housing (*Homes or Hovels*, 1944), a study of Aphra Behn (*The Incomparable Aphra*, 1948), *Railways and Society* (1943), *The Paradox of Oscar Wilde* (1949), and a biographical study of William Godwin (1946). He returned to Canada in 1949, a self-educated and recognized man of letters, but handicapped in getting academic employment by his lack of degrees. He joined the faculty of the University of B.C. in 1956.

After 1949 Woodcock became even more active — as a travel writer, an historian of anarchism, a critic of Canadian and British literature, and a political essayist. Among his works have been critical biographies of Pierre-Joseph Proudhon (1956), Peter Kropotkin (in collaboration with Ivan Avakumovic, 1950), and Ghandi (1972), full critical studies of George Orwell (*The Crystal Spirit*, 1966), Aldous Huxley (*Dawn and the Darkest Hour*, 1970), and Herbert Read (1972), monographs on Hugh MacLennan (1969), Mordecai Richler (1970), and Malcolm Lowry (1971), cultural overviews of the East and Far East (*Asia, Gods, and Cities*, 1966; *Faces of India*, 1965), of the Marabar Coast (*Kerala*, 1967) and of Canada (*Canada and the Canadians*, 1970), as well as various works in political theory including *Civil Disobedience* (1966), *The Rejection of Politics* (1972) and a superb history of anarchism (*Anarchism*, 1962).

Throughout his work Woodcock has pursued what one of his early poems terms "the humane dream" — the possibility that individual man can generate more decent and less authoritarian modes of society. His travel writings are subtly informed by the dream; most of his biographical and literary studies focus on men who have been obsessed with the degradation of man by his political structures — Huxley, Orwell, Kropotkin, Proudhon, Godwin, Ghandi. His belief that the writer participates in the social and political consciousness of his period — that even private, idiosyncratic literature is a form of political action — has contributed immeasurably to the power of *Canadian Literature* as a cultural document. Under his direction, it has not become purely a forum for dispassionate appraisal of literature as an aesthetic object separate from other aspects of life; it has offered much engaged criticism in which the living implications of the writing are recognized. Canadian writing has consequently been given invaluable assistance toward acceptance as a vital and relevant part of the total Canadian cultural dynamic.

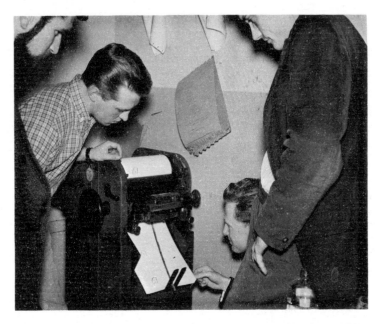

The Printing of *Tish* 19, March 1963.

Woodcock,George.   *The White Island* (poetry). London: Fortune Press, 1940.

. *The Centre Cannot Hold* (poetry). London: Routledge and Kegan Paul, 1943.

. *Railways and Society.* London: Freedom Press, 1943.

. *Anarchy or Chaos.* London: Freedom Press, 1944.

. *Homes or Hovels: the Housing Problem and its Solutions.* London: Freedom Press, 1944.

. *William Godwin.* London: The Porcupine Press, 1946.

. *The Basis of Communal Living.* London: Freedom Press, 1947.

. *Imagine the South* (poems). Pasadena: Untide Press, 1947.

, ed. *A Hundred Years of Revolution: 1948 and After.* London: The Porcupine Press, 1948.

. *The Incomparable Aphra.* London: T.V. Boardman, 1948.

. *The Writer and Politics.* London: The Porcupine Press, 1948.

. *The Paradox of Oscar Wilde*. London: T.V. Boardman, 1949.

. *The Anarchist Prince*, a biographic study of Peter Kropotkin by George Woodcock and Ivan Avakumovic. London: T.V. Boardman, 1950.

. *British Poetry Today*. Vancouver: University of British Columbia, 1950.

, ed. *The Letters of Charles Lamb*, selected with an introduction and notes by George Woodcock. London: Grey Walls Press, 1950.

. *Ravens and Prophets:* an Account of Journeys in British Columbia and Alberta. London: A. Wingate, 1952.

. *Pierre Joseph Proudhon.* London: Routledge and Kegan Paul, 1956.

. *To the City of the Dead:* an Account of Travels in Mexico. London: Faber and Faber, 1957.

. "Areopagitica Re-written," *Canadian Literature* 2 (Autumn 1959), 3-9.

. "The Tentative Confessions of a Prospective Editor," *British Columbia Library Quarterly* 23 (July 1959), 17-21.

. *Incas and Other Men:* Travels in the Andes. London: Faber and Faber, 1960.

. "A Nation's Odyssey: The Novels of Hugh MacLennan," *Canadian Literature* 10 (Autumn 1961), 7-18, reprinted in A.J.M. Smith, ed., *Masks of Fiction* (Toronto: McClelland & Stewart, 1961).

. *Anarchism:* a History of Libertarian Ideas and Movements. Cleveland: Meridian Books, 1962.

. *Faces of India:* a Travel Narrative. London: Faber and Faber, 1964.

. "Editorial Balance Sheet: Six Years of Canadian Literature," *British Columbia Library Quarterly* 28 (April 1965) 3-9.

. *Asia, Gods, and Cities.* London: Faber and Faber, 1966.

, ed. *A Choice of Critics:* selections from *Canadian Literature.* Toronto: Oxford University Press, 1966.

. *The Crystal Spirit: a Study of George Orwell.* Boston: Little, Brown, 1966.

. *The Greeks in India.* London: Faber and Faber, 1966.

, Comp. *Variations on a Human Theme.* Toronto: McGraw-Hill Ryerson, 1966.

. *Kerala:* a Portrait of the Marabar Coast. London: Faber and Faber, 1967.

. *Selected Poems.* Toronto: Clarke Irwin, 1967.

. *The Doukhobors* by George Woodcock and Ivan Avakumovic. Toronto, 1968.

. *The Trade Union Movement and the Government.*
Leicester: Leicester University Press, 1968.
. *Civil Disobedience.* Toronto: CBC Publications, 1969.
. *The British in the Far East.* London: Weidenfeld and
Nicolson, 1969.
. "Getting Away With Survival," *Canadian Literature* 41
(Summer 1969), 5-9.
. *Henry Walter Bates: Naturalist of the Amazons.* London:
Faber and Faber, 1969.
. *Hugh MacLennan.* Toronto: Copp Clark, 1969.
, ed. *The Sixties:* Writers and Writing of the Decade. Van-
couver: University of British Columbia Press, 1969.
. *Canada and the Canadians.* London: Faber and Faber,
1970.
. *The Hudson's Bay Company.* New York: Crowell-Collier,
1970.
. *Mordecai Richler.* Toronto: McClelland & Stewart, 1970.
. *Odysseus Ever Returning:* Essays on Canadian Writers
and Writing. Toronto: McClelland & Stewart, 1970.
. "Anarchism and Violence," *Canadian Forum* 50 (January
1971) 333-335.
. "Beauty and the Democratic Fallacy," *Saturday Night* 86
(January 1971), 26-29.
. *Into Tibet: the Early British Explorers.* New York: Barnes
and Noble, 1971.
, ed. *Malcolm Lowry: The Man and His Work.* Vancouver:
University of British Columbia Press, 1971.
. "How Can We Make Democracy Work Between Elec-
tions? Like This," *Maclean's* 84 (April 1971), 16.
. *Mohandas Ghandi.* New York: Viking, 1971.
, ed. *Wyndham Lewis in Canada.* Vancouver: University of
British Columbia Press, 1971.
. "Canada's October Days," *Canadian Literature* 51
(Winter 1972), 73-77.
. *Dawn and the Darkest Hour:* a Study of Aldous Huxley.
London: Faber and Faber, 1972.
. *Herbert Read.* London: Faber and Faber, 1972.
. "On Being a Writer in Canada: a personal Note," *Satur-
day Night* 87 (November 1972), 57-59.
. "Plea for the Anti-Nation," *Canadian Forum* 52 (April
1972), 16-19.
. *The Rejection of Politics and Other Essays.* Toronto:
New Press, 1972.
. "Cycles of Creation," *Canadian Literature* 56 (Spring

1973), 97-101.

. "Human Alternative to the Big House," *Maclean's* 86 (March 1973), 40-43.

, Comp. "New Wave in Publishing," *Canadian Literature* 57 (Summer 1973), 50-64.

. "Poetry Magazines of the Thirties: a Personal Note," *Tamarack Review* 60 (1973), 68-74.

ANON. Review of *Canada and the Canadians, Times Literary Supplement,* November 6, 1970, p.1288.

Cairns, John C. Review of *Anarchism, Canadian Historical Review* 44 (September 1963), 258-259.

Daniells, Roy. "Microcosm of our Moving World," *Canadian Literature* 30 (Autumn 1966), 63-64, 66.

Dobbs, Kildare. "Essayist Sees Canada as Federation" (rev. of *The Rejection of Politics*), *The Toronto Star,* Jan. 20, 1973, p.55.

Engel, Marian. Review of *Canada and the Canadians, New York Times Book Review,* February 14, 1971, p.2.

Evans, J.A.S. "Woodcock and Cook on Canada," *Commentator* 15 (April 1971), 21.

Fetherling, Doug. "The Ever-Writing Woodcock," *The Globe and Mail,* Oct. 7, 1972, p.35.

Goodman, Paul. Review of *The Doukhobours, Commonweal* 90 (April 4, 1969), 80.

Grosskurth, Phyllis. "Huxley Observed," *Canadian Literature* 56 (Spring 1973), 117-119.

Hughes, Peter. *George Woodcock.* Toronto: McClelland & Stewart, 1974. New Canadian Library, Canadian Writers 13.

Lavin, J.A. "Orwell's World," *Canadian Literature* 33 (Summer 1967), 90-91.

Pritchett, V.S. Review of *Dawn and the Darkest Hour, New York Review of Books* 7 (December 15, 1966), 6.

Stevens, Peter. "Critical Odyssey," *Canadian Literature* 47 (Winter 1971), 84-87.

Symons, Julian. "Man of the Thirties," *Canadian Literature* 37 (Summer 1968), 75-76.

Sypnowich, Peter. "The Knowledge of Failure in the Canadian Character" (rev. of *Canada and the Canadians*), *The Toronto Star,* Oct. 24, 1970, p.53.

Wainwright, Andy. "Art, a Critic, and a Whole Bloody Bird," *Saturday Night* 85 (April 1970), 33-34.

Weaver, Robert. "Remembering George Orwell," *Saturday Night* 82 (June 1967), 33, 35.

Wolfe, Morris. Review of *Canada and the Canadians, Canadian Forum* 50 (March 1971), 439-440.

Appendix A

Bibliographical material on most contemporary Canadian writers can be found in the following journals and books:

JOURNALS

The Canadian Index. Toronto: The University of Toronto Press, 1974-   . An annual index to "essays and literature in collections and periodicals" not covered by *The Canadian Periodical Index* (below).

Canadian Literature. Vancouver: The University of British Columbia, 1959-   . Contains "Canadian Literature: a checklist" annually for years 1959-1970, listing books, articles, and journals in French and English.

The Canadian Periodical Index. Ottawa: The Canadian Library Association, 1938-   . Monthly index to articles and reviews in a selected number of established Canadian periodicals.

The Journal of Canadian Fiction. Fredericton, N.B.: Bellrock Press, 1972-   . Spring issue contains an annual bibliography of Canadian Literature, including books, articles, theses, journals, book reviews, and stage reviews in French and English; indexed for subject and author.

The Journal of Commonwealth Literature. London: Heinemann Educational Books and The University of Leeds, 1965-   . Contains annual bibliography of Canadian literature listing books, articles, journals, and some book reviews.

BOOKS:
Gnarowski, Michael. *A Concise Bibliography of Canadian Literature.* Toronto: McClelland & Stewart, 1973.

Story, Norah. *Oxford Companion to Canadian History and Literature.* Toronto: Oxford University Press, 1967.

Toye, William, ed. *Supplement to the Oxford Companion to Canadian History and Literature.* Toronto: Oxford University Press, 1973.

Appendix B

Work by writers in this volume can be found in the following anthologies:

Bowering, George, ed. *The Story So Far.* Toronto: The Coach House Press, 1971, 112pp. A collection of contemporary Canadian short stories; includes Clark Blaise, Michael Ondaatje, George Bowering, bpNichol, David McFadden, Alden Nowlan.

Brown, Jim, and David Phillips, ed. *West Coast Seen.* Vancouver: Talonbooks, 1969, 212pp. The work of young poets from the west coast, including Bill Bissett.

Cameron, Donald, comp. *Conversations with Canadian Novelists.* Toronto: Macmillan, 1973, 2 vols., 160pp., 160pp. A collection of interviews with contemporary Canadian novelists. Includes George Bowering, Dave Godfrey, Robert Kroetsch, Jack Ludwig, Rudy Wiebe.

Cohen, Matt, ed. *The Story So Far/2.* Toronto: The Coach House Press, 1973, 128pp. An anthology of experimental Canadian fiction. Includes Margaret Atwood, Matt Cohen, Vic d'Or (Victor Coleman), bpNichol.

Colombo, John Robert, ed. *How Do I Love Thee.* Edmonton: M.G. Hurtig, 1970, 184pp. Favourite poems of sixty Canadian poets personally selected and introduced. Includes Earle Birney, John Glassco, Ralph Gustafson, Dorothy Livesay, George Woodcock, Irving Layton, George Johnston, P.K. Page, Louis Dudek, Raymond Souster, Eli Mandel, Milton Acorn, Phyllis Webb, D.G. Jones, Al Purdy, Alden Nowlan, Joe Rosenblatt, Leonard Cohen, George

Bowering, John Robert Colombo, Lionel Kearns, John Newlove, Dennis Lee, Margaret Atwood, Frank Davey, Gwendolyn MacEwen, Michael Ondaatje, Bill Bissett, bpNichol

Colombo, John Robert, ed. *New Direction in Canadian Poetry.* Toronto: Holt Rinehart and Winston, 1971, 96pp. An anthology of concrete poetry by young Canadian writers. Includes Bill Bissett and bpNichol.

Colombo, John Robert, ed. *Rhymes and Reasons: Nine Canadian Poets Discuss their Work.* Toronto: Holt Rinehart and Winston, 1971. Includes George Bowering, Lionel Kearns, Gwendolyn MacEwen, John Newlove, Alden Nowlan.

Denham, Paul, ed. *The Evolution of Canadian Literature in English 1945-1970.* Toronto: Holt Rinehart and Winston, 1973, 288pp. Includes Earle Birney, Irving Layton, Hugh Garner, Margaret Avison, Raymond Souster, Eli Mandel, Milton Acorn, Hugh Hood, Alice Munro, Alden Nowlan, Leonard Cohen, John Newlove, Margaret Atwood, bpNichol.

Dudek, Louis, ed. *Poetry of Our Time: An Introduction to Twentieth-Century Poetry, Including Modern Canadian Poetry.* Toronto: Macmillan, 1965, 376pp. An extensive collection of 19th and 20th century poets, with sixty pages of study aids. Includes P.K. Page, Earle Birney, Margaret Avison, John Glassco, Ralph Gustafson, Irving Layton, Raymond Souster, Louis Dudek, Eli Mandel, D.G. Jones, Leonard Cohen, Alden Nowlan.

Dudek, Louis, and Michael Gnarowski, ed. *The Making of Modern Poetry in Canada: Essential Articles on Contemporary Canadian Poetry in English.* Toronto: Ryerson, 1967, 303pp. A collection of critical and theoretical articles by Canadian poets and their editors. Includes Louis Dudek, P.K. Page, Irving Layton, Raymond Souster, Earle Birney, Desmond Pacey, Eli Mandel, Frank Davey, George Woodcock, Milton Acorn, George Bowering.

Fetherling, Doug, ed. *Thumbprints.* Toronto: Peter Martin, 1969, 70pp. An anthology of hitch-hiking poems; includes bpNichol, Bill Bissett, George Bowering, John Newlove, David McFadden, Margaret Atwood, Raymond Souster, John Robert Colombo.

Four Parts Sand. Ottawa: Oberon, 1972, 64pp. Concrete poems by four Canadian poets including Earle Birney and Bill Bissett.

Geddes, Gary, and Phyllis Bruce, ed. *15 Canadian Poets.* Toronto: Oxford University Press, 1970, 293pp. A collection designed to present writers at various points in their poetic development; includes Earle Birney, Raymond Souster, Leonard Cohen, D.G. Jones, Alden Nowlan, Margaret Avison, Irving Layton, Al Purdy, Eli Mandel,

Margaret Atwood, Gwendolyn MacEwen, George Bowering, John Newlove, Victor Coleman, Michael Ondaatje.

Geddes, Gary, ed. *Twentieth-Century Poetry and Poetics.* Toronto: Oxford University Press, 1973 (rev. from edition of 1969). Includes Irving Layton, Earle Birney, Margaret Avison, Margaret Atwood.

Gibson, Graeme, comp. *Eleven Canadian Novelists.* Toronto: House of Anansi, 1973, 324pp. Interviews of Canadian novelists, taped originally for CBC radio. Includes Margaret Atwood, Austin Clarke, Matt Cohen, Dave Godfrey, Jack Ludwig, Alice Munro.

Gill, John, ed. *New American and Canadian Poetry.* Boston: Beacon Press, 1971, 280pp. Includes Milton Acorn, Margaret Atwood, George Bowering, Irving Layton, David McFadden, John Newlove, Alden Nowlan.

Godbout, Jacques, and John Robert Colombo, ed. *Poetry/Poésie 64.* Toronto: Ryerson, 1963, 153pp. A collection of younger poets from French and English Canada. Includes Frank Davey, Lionel Kearns, George Bowering, John Newlove, Margaret Atwood, Gwendolyn MacEwen.

Goldberg, Gerry, and George Wright, ed. *I Am A Sensation.* Toronto: McClelland & Stewart, 1971, 158pp. An assorted collection of prose, poetry, and illustrations, designed for school curricula. Includes George Johnston, John Robert Colombo, Leonard Cohen, Earle Birney, John Newlove, bpNichol, Raymond Souster, Alden Nowlan, P.K. Page, Gwendolyn MacEwen, Marshall McLuhan, Louis Dudek.

Green, H. Gordon, and Guy Sylvester, ed. *A Century of Canadian Literature.* Toronto: Ryerson Press, Montreal: HMH, (1967), 599pp. An extensive collection of prose and poetry of English and French-Canadian writers; includes Dorothy Livesay, John Glassco, Irving Layton, Ralph Gustafson, George Johnston, P.K. Page, Louis Dudek, Margaret Avison, Raymond Souster, Eli Mandel, Phyllis Webb, D.G. Jones, Alden Nowlan, Leonard Cohen, John Robert Colombo, George Bowering, Lionel Kearns, John Newlove.

Gustafson, Ralph, ed. *The Penguin Book of Canadian Verse.* Harmondsworth, Eng: Penguin, 1967 (rev. edition). Includes Earle Birney, John Glassco, Dorothy Livesay, Ralph Gustafson, Irving Layton, George Johnston, P.K. Page, Margaret Avison, Louis Dudek, Raymond Souster, Eli Mandel, Phyllis Webb, D.G. Jones, Alden Nowlan, Al Purdy, Leonard Cohen, George Bowering, John Robert Colombo, Lionel Kearns, John Newlove, Gwendolyn MacEwen, Michael Ondaatje.

Helwig, David, and Joan Harcourt, ed. *73: New Canadian Stories.* Ottawa: Oberon, 1973, 175pp. Includes Hugh Hood, Hugh Garner, Matt

Cohen.

Helwig, David, and Joan Harcourt, ed. *72: New Canadian Stories*. Ottawa: Oberon, 1972, 135pp. Includes John Newlove, David McFadden, Margaret Atwood.

Helwig, David, and Tom Marshall, ed. *Fourteen Stories High*. Ottawa: Oberon, 1971, 172pp. A collection of contemporary short stories; includes Gwendolyn MacEwen, Hugh Garner, George Bowering, Rudy Wiebe, Alden Nowlan.

Kilgallin, Tony, ed. *The Canadian Short Story*. Toronto: Holt, Rinehart, Winston, 1971, 102pp. Five short stories. Includes Hugh Hood.

Klinck, Carl F., and Reginald E. Watters, ed. *Canadian Anthology*. Toronto: W.J. Gage, 1966, 626pp. A collection of Canadian prose and poetry of the past and present. Includes Robert Finch, Earle Birney, Dorothy Livesay, P.K. Page, Ralph Gustafson, Irving Layton, George Johnston, Margaret Avison, Louis Dudek, Raymond Souster, Eli Mandel, D.G. Jones, Alden Nowlan, Leonard Cohen, Gwendolyn MacEwen.

Layton, Irving, ed. *Love Where the Nights Are Long*. Toronto: McClelland & Stewart, 1962, 78pp. A collection of love poetry by Canadian poets, illustrated by Harold Town. Includes Leonard Cohen, Irving Layton, Alden Nowlan, Raymond Souster, Milton Acorn, George Johnston, Louis Dudek, John Glassco, George Bowering, Ralph Gustafson, Earle Birney, P.K. Page.

Livesay, Dorothy, ed. *40 Women Poets of Canada*. Montreal: Ingluvin Publications, 1972, 141pp. Includes Margaret Atwood, Dorothy Livesay, Gwendolyn MacEwen, P.K. Page.

Lochhead, Douglas, and Raymond Souster, ed. *Made in Canada: New Poems of the Seventies*. Ottawa: Oberon, 1970, 192pp. Includes Milton Acorn, Margaret Atwood, Nelson Ball, Earle Birney, Bill Bissett, John Robert Colombo, John Glassco, Ralph Gustafson, D.G. Jones, Dennis Lee, Dorothy Livesay, Gwendolyn MacEwen, Eli Mandel, David McFadden, John Newlove, Alden Nowlan, Michael Ondaatje, P.K. Page, Raymond Souster.

Lucas, Alec, ed. *Great Canadian Short Stories*. New York: Dell, 1971, 395pp. A survey anthology from the 19th century to the present; includes Irving Layton, Hugh Garner, Jack Ludwig, Hugh Hood, Alice Munro, Dave Godfrey, Clark Blaise.

Mandel, Eli, ed. *Contexts of Canadian Criticism*. Chicago: University of Chicago Press, 1971, 304pp. A collection of Canadian critical essays, with bibliography and introduction. Includes Marshall

McLuhan, Henry Kreisel, Dorothy Livesay.

Mandel, Eli, ed. *Eight More Canadian Poets*. Toronto: Holt, Rinehart and Winston, 1972, 88pp. Includes Margaret Avison, Raymond Souster, Eli Mandel, Milton Acorn, Phyllis Webb, D.G. Jones.

Mandel, Eli, ed. *Five More Canadian Poets*. Toronto: Holt, Rinehart and Winston, 1970, 88pp. Includes Earle Birney, Irving Layton, Al Purdy, Margaret Atwood, Leonard Cohen.

Mandel, Eli, ed. *Poets of Contemporary Canada, 1960-1970*. Toronto: McClelland & Stewart, 1972, 141pp. Includes Milton Acorn, Joe Rosenblatt, Leonard Cohen, George Bowering, John Newlove, Margaret Atwood, Bill Bissett, Al Purdy, Gwendolyn MacEwen, Michael Ondaatje.

Mandel, Eli, and Desmond Maxwell, ed. *English Poems of the Twentieth Century*. Toronto: Macmillan, 1971, 221pp. A collection of major poets in English, American, Canadian, and Australian poetry in this century. Includes Earle Birney, Irving Layton, Margaret Avison, Eli Mandel, Leonard Cohen.

Mandel, Eli, and Jean-Guy Pilon, ed. *Poetry 62*. Toronto: Ryerson, 1961, 116pp. A collection of previously unpublished poems by younger poets from English and French Canada. Includes Margaret Avison, Milton Acorn, D.G. Jones, Alden Nowlan, Leonard Cohen, John Robert Colombo.

Metcalf, John, ed. *Kaleidoscope: Canadian Stories*. Toronto: Van Nostrand Reinhold, 1972, 138pp. A collection of contemporary Canadian stories; includes Hugh Hood, Alice Munro, Hugh Garner.

Metcalf, John, ed. *The Narrative Voice: Short Stories and Reflections by Canadian Authors*. Toronto: McGraw-Hill Ryerson, 1972, 277pp. A contemporary collection which attempts to present story-writing as a process; includes Clark Blaise, Hugh Hood, Alice Munro, Rudy Wiebe.

Metcalf, John, ed. *The Speaking Earth*. Toronto: Van Nostrand Reinhold, 1973, 128pp. An anthology of contemporary Canadian poetry. Includes Milton Acorn, Margaret Atwood, Nelson, Ball, Earle Birney, George Bowering, Leonard Cohen, John Robert Colombo, Frank Davey, George Johnston, D.G. Jones, Dorothy Livesay, Eli Mandel, David McFadden, John Newlove, Alden Nowlan, Michael Ondaatje, Al Purdy, James Reaney, Raymond Souster.

Nelson, George E., ed. *Northern Lights*. Toronto: Doubleday, 1960, 736pp. A collection of Canadian short stories, including work by Adele Wiseman, Hugh Garner, Earle Birney.

Nichol, bp, ed. *The Cosmic Chef: an Evening of Concrete*. Ottawa:

Oberon, 1970, 80pp. A collection of concrete poetry by Canadian poets; includes Margaret Avison, Nelson Ball, Earle Birney, Bill Bissett, George Bowering, Victor Coleman, John Robert Colombo, Gerry Gilbert, Lionel Kearns, David McFadden, bpNichol, Michael Ondaatje, Phyllis Webb.

Ondaatje, Michael, ed. *The Broken Ark: a Book of Beasts,* with drawings by T. Urquhart. Ottawa: Oberon, 1971, 52pp. Fifty-two Canadian poems and drawings concerned with beasts; includes John Newlove, Victor Coleman, John Glassco, Gwendolyn MacEwen, George Johnston, Milton Acorn, Earle Birney, Phyllis Webb, D.G. Jones, George Bowering, Alden Nowlan, Irving Layton, David McFadden, Bill Bissett, P.K. Page, Michael Ondaatje, Al Purdy, Margaret Atwood.

Pacey, Desmond, ed. *A Book of Canadian Stories,* rev. edition. Toronto: Ryerson, 1962, 340pp. Includes Ralph Gustafson, Irving Layton, Hugh Garner, Desmond Pacey, Henry Kreisel, Jack Ludwig, Alice Munro, Alden Nowlan.

Purdy, Al, ed. *Fifteen Winds: A Selection of Modern Canadian Poems.* Toronto: Ryerson, 1970, 157pp. Includes Milton Acorn, Margaret Atwood, Earle Birney, Bill Bissett, George Bowering, Leonard Cohen, John Robert Colombo, Frank Davey, Louis Dudek, Robert Finch, George Johnston, Lionel Kearns, Irving Layton, Dennis Lee, John Newlove, Alden Nowlan, Joe Rosenblatt, Raymond Souster.

Purdy, Al, ed. *Storm Warning: The New Canadian Poets.* Toronto: McClelland & Stewart, 1971, 152pp. Includes Bill Bissett, Dennis Lee, David McFadden.

Rimanelli, Giose, and Roberto Ruberto, ed. *Modern Canadian Stories.* Forward by Earle Birney. Toronto: Ryerson Press, 1966, 402pp. Includes Hugh Garner, Henry Kreisel, Adele Wiseman, Hugh Hood, Alice Munro, John Metcalf, Irving Layton, Alden Nowlan, George Bowering, Daphne Buckle (Daphne Marlatt).

Richler, Mordecai, ed. *Canadian Writing Today.* Harmondsworth, Eng.: Penguin, 1970, 331pp. A collection of prose and poetry on literary and cultural subjects. Includes John Robert Colombo, John Glassco, Irving Layton, Hugh Hood, Alden Nowlan, Alice Munro, Earle Birney, Leonard Cohen, George Woodcock.

Ross, Malcolm, ed. *Poets Between the Wars.* Toronto: McClelland & Stewart, 1967. An anthology of five poets who wrote between the two world wars. Includes Dorothy Livesay.

Smith, A.J.M., ed. *Modern Canadian Verse in English and French.* Toronto: Oxford University Press, 1967, 426pp. A collection of

Canadian poets arranged chronologically from the late nineteenth century to the present; includes Robert Finch, Earle Birney, John Glassco, Dorothy Livesay, Ralph Gustafson, George Woodcock, Irving Layton, George Johnston, P.K. Page, Margaret Avison, Louis Dudek, Raymond Souster, Eli Mandel, Milton Acorn, Phyllis Webb, D.G. Jones, Alden Nowlan, Joe Rosenblatt, Leonard Cohen, George Bowering, John Robert Colombo, Lionel Kearns, John Newlove, Margaret Atwood, Gwendolyn MacEwen, Michael Ondaatje.

Scott, F.R., and A.J.M. Smith, ed. *The Blasted Pine: an anthology of satire, invective, and Disrespectful Verse chiefly by Canadian Writers.* Toronto: Macmillan, 1967 (Revised and enlarged from 1957 edn.), 192pp. Includes Earle Birney, Irving Layton, John Robert Colombo, P.K. Page, Raymond Souster, Leonard Cohen, Al Purdy, Margaret Atwood, Eli Mandel, Alden Nowlan, Robert Finch, Louis Dudek, John Glassco, George Johnston, Ralph Gustafson.

Smith, A.J.M., ed. *Masks of Poetry.* Toronto: McClelland & Stewart, 1962, 143pp. A selection of critical and expository writing on Canadian poetry by Canadian scholars from before Confederation to the present; includes Earle Birney, Irving Layton.

Souster, Raymond, ed. *New Wave Canada: the New Explosion in Canadian Poetry.* Toronto: Contact Press, 1966, 167pp. A collection of 17 younger poets. Includes Victor Coleman, Gerry Gilbert, David McFadden, bpNichol, Michael Ondaatje.

Stephens, Donald, ed. *Contemporary Voices: the Short Story in Canada.* Scarborough: Prentice-Hall, 1972, 182pp. Includes Hugh Garner, Dave Godfrey, Hugh Hood, Alice Munro, Alden Nowlan.

Thompson, Kent, ed. *Stories from Atlantic Canada.* Toronto: Macmillan, 1973, 231pp. A collection of stories from Nova Scotia, New Brunswick, and Newfoundland. Includes Alden Nowlan.

Vance, Bruce, ed. *The Eye of the Beholder.* Toronto: Nelson, 1970, 154pp. A collection of prose on the theme of "Man": part of the "Glimpses of Man in Time Series". Includes Alice Munro, Ralph Gustafson, Irving Layton.

Vance, Bruce, ed. *Microcosm.* Toronto: Nelson, 1970, 154pp. A collection of prose from a variety of American, British, and Canadian authors, part of the "Glimpses of Man in Time Series". Includes Alden Nowlan.

Ware, Randall, ed. *The Book Cellar Anthology of Poetry.* Toronto: Peter Martin, 1971, 96pp. A collection of work by 24 Toronto poets; includes Victor Coleman, John Robert Colombo, Dennis Lee, bpNichol, Al Purdy, Joe Rosenblatt.

Weaver, Robert, ed. *Canadian Short Stories.* London: Oxford

University Press, 1960, 420pp. A historical survey of Canadian short fiction. Includes Ralph Gustafson, Irving Layton, Hugh Garner, P.K. Page, Alice Munro.

Weaver, Robert, ed. *Canadian Short Stories: Second Series.* Toronto: Oxford University Press, 1968, 378pp. A collection of Canadian short fiction from the 1960's. Includes Hugh Garner, Dave Godfrey, Hugh Hood, Jack Ludwig, Alice Munro.

Weaver, Robert, ed. *The First Five Years: a Selection from 'The Tamarack Review'.* Toronto: Oxford University Press, 1962, 376pp. Includes Jack Ludwig, George Johnston, Alden Nowlan, Irving Layton, Raymond Souster, D.G. Jones, Alice Munro, John Glassco, Earle Birney, Eli Mandel, Hugh Hood, George Woodcock, Dave Godfrey, Leonard Cohen.

Weaver, Robert, ed. *Poems for Voices.* Toronto: CBC Publications, 1970, 97pp. The texts of six poems commissioned for CBC radio. Includes Al Purdy, Margaret Atwood, John Newlove, Alden Nowlan.

Weaver, Robert, and William Toye, ed. *The Oxford Anthology of Canadian Literature.* Toronto: Oxford University Press, 1973, 546pp. A general anthology of work from the seventeenth century to the present; includes Milton Acorn, Margaret Atwood, Margaret Avison, Earle Birney, George Bowering, Leonard Cohen, John Robert Colombo, Louis Dudek, Northrop Frye, Hugh Garner, John Glassco, Hugh Hood, George Johnston, D.G. Jones, Irving Layton, Dennis Lee, Dorothy Livesay, Gwendolyn MacEwen, Marshall McLuhan, Eli Mandel, Alice Munro, John Newlove, Alden Nowlan, Michael Ondaatje, P.K. Page, Al Purdy, Raymond Souster, Phyllis Webb, George Woodcock.

Weibe, Rudy, ed. *The Story Makers: a Selection of Modern Short Stories.* Toronto: Macmillan, 1970. A variety of stories from writers of several countries. Includes Alice Munro, Rudy Wiebe.

Wiebe, Rudy, ed. *Stories from Western Canada.* Toronto: Macmillan, 1972, 274pp. Includes Henry Kreisel, Dorothy Livesay, Rudy Wiebe.

Wilson, Milton, ed. *Recent Canadian Verse.* Kingston, Ont.: Jackson Press, 1959. Canadian poems concerned with certain recurrent problems of diction, imagery, and form. Includes Margaret Avison, Raymond Souster, Eli Mandel, Irving Layton, Ralph Gustafson, George Johnston, Alden Nowlan, Milton Acorn, D.G. Jones, Leonard Cohen.

Wilson, Milton, ed. *Poetry of Mid-Century, 1940-1960.* Toronto: McClelland & Stewart, 1964, 256pp. The work of Canadian poets who began to write between 1940 and 1960. Includes Earle Birney, Irving Layton, Margaret Avison, Raymond Souster, P.K. Page, Leonard

Cohen, Alden Nowlan.

Woodcock, George, ed. *A Choice of Critics*. Toronto: Oxford University Press, 1966, 247pp. A collection of seventeen essays from the first twenty-six quarterly issues of *Canadian Literature*. Includes D.G. Jones, George Woodcock, Louis Dudek.

Yates, J. Michael, ed. *Contemporary Poetry of British Columbia*. Vancouver: Sono Nis Press, 1970, 252pp. A collection of poets who reside in British Columbia: includes John Newlove, Lionel Kearns, Earle Birney, Phyllis Webb, Dorothy Livesay, P.K. Page.

Photo Credits

Margaret Atwood. By permission of House of Anansi, Photographer Graeme Gibson.
Bill Bissett. Courtesy of Jerry Lampert, photographer unknown.
George Bowering. By permission of the photographer, Linda McCartney.
The Four Horsemen. Photograph by Frank Davey.
George Johnston. Courtesy of George Johnston.
P.K. Page. By permission of House of Anansi, photographer Graeme Gibson.
The Printing of Tish 19. Courtesy of Raymond Hull.
Gwendolyn MacEwen. Courtesy of Gwendolyn MacEwen, photographer John M. Reynolds.
Daphne Marlatt. By permission of the photographer, Bob Rose.
Alice Munro. By permission of McGraw-Hill Ryerson, photographer Victor Aziz.
Michael Ondaatje. By permission of the photographer, Kim Ondaatje.
Audrey Thomas. By permission of the photographer, David Robinson.
Phyllis Webb. Courtesy of Talonbooks.

The author and publisher are grateful to the above for their cooperation and assistance. Thanks also go to Nelson Ball, Ian Sowton, Marty Avenus, Stan Bevington, and Victor Coleman for making books from their collections available for photographing, and to Stan Bevington for his several hours of camerawork.